Reimagining a Place for the Wild

REIMAGINING A PLACE FOR THE WILD

Edited by

Leslie Miller and Louise Excell

with
Christopher Smart

Essay Introductions by Louise Excell

THE UNIVERSITY OF UTAH PRESS
Salt Lake City

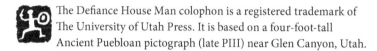 The Defiance House Man colophon is a registered trademark of
The University of Utah Press. It is based on a four-foot-tall
Ancient Puebloan pictograph (late PIII) near Glen Canyon, Utah.

"Living in a Circle of Heartbeats" was previously published as "Living in a Circle
of Beating Hearts," in *Out of the Woods: Seeing Nature in the Everyday*, by Julia
Corbett. Copyright © 2018 by University of Nevada Press. All rights reserved.
Reproduced with the permission of the University of Nevada Press.

"Love Has No Net Zero-Sum," by Erin Halcomb, was previously published in The
National Wilderness Conference Proceedings, Plenary Sessions.

LIBRARY OF CONGRESS CATALOGING-IN-PUBLICATION DATA
Names: Miller, Leslie K., editor. | Excell, Louise, editor. | Smart,
 Christopher (Journalist), editor.
Title: Reimagining a place for the wild / edited by Leslie Miller and Louise
 Excell with Christopher Smart ; essay introductions by Louise Excell.
Description: Salt Lake City : The University of Utah Press, [2018] | Includes
 bibliographical references. |
Identifiers: LCCN 2018037117 (print) | LCCN 2018041669 (ebook) | ISBN
 9781607816621 () | ISBN 9781607816614 (pbk. : alk. paper) | ISBN
 160781661X (pbk. : alk. paper)
Subjects: LCSH: Wildlife conservation—West (U.S.) | Nature
 conservation—West (U.S.) | Endangered species—Effect of human beings
 on—West (U.S.) | Habitat (Ecology)—West (U.S.) | Animals—West (U.S.)
Classification: LCC QL84.22.W47 (ebook) | LCC QL84.22.W47 R45 2018 (print) |
 DDC 333.95/40978—dc23
LC record available at https://lccn.loc.gov/2018037117

Cover image: *Bison Bluff*, 2018, by William Kranstover. Wjkart.com.
Oil on canvass.

Printed and bound in the United States of America.

Dedicated to the beasts of the western wild
and
to conserving half of our natural world.

Contents

Reimagining a Place for the Wild

Hawk in Flight, Centennial Valley, Montana 2014. Photograph by Leslie Miller.

Director's Preface

The Heart of Reimagining

Let the beauty we love be what we do.
There are hundreds of ways to kneel and kiss the ground.

—Rumi

A little more than a decade into the twenty-first century, the natural beauty of Centennial Valley, Montana, inspired a group of westerners to search for a reimagined vision of western landscapes and a new narrative for wild nature. This small contingent of wildlife advocates, dubbed the Reimagine Western Landscapes Initiative, charted a course towards understanding and reimagining the West's fraught relationship with the wild. Our goal was to use the environmental humanities to inspire the will to act for human and natural world prosperity. Through story, we would explore the connection community has with the natural world and why it matters.

Though the rough-sawn peaks encircling Centennial Valley divide the continent in two, we were confident diverse voices could bridge the disparate cries for wilderness. We invited twenty-five expert panelists, including local ranchers, nonprofit and government agents, authors, ecologists, and artists, to share their wildlife experiences and stories at the inaugural Reimagine Western Landscapes symposium, "A Place for Wildlife." The Taft-Nicholson Center for Environmental Humanities Education, in the historic stagecoach stop of Lakeview, Montana, played host and advocate to our cause.

An against-all-odds tale of survival, the story of the Red Rock Lakes National Wildlife Refuge, set in the heart of Centennial Valley, provides an enduring reminder of nature's fragility. In a remarkable demonstration of conservationism, the refuge was created in 1935 to provide sanctuary for a dwindling flock of resilient trumpeter swans. According to the United States Fish and Wildlife Service, at that time "fewer than 70 trumpeters were known to exist worldwide, at a location near Yellowstone National Park." After a miraculous recovery from near extinction, "the big-winged white swans, the jumbo jets of the avian world"—as described by Timothy Egan in his 2014 *New York Times* op-ed "New West Renaissance"—now routinely take flight over the Centennial Valley and beyond.

In spite of efforts by the United States government and nonprofit agencies devoted to the protection of wildlife and preservation of natural habitats, evidence reveals massive declines in the wildlife populations of the American West. To cite one example, the Humane Society of the United States claims that during the last decade trophy hunters in the western states have killed twenty-nine thousand American mountain lions. The West's wildlife is in peril, and our conduct needs a fresh look.

This book explores how a shared love and respect for nature—especially the indigenous, wild creatures inhabiting western landscapes—is at the heart of reimagining a place for the wild. The creative interpretation of unexpected wildlife encounters, unpredictable discoveries, and conservation practices offers an emerging role for the environmental humanities, one we champion. We believe in the power of nature to transform our lives. We trust the transformative power of language and story to reveal hidden truths.

An essay describing the pure melody of bird song at dawn, or a memoir that recounts the terror of a startled grizzly—these are worthy of our imagination and attention. When we meet a vulnerable wild animal in our backyard or engage with a keystone species on a national refuge, the story of our encounter makes a difference in the wild's fate. Without authentic stories documenting and sometimes joyously inspiring our interaction with the natural world, we are at a loss for ways to articulate and act on the essential—and existential—connection we have with our fellow creatures. We rely on the power of story to reimagine western landscapes in ways that contribute to the welfare of wild nature in the twenty-first century.

The essays in this collection speak to the diverse experiences individuals living in the Greater Yellowstone and Rocky Mountain region have with wild nature. Local wisdom and professional expertise are embodied in the text. The original narratives are told by a selection of biologists, historians, ranchers, authors, philosophers, conservationists, artists, and scholars who presented at the first Reimagine Western Landscapes symposium. Their stories reflect the inherent beauty of nature and a dedication to the complex challenges facing those who devote their lives to understanding wildlife. The essays inform our sensibilities and examine humanity's conduct as we discover our capacity for empathy in a shared commitment to saving the wild.

We cannot claim this collection to be an exhaustive representation of our relationship with nature—stories from other cultures and socioeconomic backgrounds are desperately needed—however, these voices are singing authentic notes in what we hope is a resounding chorus for improved relations with the western wild in the twenty-first century and beyond.

ACKNOWLEDGEMENTS

The catalyst for our reimagined journey began in Centennial Valley, Montana, five years ago. Friends and colleagues across the West contributed their expertise, generously donated funds, and volunteered precious time to make the Reimagine Western Landscapes Initiative come to life. Our environmental humanities workshops, symposia, and educational programs inspired this vibrant debut collection of essays and wildlife art.

This book would not have been possible without the formative vision, talent, and drive of the Reimagine Western Landscapes committee: Timothy Bywater, John Taft, Mary Tull, Louise Excell, Bill McMurrin, David Nimkin, John Alley, Tom Goldsmith, and Mona Marler. During the project's evolution we became family. The collaborative spirit of Robert Newman, former dean of the University of Utah College of Humanities, and Heidi Camp, former assistant dean, was instrumental in establishing a place for Reimagine at the Taft-Nicholson Center for Environmental Humanities Education and in the hearts of the College of Humanities faculty, staff, and partnership board. Their trust in our vision will never be forgotten.

I am indebted to Louise Excell and Christopher Smart for their expertise and the long hours they spent carefully editing each essay. As a volume editor, preparing the manuscript for publication would have been impossible without the professionalism (and patience) of Clark Kidman and the ongoing guidance from University of Utah Press editor John Alley. We are honored by the inclusion of reprints of masterworks from the permanent collection of the National Museum of Wildlife Art, and for the contemporary art generously offered by Montana artist Monte Dolack. Historic photos from the archives of the Red Rock Lakes National Wildlife Refuge contributed by United States Fish and Wildlife Service refuge manager Bill West are treasured additions. These beautifully rendered portrayals of wildlife and western landscapes enrich our diverse essays.

John and Melody Taft's dedication to protecting wild animals and their gracious hospitality in Centennial Valley throughout the Reimagine endeavors have been priceless. I am indebted to NPR affiliate KUER's Doug Fabrizio and his expert team of producers and engineers for their live broadcast of the symposium from the wilds of Montana. The heroes of the Reimagine project are the twenty-five panelists from the 2014 Reimagine Western Landscapes symposium, "A Place for Wildlife," and the writers among them who contributed to this publication. Their words have given a compassionate human voice to the voiceless wild.

Finally, I thank my lucky stars for David Bernolfo's stories, knowledge, insight, and compassion. His commitment to wildlife is beyond measure.

I am grateful and humbled by the advocacy and ongoing enthusiasm for the Reimagine Western Landscapes Initiative, which employs the environmental humanities to inspire the will to act for human and natural world prosperity.

As Anatole France once said, "Until one has loved an animal, a part of one's soul remains unawakened." My hope is for the stories in *Reimagining a Place for the Wild* to reawaken our souls and inspire a commitment to ensuring a western culture enriched by the wonder and significance of wild *life*.

Leslie Miller
Director, Reimagine Western Landscapes Initiative;
Editor, *Reimagining a Place for the Wild*

PART 1

Encounter

Understanding Human-Wildlife Connections

Waiting for Wolves

Jeremy Schmidt

A lifetime of encounters with animals in the wild leads Jeremy Schmidt to this personal reflection on wildness, which he sees as an ever-present and essential element of the human condition. Wildness is essential, Schmidt contends, because our glimpses of it, however fleeting and in whatever form, keep alive a sense of wonder and awareness of the larger world we inhabit. It is present in the wily and versatile viruses that attack our bodies, and the thousands of mites inhabiting a "dust bunny" under the sofa. Even in the absence of wolves and grizzlies, a world of wildness exists amidst human activity, and it functions outside the human construct of "civilization," often unremarkable and unseen. Wild creatures may be mutable and transient, but wildness endures.

On a small island in the middle of a big wilderness lake, I met my first wolves. They swam out from the mainland, approached through the night, and paced around my campfire. The lake was six or eight miles across, dotted with islands, so there seemed to be as much land as water. To find us, the wolves must have swum from one island to the next. They came at dusk, the way wolves are supposed to do, and paced the forest, gray shadows on the edge of the firelight. We counted four of them, just as many as us.

I was eighteen years old, on a long canoe trip in northern Ontario. My friends and I had been traveling for three weeks. We had heard wolves howling on many quiet evenings across still waters. We had gotten used to seeing their tracks, bigger than a fist, on portage trails. That same morning, while paddling slowly up the river that brought us to this lake, we had watched a wolf move through the jack pines along the water's edge, matching the speed of our canoes. Every so often he would pause to answer the howls of another wolf, somewhere off in the distance. The country seemed full of wolves. This one followed us for several hours, our shadow companion gliding through the bush, head down, eyes tracking our smooth progress. It gave us pleasure to see him.

But that evening on the island our feelings were different. We sat on a flat shelf of granite not 10 feet from the water, watching our cooking fire burn down to embers. Supper was finished, the pots washed, canoes turned over and all but the sleeping gear stowed under them. The lake glowed in that calm light peculiar to northern skies half an hour after sunset. No mosquitoes, no wind, not the slightest wave to disturb the lake's reflection of the first stars. We were tired, not talking, looking over the water.

Then, filling the silence came the howl of a wolf, deep and throaty and very close. He was on the adjacent island, a hundred yards away, hidden from us by a screen of lakeside reeds. We knew he was watching us. In a moment, we were on our feet, all with the same thought. What was a wolf doing this far out in the lake? What could he find to eat on an island?

We thought about it while night fell. The fire went to embers. There was no moon. In the dark, my three friends picked up their sleeping bags and walked toward the tent, some 200 feet back in the woods. I stayed to read by a candle. Suddenly they were shouting in alarm, shouting something about wolves attacking, calling for me to bring my flashlight and the .22 caliber rifle we had brought for shooting grouse and ducks. I ran toward them. They stood together as Roger held a hurriedly lit match above his head, trying to see by its dim light. They said they had heard animals close by in the brush, but had seen nothing yet. Swinging the flashlight in a circle, I caught dark moving shapes and reflecting eyes.

We lit a fire in front of the tent, quickly gathering enough wood to light up the forest and protect us from the attack we thought was coming. I found a large, half-rotten birch trunk still standing. I tore at it, trying to bring it toppling toward the fire. Instead, high above my head, it broke in half and the top 20 feet came crashing down in the dark beside me. That could have killed me.

No one dared risk the walk back to the canoes, so we couldn't put on a pot of coffee. With our backs to the tent, facing the fire, we sat up, watching.

A wolf came crawling toward us in the flickering light, whimpering strangely, edging on its belly toward the fire. We poised, weapons in hand. "Wait for the leap," said Tom, "then duck and slash for the belly." We had two machetes and several crude birch spears that John had carved on the spot. We decided that it was foolish to risk a shot with the .22, which might miss or provoke a serious attack.

The crawling wolf, after getting within 15 feet of the fire, paused for half a minute, then edged back into the shadows. More alarmed than ever, we agreed to take turns standing watch. Two of us stayed awake while the other two tried to sleep. I lay in the tent with my open knife in hand in case I needed to cut my way out the back, or to defend myself against a frontal attack through the door of the tent.

Of course, the attack never came. Our wolves disappeared with the first gray light of dawn. So did we.

Almost forty years later, I know more about wolves and have a better understanding of the behavior we saw that night. They were more likely curious than hungry. Other observers, with cooler heads, have described similar events when wolves approached their campfires. They claim to have enjoyed the encounters without fear, and they would say, rightly, that the most dangerous thing in my story was the falling birch trunk.

But misconceptions, in the mind of the holder, are as real as facts. The important thing to me was the sense of wildness those wolves brought with them, and the feeling they gave me of being close to the natural heart of things. I thought I knew all about it back then. I took traveling in the wilderness to be serious business. I had read Jack London's fabulous stories of woodsmen holding off packs of wolves. Caught on the winter trail, his ammunition long exhausted, the gallant Yukoner would stand in the embers of his fire and shove burning brands down the voracious, snarling throats. Any story worth its salt about Russia and northern Europe would tell in gruesome detail about packs of the gray devils enveloping sledges pulled by desperate but doomed horses. As told by Willa Cather in *My Ántonia*, wolves attack a wedding party returning from the town where festivities were held: "A black drove came up over the hill.... The wolves ran like streaks of shadow...hundreds of them." One by one, six sledges are overwhelmed, buried in a wave of fur and teeth, until only one is left moving across the moonlit snow. It carries the newlyweds and two groomsmen, Peter and Pavel. With their village almost in sight, the wolves closing in, Pavel hurls the groom from the sledge, and his bride after him. In that way, the two men purchase their escape. Ostracized, they emigrate to Nebraska, in flight from the hounding ghosts of conscience.[1]

Now I had seen them myself—the legendary red eyes in my personal firelight. Real after all. Howling in the best subarctic tradition. Not gone in some distant past. Not just legend. It pleased me to no end. The unseen became physical and stared at me across the gulf of unknowing.

Another lesson learned since then: I need not have wondered if the spirit of wildness, embodied by wolves, still existed. Wildness cannot be killed. We can never kill it. As much as humanity thinks it has a tight grip on the lives and events of our little globe—as much as environmentalists fear the final disappearance of wildness under the pressures of population, industrial growth, and climate change—we will never destroy it.

Wildness is everywhere. It is part of us. It is the matrix in which we live, and not the most bravely glittering city lights can keep the wild at bay.

Wildness is frequently likened to a grizzly bear, a powerful force that despite its strength is easily damaged. Grizzlies thrive where people are not, and those places shrink every year. If a road is built through a wilderness valley, so the argument goes, that valley is no longer wild. Something essential and profound goes out of it, like a mist fleeing before the warming sun. That much is true. Roads have devastating impact. The mood of the valley is mortally altered. Wild creatures might disappear. But wildness will not.

That cannot happen in a world where antlions—gram for gram vastly more ferocious than any grizzly—lurk under the eaves of suburban houses; where praying mantises do unholy things in our crabapple trees; where falcons, nesting atop skyscrapers, feed their young on urban pigeons.

I think it is safe to say that most creatures on Earth live their lives without regard for what we see as the clearly defined boundaries of civilization. Cockroaches, which as a species have been around some 250 million years, do not live tame. Do rats or houseflies? Or the spider on the living room ceiling? Lichens grow on marble statues as easily as on granite cliffs. Grass pushes determinedly through the cracks in concrete sidewalks. Over four hundred separate wild plant species thrive in inner-city Cleveland, not one of them the product of agriculture. On the tiniest plots of ground they appear of their own accord, growing wild. I have read that in the narrow column of air above a person's head on a midwestern summer evening, there are five thousand insects floating and flying. We look up at the emerging stars through a blur of unseen wings.

We know of about 1.5 million species on Earth, but a recent estimate puts the number of species living undiscovered at 20 to 30 million. They won't all be found—if they are found at all—under the leaves of unexplored rainforest, nor on some lost continent. Many will be found on us, in us, and around us, by the aid of microscopes and science. A single nondescript clot of debris collected under a living room chair (we call it a "dust bunny," as if we might cuddle it) supports a teeming population of some forty thousand mites. They live by eating dead human skin cells that each of us sloughs by the millions. We have shaky command even over our bodies, where viruses, the likes of hepatitis and HIV, stalk us with the same deadly efficiency as the giant cave bear stalked early hominids. At night, looking outward from Earth as if from our little caves, we confront the wilderness of space, where there might be billions of inhabited worlds.

And we think we are in control. Perhaps early hunters had the same thoughts as they carefully bound river cobbles to the ends of sticks to make clubs.

This was what Loren Eiseley meant when he wrote about hearing, from inside New York skyscrapers, the sound of sparrows tapping on air conditioners, as if testing whether he was still there: "Our time will come," he imagined they were saying. "We are waiting, more patiently than you, and someday, once again, the world will be ours."[2] Eiseley sensed the power of the wild world, still capable of ridding itself of disease. The disease in this case was the self-destructive parasite of human life.

Sigurd Olson, who saw the world in less threatening terms, wrote that when he visited Chicago and felt lonesome for his wilderness home in northern Minnesota, he would enter an empty cathedral and sit quietly. The sense of peace and openness and nearness to spirituality was the same as he could find on a remote woodland lakeshore, where he first learned to hear what he calls in his book of the same title "The Singing Wilderness."[3]

Olson wrote that one legacy of our not-so-distant past, when we lived in closer contact with the natural world, is an unconscious hunger for the music of wild places. "We may not know exactly what it is we are listening for, but we hunt as instinctively for opportunities and places to listen as sick animals look for healing herbs. Even the search is rewarding, for somehow in the process we tap the deep wells of racial experience that gives us a feeling of being part of an existence where life was simple and satisfactions real."

And if we should "actually glimpse the ancient glory or hear the singing wilderness, cities and their confusion become places of quiet, speed and turmoil are slowed to the pace of the seasons, and tensions are replaced with calm."

Olson spent much of his life (he died in 1982) in places where he could hear the singing. He heard it in the howling of wolves, in the embers of his fire, and in the flash of meteors in the night sky. He found it in mountains and forest, rivers and open tundra. But his favorite place of all was Listening Point (also the title of one of his books), the "bare gla-ciated spit of rock" in the lake country of northern Minnesota, where he built a cabin and spent many quiet hours. It was his vantage point, not only on the lake which surrounded it, but on the universe. "From it I have seen the immensity of space and glimpsed at times the gran-deur of creation. There I have sensed the span of uncounted centu-ries and looked down the path all life has come....I believe that what I have known there is one of the oldest satisfactions of man, that when he gazed upon the earth and sky with wonder, when he sensed the first vague glimmerings of meaning in the universe, the world of knowledge and spirit was opened to him."[4]

If I read him correctly, Olson was content with that sense of wonder, the feeling of nearness, the glimpse of something greater. The hunger was a good thing; to satisfy it would result in spiritual death. As far as I am aware, he never spoke of actually entering the world of knowledge and spirit. Or, for that matter, of what might come out from it.

When conditions were right, Olson heard it everywhere—the singing wilderness, the grandeur of creation. Even in cities he heard it. These emotions gave Eiseley the willies; he didn't much like standing on the brink of eternity. He didn't like being reminded of his mortal insignifi-cance. Olson was different. He took comfort from being part of a greater whole, and I like to think that he realized we can't kill it. It's too beautiful. Too big. Too determined, in its ancient knowledge and ultimate power.

I have also heard the singing, and never more strongly than the night wolves swam to my island camp. Since then they have become for me a symbol of the great music. I have often wondered if I went to the right place, the right listening point, and sat very quietly, and waited, what sort of wolves would come swimming in to sit by my fire. Maybe, if I didn't

Lobito. By Jose Solitarios. (CC-BY-SA-4.0)

run around in a panic, pulling trees onto my head, threatening to stuff burning brands down their throats, they would stay awhile and tell me wolfish stories. I'm certain those would be worth hearing.

Every so often I think I can feel them near. Or something like them. It happens without warning. An unseen door opens, the chemistry of the air around me changes, and I sense that this moment, this time in this place, holds tremendous significance. Something big could happen.

When I get this feeling, I react as if I've waked in the middle of the night to a strange footstep in the dark. A presence looms. My heart pounds. Open mouthed, so I can silence my breathing, I wait for whatever comes next. Sometimes I wait a long time. Nothing ever happens; or should I say, nothing ever has? I get cold, or start thinking about supper, and the threshold that seemed so close fades away uncrossed. I don't feel disappointed. Perhaps, as Olson implies, the glimpse is enough.

A trout stream in the Black Earth country of southern Wisconsin comes to mind. My father took me there often, when I was young, on summer evenings, with mayflies emerging into warm, humid air, trout taking them from the surface with lazy slurps, the surrounding corn-fields invisible behind high banks, the water flowing toward me through a tunnel of overhanging brush, the rattling burr of nighthawk wings in the air above, and, half a mile away, the low, labored sound of a tractor working. All the elements were there.

Yet I hardly have time to think about that stream before the memory is overshadowed by other, later recollections, all of them from big tracts of land, remote and gloriously wild. In landscapes like these the spirit of wildness strikes with full poetic force. We see it in a skein of geese flying across a gray arctic flat. An avalanche thunders down a 10,000-foot face in Yukon's St. Elias Range. Green surf pounds yellow desert cliffs on the Baja coast of Mexico. A crystal stream of water flows an inch deep and 10 feet wide through a fern-lined sandstone grotto in the Southwest. Coyotes call in the moonlit chill of a northern Rockies autumn. In Ontario, a loon's laugh echoes across still waters.

In these places, the singing is strongest. The edge between what is and what might be feels sharp and close. There's something out there worth looking for, something more than rocks and trees and wildlife; more than wolves—or whatever they are, behind and beneath the way they choose to be seen.

In Yellowstone National Park, where I lived for a number of years, there is a creek of about the same size as the one in Wisconsin. Nothing I can name sets this one apart; it resembles hundreds of others like it in the northern Rockies. But it ran within walking distance of my house, and I went there frequently with a fly rod. As often as not, the rod would go unused. Fishing was an excuse, not the real reason for being there. The creek was barely 15 feet wide, flowing at the base of a high bluff, through a series of meadows fringed with lodgepole pines. Many of the trees were dead, having been killed years before when a large hot spring changed the direction of its flow and invaded the living woodland. Now the dead trunks stood stripped of needles and branches, a forest of somber fig-ures standing knee-deep in grass and sedge.

It was late October, near the end of the day. I stood in midstream. Cold air, redolent with the pungent smell of the meadow, frosted my nose and stiffened my fingers. Cold water muscled against my rubber-clad legs.

The water moved with strength, but hardly a sound. Purling along the overhung bank, murmuring behind half-submerged tree trunks, it carried insistence and mystery. From a dozen hot springs, steam rose in vigorous columns, merging to form an increasingly dense mist that packed the meadow and gave the stark forest an air of the ethereal.

Dusk settled softly, coldly. In the forest a bull elk bugled. The sound, echoing through the fog, sent a small flock of Canada geese to wing. They took off from somewhere downstream, flew over my head, feathers whistling, and faded into the distance. Later, when I could barely make out the surface of the water, I caught a trout on a weighted bucktail streamer. The fish took it, slow and deliberate, from far under the bank and fought me silently, staying deep, not breaking the surface. Instead of using the reel, I controlled the line with my hand so I could feel the way its body worked when it ran. The fish tired. I brought him beside me. I couldn't see him in the dark. I felt my way down the taut line, into the water to the hook. It was heavy with the weight of the fish, but with a gentle twist the hook came free. I saw him go, a quick silver flash in the darkening water.

Perfect. The door opened. I stopped fishing and stood in the middle of the cold stream, motionless, holding my fly rod in crossed arms, watching the misty banks, waiting for wolves.

NOTES

1.   Willa Cather, *My Ántonia* (Boston: Houghton Mifflin, 1918).
2.   Loren Eiseley, *The Immense Journey: An Imaginative Naturalist Explores the Mysteries of Man and Nature* (New York: Vintage, 1959).
3.   Sigurd F. Olson, *The Singing Wilderness* (New York: Knopf, 1956).
4.   Sigurd F. Olson, *Listening Point* (New York: Knopf, 1958).

Living in a Circle of Heartbeats

Julia Corbett

Julia Corbett explores what it means for humans to be connected to the Others, those beings with whom we share our planet. She wonders if there are ways to "reimagine perceiving and being with animals." An inherent tension exists between the human desire for safety provided by physical and cultural boundaries, and a deeply rooted yearning to be with animals. Given that we share only one world with them, we need a shift in imagination—not only giving animals wild space, but also recognizing they are "as elemental to our being as gravity, as essential to our biosphere as oxygen, as crucial to our hearts as the blood beating in them."

"You've gotta come see this Karen!" I heard in the background. "Oh my god, look at that! Oh god, he's climbing now, oh, he's right on the porch, look, look. This is so amazing. What great pictures . . ."

Karen and Nancy were gushing about the latest photos from their "stealth cam" of a young black bear when I called them to chat about the same bear—not to gush, but to ask them to remove their bird feeders at bear-level: sunflower and thistle seeds, corn, suet. This bear had hit several area cabins and just had a run-in with my dog. I hoped this time they might be persuaded out of concern for their own dogs.

"Just bring the food inside until the bear moves on," I said.

"Well, I don't know," Karen said slowly.

Karen and Nancy's cabin is a half-mile from mine—as the bear walks—in the high elevation woods in western Wyoming. I summer here, far from the heat and pollution of Salt Lake City, where I teach during the school year. And my summers in the woods typify all the singular experiences and joys of watching wildlife; the encounters expand my human world into something much more brilliant and real.

There's good reason why many people want to watch and get close to animals: of all the elements of the beyond-human world—geosphere, hydrosphere, atmosphere, and biosphere—it's the beating hearts in the biosphere to which we connect most deeply. As human ecologist Paul Shepard wrote, "Being human has always meant perceiving ourselves in a circle of animals." From prehistoric times to present ones, adventure among the Others (as he calls them) has remained central to our lives. For reasons historical, spiritual, and biological, we cannot be fully human without them.

Even though animals permeate our lives and culture, they are often inconspicuous in our everyday routines, occupying a physical and mental space that's tucked back from consciousness. When we seek animals out, there's an ironic dance with distance: the closer we try and get, the further and sparser they may seem. So what influences our cultural perceptions of animals, and how do those perceptions influence the consequences of our connections with them? Are there ways to reimagine perceiving and being with animals? Those were questions I entertained during the summer of bears.

The bear first visited on my very first morning at the cabin in May. My golden retriever, Maddie, woke to a sound and planted her paws on the bedroom window sill. I put on my glasses. A young black bear pushed the last of the birdseed into a pile with its paws and lapped it up with a dark tongue. The feeder, hung just eleven hours before, sprawled on the ground.

I was proud of my feeder site: a lone, slender branch on a Douglas fir 12 feet off the ground, stretching almost 4 feet from the trunk. No bear in my decade of bird feeding had reached the feeder (some had tried), but this was "smarter than your average bear," and smaller—I guessed a two-year-old, lightweight enough to shinny out the branch. The bear was also a repeat offender, judging from the blue plastic ear tags. I took some pictures through the window.

In an exercise in my environmental communication class, I ask students to list animals (broadly defined) on two blackboards, one labeled "good" and one "bad." Quickly and with relatively little disagreement, they fill both boards. Then we examine what lies behind our gut reactions; what is it about charismatic megafauna that we like and about insects we don't?

Over twenty different factors influence whether we like or dislike certain animal species, such as size (we prefer large over small), intelligence, mode of locomotion (we like animals that walk instead of slither), and evolutionary closeness to humans (we like chimps). We prefer zoomorphism (animals that bond to humans), animals with individual personalities, and animals with relationships to human society (such as pets, farm animals, game, and exotic animals). We like animals with similar social habits, such as parenting, pack loyalty, and helping each other. We're less magnanimous toward animals capable of harming us or our possessions, like crops or gardens. The students put black bear on the "good" board and grizzly bear on the "bad."

A mother black bear poking her nose through our station wagon's triangular vent window on a family vacation was my first encounter with a bear. Her cubs stood well behind her, watching. It was thrilling, and a little scary, but mostly thrilling. At Yellowstone National Park in those days, black bears were park panhandlers, looking for picnic baskets, like Yogi Bear and Boo-Boo. To me, that mama bear was feeding her cubs, a good animal. She stood upright on the soles of her back feet and used her front paws to take the marshmallows and bread slices offered through car windows (though our parents didn't allow us to).

Whether bears or birds or bees, animals are a key metaphorical device we use to express core feelings and perceptions about the nonhuman world. If an environmental group wants to "save" a forest from some threat, they focus on an animal who's an iconic symbol of that place. Sentient beings with beating hearts are symbolic barometers of our fundamental beliefs and valuations of nature—in ways that trees or rocks or rivers are not.

Maddie and I watched the bear leave the grounded feeder and walk toward the bedroom window. When it saw us, it stood and stared at us and sniffed the air. Maddie gave a soft, low growl. I banged on the window and yelled, "Go on! Get outta here!" The bear resumed walking and proceeded to circle the cabin, finishing at the bird feeder with a few more mouthfuls. Then the bear walked over to my car and put its front paws on the passenger door and sniffed. It then galumphed past the shed and disappeared over the rise. I made coffee and called my closest neighbors to be on the lookout.

Professor Stephen Kellert at Yale University famously described nine different attitude orientations toward animals from a sample of three thousand people in the US.[1] Roughly a third of the respondents were strongly Humanist (interest and strong affection, particularly for individual animals) and another third had Negativist-neutralist attitudes (an active or passive avoidance due to indifference, dislike, or fear). One-fifth of people were strongly Utilitarian (concern for practical and material value of animals) and another fifth were Moralist (concern for right and wrong treatment). The least common attitude orientations were Aesthetic, Naturalist, Ecologist, Scientist, and Dominionist.

In Kellert's study, some individuals were strongly disposed to more than one orientation, which is true for several friends of mine. Camille is a Humanist in her love of individual animals (including pets) and also a Moralist in her concern for animal treatment. Pete is a hunter and thus strongly Utilitarian, but he's also a Naturalist, with his love and knowledge of wildlife and the outdoors. Susan is a painter and thus interested in the artistic and symbolic characteristics of animals (an Aesthetic), and also an Ecologist, concerned for the interrelationships between animals and habitats. Why are such attitudes important? These feelings guide our everyday portrayals and communication about animals, and the destiny of many particular species depends on people's subjective feelings about them, whether mountain goats or monkeys.

A simple model for understanding attitudes toward animals compares two dimensions: affect and utility. The affect scale ranges from love, sympathy, and identification with animals at one end, to fear, loathing, and lack of identification at the opposite end. The utility scale ranges from very beneficial to human interests to very detrimental; that's very anthropocentric, but it's how many people view both wildlife and the whole natural environment. If you overlap the two scales in a cross, it creates four quadrants.

I tested this model for bears and a much smaller animal I found in my car's glove-box, a deer mouse who looked up with dark eyes and wiggling whiskers from a round, multicolored nest made from the upholstery stuffing beneath the car seats. So that explained the bear's interest in my car. When mice first discovered the glove-box several years ago—to which I was alerted when a bear and her three cubs all put their paws on my car—I pestered the Toyota dealer until they devised a wire mesh to attach behind the cabin air filter, their entry point to the glove-box and the car. It did the trick, until the mice chewed clean through the metal mesh. I cleaned out the new nest and set a mousetrap with peanut butter.

On the affect and utility index, how would I score bears and mice? I like both and have sympathy for both, though I identify less with mice than bears. The utility scale is harder; both species crossed my path, not by happenstance but because of what my presence offered them. It was beneficial to my human interest to see them both intimately; animals that don't typically cross one's path. Losing the bird-feeder contents was not that detrimental, and I feel solely responsible. The presence of mice is more damaging; I don't miss the upholstery stuffing but the smell of mouse urine and feces is foul and worse when I use the vent fan. And, I hate checking the trap each morning, hoping not to find a silent silky body pinned there. But I grant the bear a good utility score for alerting me to the mice and not ripping off my car doors to find them.

Five days later, Maddie and I awoke to clanking on the porch. The same blue-tagged bear pawed at the fresh moose antler on top of the grill. On a walk the day before, Maddie had raced past me, clutching the heavy antler prize tightly in her jaw for the half mile back to the cabin. When she let me hold it—a good-sized, palmated paddle—I discovered how she discovered it: it reeked, probably from some critter's scent marking. So I parked the paddle on the grill, intending to wash it the next day. Guess the bear thought it reeked, too. I banged on the glass, and the bear startled and ran to the dead-end portion of the porch, high off the ground. It sat cowered in the corner, head tucked in, looking scared and staring right at me. Poor thing. I waited until the bear rose to all fours, then I banged again and it galloped off the porch and down the meadow.

Black bears have come to cabins since people have built cabins, attracted by all manner of smells, provisions, and plantings. I admire how bears emerge from their dens and let their appetites walk them through the seasons, first dining on winter-killed carrion, new grass, and aspen catkins.

Next come grubs, rodents, dandelions and stream-side frogs, snails, and fish. By late summer, berries are dessert. I once watched a black bear for an hour as it dexterously ripped apart a large decaying pine log and delicately lapped up all the beetles, grubs, and ants inside. Black bears, like many species (including us), are opportunists with an adaptable omnivorous diet. Their foraging patterns easily divert for "anthropogenic attractants," such as bird seed.

The attributes of a species—like the food-driven curiosity of black bears—are just part of what influences our attitudes toward them. The attributes of the human observer (such as education level, sex, income, residence, and experience with animals) also play a part. Women have stronger affective perceptions than men, as do urban dwellers versus rural ones. Children who have relationships with animals focus less on utilitarian aspects and have more positive emotions about animals. For kids and adults, direct, participatory contact with animals, such as bird watching or hunting, is tied to greater appreciation, concern, and knowledge. Levels of education and wealth are harder to generalize in terms of animal attitudes. In some studies, growing up in a rural or urban area was more predictive of attitudes than education or income.

It's just as hard to generalize what people know about animals, except to say, it isn't much. Overall, we know most about pets, animals that harm people, and wildlife involved in emotional public issues (think wolves and grizzlies). The people least knowledgeable about animals live in cities of more than a million residents. Knowledge of wild animals in the US is pretty abstract and indirect, informed more by mass-mediated images and pop culture than by personal experience. For many, the generic "bear" or "trout" is the level of recognition; a specific species reference, "black bear" or "cutthroat trout," suggests greater cultural importance.

So where do our cultural cues and animal facts come from? Folklorists Gillespie and Mechling identified seven sources that inform public beliefs about wild animals: conversational genres, oral narratives, children's literature, popular and commercial culture, public performances, elite culture, and scientific discourse.[2]

Pop culture and entertainment affect perceptions enormously, from Animal Planet to PBS. On a class field trip to the zoo, where my students listen to how people talk about the animals, we hear kids reference animals according to which Disney movie they appeared in. A mom told her toddler who got excited by the "big kitty" cougar that "no, that's a bad kitty." (Studies find that most people learn virtually nothing about animals at the zoo.) We are surrounded by animals in advertising, as sports mascots, as home decor and on clothing and jewelry, in news stories, YouTube videos, and digital photos shared on Facebook and email.

Powerful pop culture portrayals rely on a stereotyped and topical shorthand to represent a particular animal—sharks are manic killers, swans are regal, ladybugs are cute—which conveys every fear, admiration, envy, and longing we possess. Animals in advertisements "work" because in just seconds, shared meanings (even ignorant ones) of jaguars or pandas are exaggerated and exploited to sell you products. It's difficult (perhaps impossible) to parse the human-generated symbol of a particular animal from the living and breathing animal symbolized. As Adrian Franklin said, "When we gaze at animals, we hold a mirror up to ourselves."[3]

We don't think twice about stereotyping an entire animal species, yet work to avoid stereotypes within the human species—Mexicans, gays, the homeless. Any stereotype makes it easier to marginalize, hate, and fear a large group and see it as a threat to the established order. We stereotype that cougars or bears are a certain way, largely because it's unlikely that we can differentiate individuals and their behavior. Thus, when one cougar attacks a pet or a jogger, fear and loathing applies to the entire species.

Conversations and stories shape our beliefs of what animals are like. In our speech, animals are verbs and nouns representing countless human conditions. As Shepard notes, "We duck our heads, crane our necks, clam up, crab at one another, carp, rat, crow, or grouse vocally. We…lionize and fawn.… We fish for compliments, hog what should be shared, wolf it down, skunk others in total defeat, and hawk our wares. We outfox and buffalo those whom we dupe; we bug and badger in harassment. We hound or dog in pursuit, bear our burdens, lark and horse around in frolic. We bull, ram, or worm our way, monkey with things, weasel, and chicken out. We know loan sharks, possum players, and bull-shitters."

And we see ourselves in animals' experiences. My friend Flo came to my cabin one Sunday to watch a nest of woodpeckers from my deck. The red-naped sapsucker parents arrived with food in quick intervals, prompted by the continuous hunger-begging peeps of the chicks. Between feedings, the growing chicks poked their heads out the hole, surveying sky and earth. Suddenly, one chick clambered out and walked up the trunk, swiveling its neck to see the world and testing its beak on the aspen

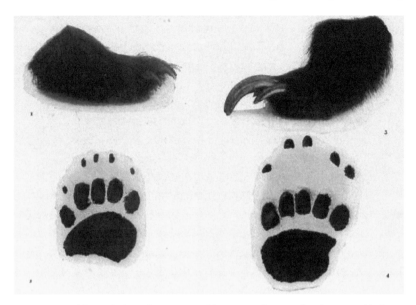

Bear Prints and Paws. Artist unknown, 1909. The paws and prints of an American black bear (*Ursus americanus*), native to North America, and a brown bear (*Ursus arctos*), often called a grizzly bear. From William H. Wright, *The Grizzly Bear* (1909).

trunk. In a couple minutes it flew away, perfectly, on untested wings and landed in a fir downslope. Shortly, the second chick repeated the fledge. One parent returned and searched for the chicks, poking her head in the hole, walking around the trunk and back to the hole where she clung for several more minutes. Wow, we thought, empty nest syndrome! Flo, whose adult daughter had flown back east that morning, said, "I know how the adult sapsuckers feel. No matter how old they are, I always hate to see my kids leave."

Some argue that our attitudes toward animals are not merely the result of digital images, plush toys, and beer commercials but of ancient influences. Biologist E. O. Wilson claims that our evolutionary heritage gives us biophilia as well as evolution-derived fears and prejudices toward certain animals. Shepard argues that our very brains and bodies evolved through participation in the animal world as both prey and predator, thus animals are justifiably at the heart of human symbolism. The "reciprocal mental evolution" of humans and animals made each grow and evolve. The gift of the mind enabled early hunters and gatherers to identify aspects of themselves in many species. For many Paleolithic peoples, it was the bear who became a model of ourselves.

Three ponderous, moist piles of bear poop lay in the middle of the game trail. Maddie and I had walked down the meadow below the cabin for a hike one sunny afternoon in late July. The blue-tagged bear hadn't returned in almost three weeks, but Maddie lost her bear-bell in the brush the week before, and a grizzly was reported recently near the highway about seven miles away. We returned to the cabin for my bear spray.

The phone rang; it was my friend Sara. Outside, Maddie barked excitedly. Since she is not a barker, I figured it was someone coming up the driveway, but all I saw was Maddie trotting up the drive, looking behind her. Sara and I kept talking. Maddie's paws scratched at the front door, also not typical. I went to let her in but she wasn't there. I returned to the back door. At the far side of the driveway, a bear stood with its front paws on a tree trunk, but no Maddie. "I gotta go, there's a bear!" and I threw the phone down. When I opened the back door, I saw Maddie by the woodpile, 10 yards from the bear. I called her and she came flying up the stoop, glancing back. The blue-tagged bear ambled past the woodpile, past the fir that once held the feeder and toward the stoop. When one paw thumped on the bottom step, I slammed the door several times, yelled, and pounded the glass. I couldn't read the bear's expression, but there was no fear or aggression. It padded down the steps and strolled over the ridge. I don't know if the bear chased (or frightened) Maddie or if Maddie chased (or was ready to chase) the bear. My heart pounded. In the intensity of the moment, it didn't occur to me to use the bear spray.

When I called him, Zach from Game & Fish asked if I knew the number on the bear's blue tag. I enlarged some photos and found it. Now I could call it a "she." She was a two-year-old female who was trapped as a one-year-old last summer after causing problems several miles west at my friend Phyllis's cabin. The bear was transported and released in the Upper Green River Valley—a couple of hours away as the human drives, or thirty miles of mountainous terrain as the bear walks. Phyllis fed all sorts of critters for many years, winter and summer, and no one could convince her not to. Phyllis died in March and left her property and cabin to animal welfare groups. And now her bear was visiting me.

When I learned the bear's story, I felt differently about her, this young girl bear I decided to call "Phyllis." In her short life, Phyllis had learned that cabins are sources of food, that people mostly stay inside those cabins and don't hurt you. Many one-year-olds den with their mothers a second year, but Phyllis hibernated and survived on her own in the wild Upper Green. Amazing. No wonder she trekked back to familiar ground. Zach said the sooner a cabin-visiting bear is relocated, the better chance it has of "reforming." It wasn't good news that Phyllis was back.

When I called Game & Fish, Phyllis became newsworthy. Until then, Phyllis was doing what she did every day of her normal bear life—sleeping, roaming, eating, pooping—no "news." Instead, wildlife make the news when a human is making claims about them, or when boundaries—symbolic or real—between humans and animals are blurred or are breached. Moose visits strip mall, insects visit crops, duck nests downtown, bird collides with plane, black bear has run-in with a golden retriever. That's an important thing to remember about the quality of "news," but also about the long, languid stretch of "normal" in the everyday lives of animals.

Government wildlife officials, like Zach, are the most predominant "voice" for animals when those animals make the news. Years ago, I analyzed news coverage of wildlife in four urban and four rural Midwest newspapers. About 60 percent of all quoted news sources were government employees, and 80 percent of all stories were about game animals. This reflects the dominance of game animals in wildlife management, the role of state wildlife departments, and the big animals we simply prefer; it also parallels where wildlife management dollars are spent. Only 13 percent of the news stories concerned threatened or endangered animals. Almost a quarter of all environmental news is about wildlife.

The dominant themes differed in urban and rural wildlife stories. Urban newspaper stories focused on animal "stewardship," which makes sense in cities where people see wildlife infrequently or as a deliberate by-product of outdoor activities, and when their contact often lacks utilitarian value and a connection to livelihood. The predominant story theme in rural newspapers was "utilitarian," which makes sense in a place where residents live physically closer to wildlife, directly contact and interact with them, and where many jobs depend on "natural resources." Rural Americans greatly value animals (wild and domestic) for what they provide, and dislike them for what they take or harm.

The day after Maddie's encounter, Zach towed a bear trap up the driveway. While we talked, Maddie nosed cautiously toward the round metal tube, then sprang back with fright, which she repeated several times. "She smells 'em," Zach said. He positioned the trap halfway down the long drive, near a big woodpile, out of view of the cabin. He baited it with two pieces of fresh trout and grain pellets, and mounded fresh dirt below the opening to catch paw prints.

The trap stayed for four days, but the only creature caught was a golden retriever who couldn't resist the fish. Zach replaced the fish and reset the door. When Zach came to remove the trap, there once again was no fish, but no paw prints in the dirt either. "Probably ravens," he said. Clever ravens. The day after he pulled the trap, Phyllis appeared on Bill and Jane's porch, my nearest neighbor a half mile south. Jane was upset she didn't get pictures.

The choices for solving human-bear conflicts, a common wildlife management problem, are: try and change the bear's behavior (trap and relocate), kill the bear, or change the humans' behavior. Changing the bear sounds good, but even early intervention in Phyllis's case did not work (and she likely is now trap wary). And I've learned that changing the humans is even more problematic. Karen and Nancy won't alter their big array of bird-feeding stations, nor will a dozen other neighbors. Two neighbors feed their cats outside. Zach once spoke to our homeowners' meeting and posted roadway signs about removing food sources when bears are present, but little changed.

My neighbors' sentiments about bears matched those reported in some bear-human management studies I read. Most people like black bears, enjoy seeing them, and appreciate their place in the ecosystem. People perceive them as "highly intelligent and aesthetically appealing." But sentiments are mixed about the threat bears pose and what "management actions" are appropriate. One neighbor (who cooked her bacon outside and didn't secure her garbage) was ready to shoot any bear on sight. Some neighbors warned me not to call Game & Fish for fear the bear would just be shot. And a great many continued to refill bird feeders, either unaware of the phrase "a fed bear is a dead bear" or oblivious of their connection to it.

When animals, like black bears, foxes, coyotes, deer and others, cross precarious human boundaries (invisible to their eyes), they are perceived as elusive wild creatures or destructive intruders. But a bear's "trespass" is partly mitigated by our ecological concern for their continued survival, and by their pervasive cultural presence: bears appear in comic strips and cartoons, survival stories, urban legends, TV commercials, and cabin decor.

At my Summer Solstice party several days after the bear trap rolled away, Jennifer brought me a straw ornament of a bear as a hostess gift. I hung it near the kitchen sink.

The decor of most Wyoming cabins includes multiple representations of "woodsy" animals: bears on kitchen towels, antler coat racks, moose light-switch plates, couch throws with trout, bear toothbrush holders, elk fridge magnets, antelope coffee mugs, owl clocks, and artwork and photographs with these animals. Cabin clothing and jewelry also are animal adorned.

These tchotchkes often repel me—the Disneyfication of a woods full of far more than charismatic megafauna and game animals. How tawdry using animals to hock consumer goods whose very production shrinks habitat and pollutes and warms our world. Why depict cartoonish moose standing on two legs? What's with pillows in animal shapes? And a dopey bear to hold the toilet paper—really? Stores in every touristy town sell these things.

Yet, I haul home moose paddles, elk antlers, jawbones, and feathers of every description. Egg shells, fossils, and assorted teeth line my bookshelves. It's the naturalist in me, my attempt to touch corporeal remnants of the Others and feel I know them. In a way, they are as much collective markers of a specific place, a habitat, as the manufactured wildlife knickknacks, a way to feel we possess these woods and the Others who live in them more fully. Both types of fetishes may give us an exaggerated (even false) sense of intimacy, that we somehow "know" bears or owls or moose. It speaks to the hunger we have for animals, the desire to have them near, whether actual fragments or stylized and "humanized" versions of them.

By contrast, we modern humans are so adrift in our standardized spaces, living in cities and towns that are almost interchangeable and not solidly oriented to landscape or native creatures. While driving across Idaho recently, I exited to get gas and lunch, and for a moment I had no idea where I was because all that I saw—storefronts, billboards, parking lots—were things I saw everywhere, anywhere. Thus, we envy animals' complete possession of their place, their ease and confidence of movement and deep knowledge of it. The Others live lives congruent with and rooted in their surroundings, with skills and abilities perfectly honed to it.

Many of us spend our lifetimes trying to get close to animals, in hopes that our meetings will magically bridge the chasm between their world and ours—as if these are somehow two separate places and not one in the same.

As June blossomed and deepened, I missed the birds. I caught glimpses in the aspens or heard them sing in the morning, but without the feeder I rarely saw some species. Then I spied in a closet a small plexiglass feeder with suction cups to hang on a window (a gift I never used). Ah-ha: I could attach it to the office window that was 12 feet off the ground and above the cement walk-out basement; there was nothing for a bear to hold on to and climb.

I filled it with sunflower seeds and immediately the evening grosbeaks materialized, as did the Cassin's finches, black-headed grosbeaks, pine grosbeaks, and pine siskins. And what a view I had from my desk in front of the window, no binoculars necessary! Their slender talons clutched the rim, their beaks frenetically opened the shells, their heads cocked when I spoke to them. I witnessed pecking order; the female evening grosbeak ruled the plexiglass roost, and the tiny nuthatches waited. I was a voyeur with a box seat on the bird world; I just had to move slowly or they scattered.

There is magic in the wild and close encounter that's hard to name or replicate. The best nature documentary is incomparable to seeing cow elk dance in my meadow, or startling a sandhill crane when I hike. It's like the difference between seeing a mountain peak in a postcard versus hiking there yourself; with all the exertion, anticipation, and engaged senses, you see and feel the mountain in full color and context. With animals, it's powerful, intoxicating even, to be in their presence, to know you're sharing the air, the light, the moment. The magic is also the serendipity and uncertainty of the encounter, and even the possibility of danger. The Others define and create the moment as much as I.

At a recent writing conference at a church camp in Oregon, the first time I saw a deer grazing outside my yurt, I wanted to grab my camera. But when I realized that the plentiful deer didn't so much as look up when you spoke or approached, I lost interest. They were not confined, but they weren't the "wild" Other—they didn't count.

Like most photographers, I often snap wildlife photos when the animal looks at me. It's seductive to think they returned my gaze, that we shared a moment of mutual recognition and they saw me like I saw them. However, when the ungulates grazing my meadow early and late look up at me on the cabin deck, it's to judge my threat; it's a look of alert caution, nothing more. Their interest is eating (like the bear's) and I am judged as impeding that or not. They may recognize me as a human animal, but that's a species that mostly means danger to them. If I want to watch them, I must keep my distance.

One sure sign of spring for me is not just the smell of warm wind, gathering light, and robins sparring in the backyard—it's when the nest cams go live. For years, I placed the peregrine falcon web cam in Rochester, New York, in the background on my laptop. The falcon vocalizations alert me to activity: male bringing food to the female, the pair trading incubation duty, a fresh piece of pigeon arriving for the nestlings. I also tune in to several bald eagle nest cams along the California coast.

A new one-stop web cam site is Pearls of the Planet, the media division of the Annenberg Foundation, with wildlife cams around the world: puffins, osprey, snowy owls, penguins, pandas, and my favorite, the fishing brown bears of Katmai National Park. The site's founder told the Associated Press, "What we are doing is building out the zoos of the future, where animals run wild and people from everywhere can feel connected to the experience."[4]

The animals are wild and the video feed unedited, which gives the viewer critter-life in real time, with long expanses of normal quietude in their everyday lives. Hanging out. Sleeping. Flicking away flies. Looking around. Grooming. More sleeping. Even for fishing bears, there's lots of standing around in the water, watching, waiting, interspersed with occasional tiffs over riverbed turf. After enough cam viewing, a viewer learns what's involved in feeding chicks, catching rodents, and fishing for salmon.

In our culture today, virtual electronic encounters are touted as making us more connected, as bringing us together and shrinking the world. Yet I question whether I'm "connected" to the experience of fishing bears beyond the camera and internet connection. The cams do allow me to enter their watery restaurant as a silent voyeur half a world away. But there's no investment on my part, no consequences. I didn't journey across time zones, I'm not sitting on the bank in the constant buzz of mosquitos, I can't smell the rotting fish, and I'm in no danger from these talented carnivores. Do I have a stake in any outcome—theirs or mine? I'm entertained, I'm in awe, but am I "connected"?

Compared to watching bears fish at the Anan Creek Preserve near Wrangell, Alaska—no. I took my dad on a small-boat cruise of the Inside Passage, and Anan was an optional day trip. We were instructed to leave anything that even smelled edible (gum, suntan lotion, soda) on the boat. We marched single file behind a burly woman with a rifle—no stopping!—along a wooden boardwalk to an enclosure of sorts. A series of wooden decks with railings overlooked a stretch of Anan Creek where an ensemble of black bears and brown bears fished for migrating salmon. No loud talking, no camera flashes. Sign up for fifteen minutes down in the blind at the river's edge. If you need to pee, a guard with a rifle will escort you to a porta-potty; open the door and wave when you want to be escorted back.

For four hours, we were bewitched by bears. Bears staked out fishing holes—black bears upstream, brown bears down. Cubs cavorted and climbed trees and napped in them. The smell of broken salmon wafted up to us, along with the rush of rapids where the bears fished. Above the rapids in a stretch of calm, shallow water, exhausted salmon who had run the gauntlet prepared to spawn. We identified bears with great fishing skills and those who missed a lot. Some bears walked their fish up the bank to eat the guts and brains, abandoning the rest for the long line of scavengers. Some bears ate their catch on a rock in the river before turning back for more. When a bear ambled by close (the guards on alert), I saw duff in its fur, smelled its dusky body. Though we were just yards from them, we felt invisible—that's how focused they were on the feast.

Compared with my complete sensorial engagement at that creek, the web-cam fishing bears are dull and flat like the screen. But I realize my Anan experience was one that a privileged few ever experience. I also realize that our presence likely changed the scene itself in some way.

I remember when radio telemetry "revolutionized" wildlife biology, allowing biologists to attach small pieces of electronic equipment to a captured animal to track its location once released. Oh, the reams of data collected: cougars roaming great distances and birds migrating vast oceans. Biologists said it minimized animal disturbance and slashed hours in the field. Then came web cams, which ramped up the viewing several notches. Then came the drones.

One May, some tourists buzzed a herd of bighorn sheep in Zion National Park with a drone, causing young sheep to become separated from the herd. The park ranger said they encountered people using drones in the park several times a week to get close to wildlife. Other national parks reported visitors disturbing nesting birds with drones. In June, the National Park Service (NPS) announced it was prohibiting drones in all national parks because the devices annoy visitors, harass wildlife, and threaten safety. Former NPS Director Jonathan Jarvis said they would educate visitors about how drones disturb wildlife. (Just like managers educate cabin owners about bears? I wondered.)

Wildlife biologists say that drones are once again revolutionizing their work. I trust that biologists are more sensitive about disturbing animals with "conservation drones." But is that even possible? To a wild creature, drones in anyone's hands are paparazzi, an alarming buzz of unwelcome and unsolicited attention. It reduces the vital private space animals need to thrive, and reduces the space doubly with the noise they bring. Like electronic dogs hounding a fox.

Biologists might argue they "need" drones to learn and understand animals in order to better protect and manage them. It's a typical anthropocentric perspective: animals need us and our knowledge, and any drone disturbance is therefore justified in the name of the larger animal (if not public) good.

Animals need quiet privacy and deep retreat; they know this and they seek it. And if we recognized that we are one among them (not the other way around), we would know that we need quiet privacy and deep retreat, too. But our "modern" society is hell-bent in the other direction, ever more oblivious to privacy: we give it away on Facebook, through "cookies," the Google Earth camera that snaps close-ups of our homes, and drones invading our private airspace. People "retreat" into earbuds and constant e-connections, which is not retreat, deep or otherwise.

The wrong question is "How close can or should we *get?*" to animals through any means, drones or otherwise. The deeper question is "How close can we *be?*" in a way that is irrespective of distance. We live in a circle of animals, one community of countless beating hearts, whose fates are far more intertwined and synchronous than we can fathom.

Though I didn't see Phyllis again that summer, I have no doubt that she (and other bears) traipsed across the area all summer. I was content with bear signs to know they were near: poop in the woods, a paw print in mud outside the basement door, another print in the road. By August, a bear or two smashed through the raspberry bushes a mile up the road, depositing crimson piles of evidence nearby.

When neighbors came together, we told stories of bears, stories that reminded us that the Others were fully present and proximal in our lives. Gail's bear tore down a bird feeder. Anne's dog, Gus, chased off a cub on their deck one morning. Tom got pictures of a bear on his cell phone, though he wasn't sure whether it was "my bear." Karen and Nancy got pictures of a bear visiting their porch on their stealth cam eight times. Only after the last visit, when their dogs cornered the bear and a shotgun blast in the air was necessary to end the confrontation, did they bring all their bird food inside.

But I also was uncomfortable with our stories because the bears remained objects of our human gaze, a bit like circus bears who came to our cabins to perform for us, but sometimes crossed the line from desirable to unwanted, from close to too close, from rewarding to costly. We were turning them into panhandlers, threatening the very creatures we so enjoyed.

Humans seem to feel safest with boundaries: inside/outside, private/ public, wild/tame, nature/culture. Yet any such division demarcates two separate worlds—when there is only one world available. And we long to be in that same world with the Others, a longing that is a deep-rooted piece of who we are, as imbued in our language and dwellings as in our hearts.

Recently, a friend and I spoke about diminishing wildlife. She asked, "Well, what can we do without changing our lives?" First, I said, we change our minds. Bears, deer, moose, birds—all are autonomous subjects in charge of their own destinies, not objects of human control. They don't need us; if anything, they need far less of us. The Others will continue living their animal lives as long as they have the space and provisions to do so, space and provisions that are rapidly disappearing.

What we need is a cosmology that is able to see ourselves as just one species among Others in a global circle of circulating hearts. A cosmology that holds as its general universal law that the Others are as elemental to our being as gravity, as essential to our biosphere as oxygen, as crucial to our hearts as the blood beating in them. That's how big a shift we need—a shift more crucial each day we change the biggest general law of all, the climate.

In his book *The Others,* Paul Shepard composed a letter of reply from the animals to the humans, which concluded: "We are marginalized, trivialized. We have sunk to being objects, commodities, possessions. We remain meat and hides, but only as a due and not as sacred gifts. They have forgotten how to learn the future from us....Their own numbers leave little room for us, and in this is their great misunderstanding. They are wrong about our departure, thinking it to be part of their progress instead of their emptying. When we have gone they will not know who they are. Supposing themselves to be the purpose of it all, purpose will elude them."[5]

One late summer evening after a sudden heavy cloudburst, a black bear lumbered up the steep meadow. The storm had sent me inside to cook veggie burgers, and when the pan got too hot and smoked, I opened a window. The bear was large and rotund, far larger than Phyllis and without ear tags. It rounded the big Doug fir 20 yards below the kitchen door and then stood, sniffing the air, its massive paws and pencil-thick claws resting on its belly below its beating heart. It fell to all fours and took a dozen more paces up the meadow, stood again, and sniffed again. I stood in the kitchen grinning, my hands clutching a dish towel. The bear turned and in a few large strides, cleared the ridge and disappeared. Thump, thump, thump went my heart.

NOTES

1.   Stephen R. Kellert, "Contemporary Values of Wildlife in American Society," in *Wildlife Values*, eds. W.W. Shaw and E.H. Zube (Center for Assessment of Non-Commodity Natural Resource Values,

Institutional Series Report Number 1. U.S.D.A., Rocky Mountain Forest and Range Experiment Station, Fort Collins, CO, 1980b), 31–60.

2. Angus K. Gillespie and Jay Mechling, eds., *American Wildlife in Symbol and Story* (Knoxville: U of Tennessee P, 1987), 8.

3. Adrian Franklin, *Animals and Modern Cultures: A Sociology of
Human-Animal Relations in Modernity* (London: Sage, 1999), 62.

4. Charles Annenberg Weingarten, "Live Camera Shows Arctic Snowy
Owl, Chicks in Nest," The Associated Press, July 03, 2014, http://www
.cbc.ca/amp/1.2695115.

5. Paul Shepherd, *The Others: How Animals Made Us Human* (Washington D.C.: Island Press, 1997), 333.

Field Notes from Twenty Years of Living into a Story of Grizzly Reconnection

Steve Primm

We believe in science. A wide range of public policy decisions are based largely on scientific data, and we look to science to be the wise arbiter when opinions clash. Steve Primm's decades of experience in large carnivore conservation have convinced him that science alone cannot provide our justification for sharing large swaths of the western United States with grizzly bears; reason falters when we are asked to live among fierce, predatory giants like grizzlies. Primm asks us to examine our authentic motives for choosing grizzlies, motives which are, he suggests, emotional; we desire connection with creatures unlike ourselves and to experience "surprise, wonder, and an autonomous wild world; away from control, predictability, sameness, and scripted-ness."

THE BEGINNING:
MAPS, AND ALL THAT THEY PRESUME AND SIMPLIFY

The Continental Divide draws southwest Montana's shape, winding along high ridges and dipping down to gentle passes. From Lionhead to the Centennials to the Italian Peaks, back up along the Beaverheads, to Lost Trail Pass: this is the only place where state lines follow John Wesley Powell's idea of laying out jurisdictions along watershed boundaries. (In my Montana-centric worldview, I mostly fail to see that it also draws Idaho.)

It was in the early 1990s when I first started seeing the maps. With a science-y sort of gravity, the primitive computers of the day showed us stippled "linkage zones" for grizzlies and other wildlife along those ridge tops.

The thinking was that isolated grizzly populations—notably Yellowstone's—were doomed, stranded in an impassable sea of human activity. With no grizzlies from outside populations arriving to mix up the gene pool, the world's most studied, most famous grizzly bears would decline ignominiously as inbreeding turned them into vitiated freaks.

So, the thinking went, grizzlies need long, thin wilderness areas so they can reconnect.

The academic talk burbled along: Were these "corridors"? Were they good or bad? Would bears use them? Would it be better to have a single mega-reserve or—following the notion of not putting all one's eggs in one basket—several little ones? Were wolves more important than bears? Journal articles blizzarded about the topics. Rival science gangs postured and posed at conferences, Montagues and Capulets in sensible shoes.

The debates grew tedious, especially once I began to doubt that anyone had any kind of plan for making this reconnection so. Someone needed to go out to these places and see what they looked like, for real.

Still, the going out and looking part was about science: "ground truthing," so we knew our GIS models were accurate. Automated cameras, "hair snares" (to gather follicles for DNA studies), and line transects to document which species were where. The maps, meanwhile, grew prettier and more accurate. One could "fly" through mountain passes and down valleys using Google Earth.

Clearly, all of this studying and fact finding was a necessary step—there's no point in talking about grizzlies in places they will never be. But like unfamiliar terrain gradually revealing itself at dawn, I started seeing that there was a lot of ground to be covered, and that science wasn't the vehicle for it.

There is still a notion that somehow reality really does correspond to the departmental divisions of a university. In the realm of wildlife conservation, things seem to go even further, envisioning the world as an assembly line: Biologists take on the main tasks, figuring out what's important and what needs to be done. Then, the issue moves along the conveyor to economists, sociologists, and other "soft science" folks to do their bit—namely answering some ancillary questions about how much people would pay to see a grizzly, or how they feel about having mountain lions in their neighborhood. (Maybe, just to unwind in the evening, a serious person might curl up with some poetry or art, but only as a diversion. To take it seriously might threaten one's objectivity.)

It became increasingly clear that the world was a glorious mess that wouldn't sit still long enough for any one academic discipline to nail it down, let alone conduct controlled experiments on it. The best we could hope for would be little fragments of hard-won knowledge about tiny subsets of this roiling cacophony.

Still, I clung to the idea that my marching orders ultimately came from science. I resisted any suggestion that wanting grizzly bear populations reconnected was in some way "an aesthetic preference" or romantic or emotional. I scoffed at these critiques, haughtily declaring that the critics didn't understand population viability or conservation biology. My armor was heavy and cumbersome, and I had a creeping sensation that it wasn't really going to protect me.

Because I wanted to be rational and reasonable and professional, I cringed at heartfelt accounts of grizzlies, of connection, of how grizzlies made one feel. I fretted that "our side" would be too easy to dismiss, too easy to lampoon, too vulnerable. I distanced myself from poets and mystics, because I wanted to be taken seriously.

The cracks first appeared when people I regarded as cranks started suggesting that we just truck grizzlies from one wildland complex to another to negate the need for corridors. "Ha!" we all thought. "They just don't understand the science, or maybe they just don't like grizzlies. Or both." I labored mightily to develop a working understanding of terms like "demographic stochasticity" to counteract such foolishness.

But really, the cranks had a point. If we were just looking to maintain a certain number of grizzlies and guard them against the perils of inbreeding, and we don't care how it gets done, we could reach our goal by shuffling bears around in trucks.

Not caring how we reach our goals is how we end up getting bacon from pigs that never set foot on soil and almost never see the sun. Caring about the means puts the poet, the oracle, back in the circle to guide our deliberations. Caring about how we sustain our grizzlies—rather than just having some number of them—sets us in a broader conversation about how we aspire to live in this place, as stewards, as neighbors. This notion had grown alien to me early in my endeavors. The sway of science, as well as my origins in the mostly cultivated Midwest, made these questions unfamiliar to me.

Where I live and work, there were very few grizzlies twenty years ago. Since then, grizzlies have steadily filled the void. First came younger males, curious, hungry, and trying to stay out of the path of older bears. Then, as Greater Yellowstone's grizzly population steadily grew through the 1990s, mother grizzlies and their cubs roamed out to our big valleys. Government biologists gradually stopped saying that the local grizzlies were "transient," and started calling them residents.

In the frantic fall of 2001, big and little grizzly tracks crossed our trail in a lonely canyon high in the Gravelly Range. I was riding with the Forest Service, checking hunting camps and visiting with folks about what they were seeing. In the gloaming that November evening, those fresh tracks snapped me wide awake, made me forget the cold. She was in there, in the dark canyon, somewhere within earshot.

The GIS maps, the hypothetical home ranges superimposed on the landscape—all that speculation, all that "objective" planning, seemed so far away. She is here, and in all likelihood she will winter here, ensconced with cub in some secret, well-built den.

There is a dispassionate, nuts-and-bolts, follow-the-manual element to helping this happen: bear-resistant garbage cans, 7,000-volt electric fences around chicken coops, training folks in the use of bear pepper spray. Hundreds of garbage cans, thousands of horseback miles, and two decades in, though, I can no longer dodge the "why" of doing all this. There is a "why," and it's much richer than "because science says we have to."

Science can help you define what you're trying to sustain, can help devise ways of sustaining it, can help you measure progress toward sustainability. However, it can't tell you what to sustain, for how long, and at what level of risk. The answers to these questions depend on what we care about and what we connect with emotionally. Scientific observations can deepen our knowledge, which should deepen our connection, too. But the heart of caring comes from emotional connection.

We still teach young scholars that science will tell us what to do—I know because I encounter them, like dispersing young rabbits, every summer. Still mimicking the assembly line, we tell them the next step is going out into the provinces to "educate" people about these truths. If we're feeling wise, we warn them that people are stubborn and irrational and as likely as not to reject science.

Once you abandon the underlying premise (that science will tell us what we ought to do) though, you confront the terror of complexity, serendipity, maybe even nihilism. There is no simile here: one really is an apostate, walking away from one's religion. "Surely you don't mean that!

Are you just being provocative?" is the feedback you'll get early on. Then they'll start to question your intelligence, or integrity, or both. Maybe you never got it in the first place? Maybe you're not cut out for science.

There are sincere attempts to argue that we "need" grizzlies to perform some service for us. Maybe they till up the ground and help along the nitrogen cycle? Keep elk populations in check or on the move? Something, anything besides saying that we want grizzlies because they're powerful and amazing and make us feel something we never feel otherwise.

GRIZZLIES: THE WILD IS CONSEQUENTIAL

Ecologists of a certain stripe like to talk about how no one part of the ecosystem is more important than any other. There's certainly some truth to that—step into an anthill if you want the ants' opinion on how important they are.

There's the big-picture, conceptual view of every creature, element, or process acting out its own role. Then there's the embodied viewpoint of an individual creature recognizing the here-and-now tangible risk of having something out there that could hurt you, maybe eat you. As industrial-age humans, we're really cut off from experiencing that, suffering instead from a generalized, abstract anxiety. (I had to stop watching television because it seemed to be an anxiety churn. Fear the weather! Fear brown people! Fear teenagers! Fear cancer! Fear being indigent in your old age! And so on.)

One characteristic of this corner of the Rockies is the expanse of rolling sagebrush country—miles and miles of it. Huge swaths of it—100 square miles here, another 100 square miles over the mountains. We get used to thinking of grizzlies living in the woods, and it's a surprise to find them living out here. Then again, they evolved on the glaciated plains of the Eurasian land mass in the Pleistocene, and they still thrive in the treeless Arctic mountains of Alaska. The high sage uplands of the Missouri River headwaters aren't that dissimilar.

There is no way to talk about wanting grizzlies back, to talk about their wild and free spirit, how sublime, without also saying a word for those who get hurt. This is serious business. Out there in a huge sagebrush basin, where for much of the year there are almost no people, grizzlies roam the open country. They use terrain and willow bottoms should they actually feel the need to hide from anything.

Grizzly Bear, Denali National Park and Preserve. Photograph by Daniel A. Leifheit. (CC-BY-2.0)

And some of them maybe don't feel the need to hide, nor to run.

We don't know for sure what happened. We may never know. The man, well loved and respected in his community, was hunting with his father out in one of the vast rolling expanses of sagebrush. Islands of timber sometimes held black bears, and that's what the man and his father were after.

All we can really know for now is the outcome. A big male grizzly attacked the man, destroying his face, breaking both arms, severing fingers. The grizzly died from a gunshot wound. The man's father amazingly enough transported him for miles on an ATV and managed to call for help and keep his son alive. Their day ended a time zone away, in Seattle Harborview Hospital. The man has been there since, surgeons putting him back together and treating him against the threat of rabies.

Other people have stories like this man's. I have met some of them, just in the course of living here. A younger version of myself did not know enough about pain to recognize what they carried, as someone who knows nothing of a trade could not tell a novice from a master.

The ones who have been bit in the face, one imagines, remember every time they pass a store window or comb their hair or brush their teeth. Some have carried on; some had to stop living.

I hear a younger version of myself offering glib answers about how one can be safe around grizzlies. I hear people far removed from grizzly country spouting bravado, telling people not to be afraid. But there's a reason to be afraid; there's a basis to the mortal terror grizzlies evoke. The man in the jaws of the bear, the man in multiple half-day surgeries in Seattle, his life forever altered. His story is at the root of that fear.

The man's story of survival, and contemplating the long, uncertain journey that lies ahead of him, seems maybe more terrifying than the fatalities, with their comparatively tidy endings.

The man is the first one that a grizzly has gravely, seriously injured in this newly reinhabited grizzly country west of Yellowstone. Grizzlies here, west of the Madison River, have inflicted a few other injuries, but scarcely any more severe than, say, a bad bicycle wreck. But the man was almost killed in a place where people had come to not expect grizzlies.

We want grizzlies back, we want them in large, robust, self-sustaining populations. We want, we want, we want. Do we realize what we're asking for?

I sat in confessionals regularly between the ages of seven and nineteen. Now, with over two decades of working, mostly full time, to see that grizzlies can live in more places, the old familiar urge for atonement tugs at my conscience. What have we done? The man—who still sleeps every night in Seattle Harborview, some two months later—is not a case study, not a cocktail party anecdote, not a receptacle for blame. The man was out on a lovely June day in wild country with his father, sharing time together.

I am rattled, my convictions wobbly. I am digging deep to make sense of what we in the grizzly conservation world are doing. My toil gets me this far: grizzlies are what they are. And there is no getting around the paradox that the very qualities that draw us to grizzlies are the very ones that make them utterly unacceptable to others.

We could have demilitarized zones—no-man's/no-bear's lands—so there would be no ambiguity about whether one was exposing oneself to risk of a grizzly attack. We could go back to poisoning, trapping, even add aerial gunning and infrared drone detection to rid whole mountain ranges of grizzlies and keep them that way.

What then of lightning, hypothermia, rocky trails, falling trees? What of yellow jackets and bumble bees? Avalanches? We could start with grizzlies, because they're big and not very prolific. But why would we stop there? What would keep us from going after mountain lions next? How about skunks or rattlesnakes?

Maybe these trails of thought lead us back to why we do conserve grizzlies and honor their wild freedom: we turn from control, from seeking to vanquish risk, ambiguity, and fear itself. Start with grizzlies, as a way of exulting our commitment to this path.

THE FAR HORIZON: LETTING GRIZZLIES BE

At the fiftieth anniversary of the Wilderness Act, we reflect on what we have set aside, saved from the bulldozer and the chainsaw. To reinforce the rightness of wilderness, we emphasize how much we need these places, how they restore us, heal us, give us hope. Aldo Leopold, Wallace Stegner, Edward Abbey—all of this resonates.

Yet, for all the pretty talk, it still sounds like it's all about us.

But what about—if we can presume—doing something for grizzlies? Or is that still ultimately doing something for us, a monument to ourselves? Is it still an aesthetic whim to choose to give bears room, room to be bears, places where they won't be lonesome for other bears?

Sure, we run smack into philosophical problems of ever being able to get outside of our own skulls, or to outrun our own motives. So we do the best we can, and we come back to: get as far along the continuum as we can toward wildness, as far away from gardening or feedlots as possible.

Certainly, there is a huge difference between fattening cattle in a feedlot—computer-measured customized rations, hormone implants, broadspectrum vaccines—and moving a few grizzlies around Montana every decade or so to keep the gene pool stirred up. Taking charge of a few inputs (say, piling up dead bison to help grizzlies stay well fed inside Yellowstone, in spite of climate change) is very different from controlling virtually all inputs, such as in a greenhouse.

Here's where the poets come in: as long as we have choices, we should choose the wilder path. We should step back and let grizzlies have autonomy and dignity. As the storytellers aver, grizzlies will go down fighting for those things anyway.

In doing this, we aspire to live in such a way that adds one's own tiny weight to tilt this life toward surprise, wonder, and an autonomous wild world; away from control, predictability, sameness, and scripted-ness. This choice busts free from the seminar rooms and into frightful relief when grizzlies bump into people—we've literally got skin in the game, and there are consequences.

It's time to stop hiding and get it out in the open as to why we would choose to give grizzlies more. It is clearly a choice: the historic range maps show that we can choose to get rid of them and have done so down the length of the continent. We should open up ourselves and be vulnerable, be radically honest—it is enough to say we want these things, we choose to make room for this awesome, terrible being on the landscape.

There is a pragmatic side to this as well. The conceit that our goals are backed by the authority of science, a mandate rather than a choice, is rotten ground to stand on. It falls apart under scrutiny, to say nothing of making one's voice inauthentic. Be vulnerable, authentic, and real. We must, because many do not agree that grizzlies should have more room. We cannot begin the conversation with self-deception and poorly understood motives.

We fear being called out for romanticism, for trivial desires that have nontrivial consequences for others. So we pretend that Moses brought the maps down from Mount Sinai with the tablets, so we don't have to own our desires.

It's a delusion that folks we need to work with can see right through. Ranchers, hunters, rural citizens—although it's scary, we need to be forthright about where we're coming from. We need to offer up the authentic vision, in a way that shows empathy and realism about the downsides of having grizzlies as neighbors. We weigh these costs against a veiled bundle of benefits when we cling too much to science, wanting to appear "reasonable." Grizzlies have their own reasons.

Reimagining the Range of Wild

Biodiversity in the Greater Yellowstone Ecosystem and Its Relevance in the World

John D. Varley

The nineteenth-century poet Francis Thompson writes, "All things by immortal power / Near or far, / Hiddenly / To each other linkèd are, / That thou canst not stir a flower / Without troubling of a star." Thompson seems to intuit the interconnectedness between the tangible and immediate flower and the unseen, distant star. Likewise, John Varley skillfully asks us to consider a universe of microfauna that falls outside our gaze and awareness—a universe no less vital to the planet's well-being than its "charismatic megafauna."

All this I tested by wisdom and I said,
"I am determined to be wise"—but this was beyond me.
Whatever wisdom may be, it is far off and most profound—Who can
discover it? So I turned my mind to understand, to investigate and to
search out wisdom and the scheme of things.

—Ecclesiastes 7:23–25

INTRODUCTION

For me, this story is a tale of the search for wisdom, and perhaps more importantly, wonder. If I do my job well, perhaps the story could be one of wisdom and wonder for you as well. I spent almost an entire career—almost four decades—working for and with some of the most glamorous wildlife in our nation and probably the world. Wildlife species whose images come immediately to mind for most of you: native cutthroat trout and all their cousins for starters, and then later, gray wolves, grizzly bears, elk, bison, and whooping and sandhill cranes—to mention a few. Each of these creatures has great stories associated with its life and management in the Greater Yellowstone. At times I was immersed in fire ecology, brucellosis, invasive exotic species, bio-prospecting, and snowmobiles, among many other issues, and each is novel-ready simply because each is so interesting. But here I bring you a story I believe is a story of wonder because, while you all are familiar with these creatures, few of you have heard of or know anything about any of the remarkable species I am going to introduce to you in this essay.

In part, this is a story about the real range of species diversity and how our society ignores the largest component of the world's biodiversity. These creatures are parts of biodiversity that have only been discovered recently, and science knows little about most of them. Fortunately, for a few of them enough is known to begin to tell a story, and it is a tale about life that resides in us, all around us, everywhere on earth, and could resemble life in other worlds. Not only is this life ubiquitous but also early evidence from scientists suggests that the human race may depend on this part of the biological world for its own survival.

First, I want to be very honest regarding my topic. It's a self-selected subject, so I have no one to blame but myself. Over a four-decade career in Yellowstone National Park I entertained a host of visitor questions, and not a single visitor, administrator, or judge—certainly not a politician or even a scientist—ever asked me, "How would you describe the range or breadth of biodiversity in Yellowstone?" (FYI: Unquestionably, the most common visitor question is "Where is the nearest restroom?")

It was not as if I was anxiously awaiting the range-of-biodiversity question either. In fact, it is quite likely that it is a question that has not yet reached its time for discussion. Many in science believe we are only on the threshold of a biological revolution, and it could well be premature or even folly to anticipate its scope.

But still, if for no better reason than clarity—because as a people we are generally a nation of counters or measurers—we should be curious. Just look at counting in our national sports. Perhaps the most obvious example, baseball is considered a favored national pastime and it's statistically outrageous. Similarly, I come to you from a world of bureaucrats and scientists and can attest that for both groups counting or measuring is a serious part of their daily activities, and much of it is also outrageous.

In my Yellowstone experience, most of the nature-related questions involve counting: the number of bird or fish species, how many elk live there, the number of geysers, the minutes until Old Faithful erupts, or the miles to Grand Teton National Park. All of these questions, generally, have straightforward answers that include a number.

Further disclosure: If I had been asked the "range or breadth" question at any time in my career, my answer would have been "I don't know." By the time I retired from Yellowstone National Park I might have answered, "I don't know, but it's big, really, really big." The quality of "bigness" is one of the many reasons it's an interesting question to ask and a natural question to reimagine. But it may also be a little bit like Fantasy Football in that a little bit of hard data is the basis for totally make-believe games, with fantasy winners and losers. This seems like an activity that only gamblers could love, but also warns me to be careful defining—or even reimagining—"really, really big."

SPECIES OLYMPICS

There is an ad hoc group of scientists scattered around the world involved in an informal sporting contest to identify which place on earth hosts the greatest biodiversity. They favor using the number of known species, also known as "species richness." For many years the tropical rainforests have been assumed to be the champions of biodiversity, largely due to the richness of plant, insect, and bird species. At some time in the distant future, when all species are counted, the rainforests might still reign, but first we must count all of the species in the rainforests that have never been identified—in the microscopic world, for example, which is the most diverse and has the most species in the living world but very few have been identified. In other words, we have been fairly efficient at identifying and counting the species at the top of nature's food chain and woefully inadequate at identifying and counting the species at the bottom. The reason this is important is that organisms at the bottom of the food chain are by far more numerous, not only in terms of the number of species, but also in population numbers and biomass, so we have to reimagine the chain with the largest link at the bottom end and the smallest link at the top, and as the phrase "food chain" strongly implies we are deeply interconnected, probably in ways that are as yet unknown to science.

To give you an idea of how this works, scientists assert that one microorganism species that is widespread in the world's oceans, *Prochlorococcus marinus*, is the most important producer of oxygen of all photosynthetic species across the globe. These little fellows, who are classified as *Cyanobacteria*, put all of the world's forests, shrub- and grasslands, and marine algae to shame in the production volume of oxygen. It is also widely believed that it was the marine *Cyanobacteria* group, perhaps even including *Prochlorococcus,* that provided the earth and all of us oxygen-dependent breathers the original concentrations of oxygen to live. The beginning of oxygen in our atmosphere happened 2.3–2.4 billion years ago, and scientists call it the "Great Oxidation Event."

Now it turns out that *Prochlorococcus* are not fond of the acidification of our oceans caused by the excess atmospheric carbon dioxide oceans are currently consuming. In the places where this is happening, there are fewer and fewer *Prochlorococcus*. I believe that all of us should be concerned about the health and well-being of the oceans, and of *Prochlorococcus*, with as much fervor as we give to wolves, tigers, and elephants, because they manufacture the oxygen necessary for all of us—including wolves, tigers, and elephants—to breathe.

For years there were scientists telling us that we should be concerned about the preservation of the tiny things, not because of any esoteric "sanctity of life" arguments, but perhaps more crucially, because their activities might affect humanity. For many years, scientists never were able to say *which* tiny things might do this but now with *Prochlorococcus*, they have, and it should be everybody's hero.

Also, not too long ago some scientists studying whale falls—places where a dead whale lands on the ocean floor—discovered a remarkably large assemblage of species, microscopic to large, consuming the whale, or consuming the amassed organisms feeding on the whale, and consuming the consumers consuming the consumers, and, well, this goes on ad infinitum until you reach a living whale. It was a superb depiction of a large, complicated food chain. These scientists proposed that whale falls might be the champions of biodiversity. It sounded plausible to some of us but note, however, that the whale fall contenders changed the parameters from a large geographic area and ecosystem type (i.e., rainforests) to a tightly focused specific habitat within an ecosystem—but these definitional semantics are endlessly arguable.

Just as interesting, perhaps, is the case of the scientists who study agricultural soils. Here we must ask whether the ag-soils they are studying are ecosystems or habitats. They could be habitats, but anyone who has driven through the corn belt might favor calling them "ecosystems." I will forego a guess. Regardless, some of these soil scientists have contended that these types of soils may have the greatest diversity yet measured, and they make a good case. But the foul I would call here is that agricultural soils are by far the most studied areas in the entire soil arena, possibly the most studied of any habitat or ecosystem. If rainforest soils received the same level of study, would they be the soil champions? We don't know, because rainforests have not received anywhere near the scientific attention that agricultural soils have received.

When compiling biodiversity lists of any large geographic location, like rainforests or agricultural regions or even smaller regions like the Greater Yellowstone ecosystem, it is important to note that for each place there are huge holes in the knowledge about them due to their complexity and the poor funding of the scientific effort it takes to fill those holes.

Knowledge gaps or holes, themselves, appear in unexpected places. For most places, bird species lists are the first biodiversity measurements to occur because they are relatively easy to identify and a horde of laypeople assist science in the effort. All of the ecosystems mentioned thus far have very accurate—some would say complete—bird species lists. One hole here is that no one has compiled lists identifying the resident microorganisms within the same birds, and I believe that when that is done it will show that tiny species living within the birds outnumber the bird species by orders of magnitude.

When the human genome was first constructed, perhaps you saw in the news that something around 20 percent of the genes represented were not human genes at all but were instead the genes of resident microorganisms within the human body. This is a feature with the human genome that science is still sorting out but it has highlighted for the first time the scope and importance of tiny creatures in the human organism. The human skin alone, for example, has an impressive biodiversity of bacterial and *archaea* (single-celled organisms without nuclei) members and fungi species, not to mention our eyebrow mites!

The Greater Yellowstone ecosystem contains some major holes in its species list, too. We have no or little data from many habitats in the area. For fun, let's say elk or bison stomachs, which preliminary evidence shows are likely distinctive habitats for a suite of remarkably diverse microorganisms. Also, to my knowledge there are zero species of any kind known from Greater Yellowstone tree canopies, or forest soils, or cliffs, or caves—just a few obvious examples. In other parts of the world, including northern Montana, cold floodplain groundwater has been recently shown to be populated with small animals, including crustaceans, almost totally unknown to the scientific community. No one has looked for them in the Greater Yellowstone, but if anyone did look, I'd imagine they are there as well.

The big holes in our knowledge of Greater Yellowstone species richness exist, in part, because of human preoccupation with what has been termed the Greater Yellowstone's "charismatic megafauna," which surely includes wolves, elk, bison, and grizzly bears, but might also include cutthroat trout, trumpeter swans, mule deer, and longhorn beetles. It is a long and arguable list. "Charismatic megafauna" is a useful term because, simply put, it describes species that people come to the Greater Yellowstone to see. There is lesser mention by people of "charismatic megaflora," which might include forests and wildflowers and—if I had my way—the whitebark pine, or "charismatic geothermal features," which certainly would include Old Faithful at the top of a long list. However, no one comes to Greater Yellowstone to see charismatic microfauna, except for a small group of eccentric scientists. Speaking in defense of the tiny things, one of these scientists, Montana State University microbial ecologist Dr. David Ward, once said, "Everyone comes to Yellowstone wanting to see a grizzly bear or a gray wolf and few get to see them, but everyone comes to Yellowstone not expecting to see bacteria and *archaea* and yet, everyone does see them." I would add that most actually see them but are mostly unaware they are seeing them, although park service naturalists are slowly changing this oversight. Surely everyone sees the brilliant colors associated with geothermal features, especially hot springs, and most of the coloration represents colonies of bacteria and *archaea*. It's true—you cannot see an individual bacterium with the naked eye, but you can easily see a billion of them, and they come in a great range of brilliant colors.

Later, I will tell you how scientists have revolutionized biology so that they not only look through microscopes to see individual bacteria but now also "see" a bacteria's genes and how they line up as the blueprints for an organism's physiology and its life, or "livingness," as Stephen Colbert might put it.

First, let me tell you a little bit about my qualifications for talking about these subjects and Greater Yellowstone as well. I was a child in 1948, when I first visited this wonderful part of the planet. As with most children who visit this region, my memories are vivid, long lasting, and life changing. Looking back over that first visit and the many visits that followed implanted something intangible in me that encounters in many other places did not—and it made me a devotee of the Greater Yellowstone.

This, I discovered, required signing on as a lifelong student of the Greater Yellowstone. It wasn't a conscious decision on my part but more of an "it just happened" event, as I spent more and more time and energy encountering and experiencing the place. Later, as my new wife, Anita, and I were planning our honeymoon, Greater Yellowstone was almost an automatic addition to the road trip.

Much later, in the fall of 1972, I found myself with a young family, moving from Utah to a brand-new job in Yellowstone Park. By that time I had in my possession two degrees from the University of Utah that, as I look back, superbly prepared me for work in the aquatic sciences field, with emphasis on fish, especially trout. I loved everything about trout and, if you don't know yet, the Greater Yellowstone is a world mecca for trout—and trout hands-down qualify for charismatic megafauna status in my view.

As a child or young adult I would never have guessed that I would spend almost an entire career in Yellowstone. Nor would I have guessed that I would retire to a place within the Greater Yellowstone, or that at this age I would still be performing part-time research on Yellowstone Lake with the National Park Service and Montana State University and others. It may turn out that instead of spending a career in Yellowstone, it could be most of a lifetime, and I feel very grateful about that course of events. I've spent my life there as a practitioner of science and a science administrator and—as some around me know all too well—an annoying advocate for science-based resource management to anyone who would listen.

WHY SCIENCE?

The protection of parks and similar conservation reserves has always been the park manager's first line of defense. Whether we consider Yellowstone or Yosemite in the 1870s–90s, or a newly created park in Alaska, South America, Africa, or Asia, the first thing a park manager must do is deploy rangers to protect the park from poachers and squatters or anyone else who is bent on exploiting the park's resources. It's the first and most basic requirement of park management. While this is still true in all parks, they now also face new, more insidious and stealthy threats than Yellowstone's early leaders could have possibly dreamed of.

Polluted air from eastern Asia can filter over Yellowstone in just sixteen days. Pollution from our own West Coast can arrive tomorrow. The Everglades and a number of other parks and reserves are affected by being at the tail end of very sick rivers. Tree species in the Great Smoky Mountains are dying from sick air; Everglades panthers, from mercury poisoning and being run over by cars; and Yellowstone Lake cutthroat trout, from the unfortunate introduction of several exotic, invasive species. Global climate changes are occurring in essentially all parks and also threaten the entire earth.

These days the meaning of "park protection" has had to evolve into an entirely new definition that goes far beyond the type of protection practiced in the simpler, earlier days. Now, in addition to rangers, park protection involves scientists and technical experts. These specialists are essential to park managers, as these environments each grow their own complexity.

YELLOWSTONE, THE POLYMERASE CHAIN REACTION, AND THE BIOLOGICAL REVOLUTION

Long before *Prochlorococcus marinus* was even known to science, the discipline of biology as taught to me in college began to unravel seriously in several arenas important to my career—mostly genetics and the identification and classification of organisms. It began slowly in the 1970s, and by the late 1980s and early 1990s the unraveling picked up steam, and

Excelsior Geyser Crater, Yellowstone National Park, 2017. Photograph by Leslie Miller.

Yellowstone was flooded with a different type of biological researcher, who had new language and tools.

Unbeknownst to most of us, including me, a scientific breakthrough had occurred, and a biological revolution was beginning to change things seriously. The breakthrough involved a laboratory chemical reaction called the polymerase chain reaction, or PCR for short. PCR had been kicking around laboratories for some time but it never got to be anything big or important because the process called for adding heat to start the reaction, which broke down the enzymes (catalysts) that made the reaction work. In California, a scientist named Kary Mullis was puzzling through the PCR experiments, wondering how he could find an enzyme/catalyst that would not break down at high temperatures. He had the bright (later, Nobel Prize–winning) idea that maybe recently discovered hot springs organisms could have enzymes that might work in PCR. It turned out he was right. The hot spring thermophile (meaning a heat-loving organism) that gave him the right enzyme was *Thermus aquaticus*, a bacterium originally isolated from Mushroom Pool in Yellowstone National Park. The enzyme, now known as TAQ polymerase, was named after the organism that had shown Mullis the light (T from the genus name *Thermus*, and AQ, the first two letters of the species name *aquaticus*). In a takeoff of *Time* magazine's "Man of the Year," the authoritative journal *Science* named TAQ the "Molecule of the Year" for 1995.

The newly operational PCR-TAQ process now gave scientists the ability to take DNA from any living organism and clone, or exactly duplicate this tiny quantity overnight into an amount of DNA large enough to be studied. It's like taking a single page of, let's say, a poem, and using a yet-to-be-invented photocopier that gives you a billion exact copies of the poem by the next morning. By itself, this was a remarkable achievement. For biologists, it was truly earth shaking because for the first time ever it gave them the ability to explore the largely unknown world of genetics with levels of precision and depth never before possible.

Why should you care? Perhaps you should care because the polymerase chain reaction starring TAQ polymerase is now playing in a laboratory near you. In case you missed it, it may have been playing under its common alias: DNA fingerprinting. So, for instance, if there is a suspected rapist, to use a lurid example, and he leaves one sperm cell behind, and if the police capture it, it can be cloned into billions of exact copies overnight. In turn, this allows the typing, or precise characterization, of the perpetrator's DNA, and could bring a conviction in court.

But the magic of PCR works in the reverse too. We are seeing more and more news reports of humans leaving prison because the convicted person's DNA did not match the DNA left behind by the perpetrator at the crime scene. Sometimes the DNA has been patiently waiting in police evidence rooms for decades, and it can still be cloned. So PCR works for exonerations as well as convictions. God bless TAQ polymerase!

But the criminal forensic applications you may now see regularly in TV police shows simply represent the tip of the iceberg. DNA recovery is now routinely done from murdered people dug up from mass graves or a soldier's bones found in the forests of Viet Nam. In medicine, PCR can identify, overnight, human infectious agents ranging from a child's strep throat to infections by HIV or Ebola.

The PCR–TAQ process also revolutionized the world of basic biology. It enabled scientists to construct for the first time the entire human genome and to begin to understand why people are different from each other or why, in other respects, we are all the same. It allows medical doctors to understand which of our diseases and afflictions are rooted in the DNA our ancestors gave us, and which diseases are independent of ancestry. Laboratories can now give you a map of where on earth you came from and, because your ancestors often came from different places, give proportions of each contributor to your genetic heritage.

Clearly the PCR-TAQ duo revolutionized basic and applied biological sciences, but it created new industries too. The duo is generating billions of dollars in business applications worldwide. Much of the current ongoing research on all species, but especially microbial species, seeks to find the kind of molecules that, like TAQ, can assist different biological processes that can aid or abet the biological revolution.

My story may not be as stupendous as constructing the human genome or catching rapists or Ebola detection, but it is a spin-off of the larger PCR-TAQ revolution in biology. All of these advancements carry great stories worthy of telling, but there is a lesser-told story that interests me the most, and few people are aware of it. It is appropriate and meaningful to me because it is a natural extension of the discovery and isolation of *Thermus aquaticus* in Yellowstone by Dr. Thomas Brock, who gave us our first taste, so to speak, of the wonderful world of life in hot water.

I think almost everyone has some basic understanding of habitat. We know, for instance, that there are places on Earth where people cannot live (without technology), like Antarctica or the ocean floor, and that there are other places where we thrive, like California. So ideal habitat for humans, again without technology, would be decidedly terrestrial, and let's guess between the latitudes of about 60 degrees north and 60 degrees south. That's a very large and broad habitat in which a species can prosper, and we don't find—with a few exceptions, like houseflies—many other species as fortunate as humans. Most other species are far more limited in their habitat. Our closest relatives in the animal world are said to be the chimpanzees, who, even before humans began to influence their populations, had a small habitat compared to humans. And small is closer to the norm for any given species.

For example, the habitat of Ross's bentgrass (*Agrostis rossii*) is only found scattered around some of Yellowstone's geothermal basins, which if mapped and added together might only be a few acres. While that is an unusually small habitat for a species (especially for a grass species), the average size of a species habitat tends toward a smaller size, as opposed to the gigantic habitat of humans.

It's interesting that there was a time when the sole habitat of our new friend *Thermus aquaticus* was thought to be Mushroom Pool in Yellowstone, but scientists later found it in many Yellowstone hot springs, and still later they found it residing in home water heaters across a broad geographical area. This is an example of a basic and important tenet in biology: for any given habitat, that habitat selects which species live there and which species do not. Now, let's put that theory to harder work.

Yellowstone Park has over eleven thousand distinct geothermal features, and they mostly come in the form of geysers, hot springs, mud pots, and fumaroles (that emit hot gasses). There are even more geothermal features in the lands adjacent to Yellowstone. While the features are all hot, they have a huge temperature range, from about 60 degrees Fahrenheit to over 220 degrees Fahrenheit. It's interesting that for most of the twentieth century scientists believed that life did not exist above 140 degrees Fahrenheit, but Professor Tom Brock and his students blew the lid off that notion in Yellowstone. I was late getting the message. When I was a Boy Scout, one of the first things I learned about the outdoors was that we need to boil drinking water to kill all the organisms in it, yet in Yellowstone organisms thrive in boiling water.

By now you may not be surprised to hear that the habitat with the greatest number of known species is hot, or geothermal, water, some of it nearing, at, or above the boiling point. In Yellowstone's geothermal waters there are thousands of known species and, for the most part, we don't know much about them beyond their alphanumeric identifying number.

These geothermal features also have extraordinary variability in the acidity–alkalinity measure known as pH, which ranges from 0 to 14, with 7.0 being neutral. Yellowstone's geothermal water ranges from ultra-acidic (at or near zero on the pH scale) to highly alkaline (pH 11.3).

Because the pH scale is a logarithmic scale, that is a huge range and is unusual to find in untrammeled nature.

In addition, most of these features have their own distinctive, if not unique, geochemical signatures as a result of differences between the hotwater interactions with soluble minerals deep within the earth's crust. Virtually all geothermal waters are rich in minerals but the makeup of the types of minerals in each feature is quite varied. Naturally occurring minerals at toxic concentrations (e.g., arsenic, mercury) are not uncommon, and radioactive minerals occur in some springs.

Now, let's do the hard work. When you put eleven thousand geothermal features into an equation with the three variables of temperature, pH, and geochemistry, the calculated result is that there is an infinite number of possible habitats available for different thermophilic organisms to establish themselves, grow, and evolve. That is what science predicts, but is that what scientists are finding?

By about 1990, prior to PCR-TAQ becoming accepted science, scientists had identified thirty-eight species of organisms belonging to the domain *Prokaryota* (bacteria) and *archaea* species they thought at the time were bacteria, in all of Yellowstone Park. (It was a little after 1990 that *archaea*, as a life form, were first recognized as having their unique domain, *Archeota*. They were first discovered in Yellowstone hot springs). Since the use of PCR-TAQ began, scientists have identified thousands of what they are calling OTUs (operational taxonomic units), which they believe are the equivalent of species, and the list continues to grow rapidly. In fact, if there is an infinite number of hot habitats, and with the number of new species or OTUs discovered growing rapidly, some scientists have suggested that Yellowstone geothermal features may ultimately be a contender for greatest biodiversity richness—but that remains to be seen.

YELLOWSTONE THERMOPHILES UNMASKED

When we compare the normal world of humans and the thermophile world, there are few similarities. To simplify, in our world plants eat photons from the sun and make them into useful compounds to live and reproduce, and then serve as prey for a host of predators to consume. Humans have the ability to consume plants directly as well as the animals that eat the plants. In contrast, while Yellowstone's thermophiles do have photosynthetic members that depend on the sun, many other species have adapted to eating bizarre food items, such as sulfur, iron, arsenic, and others. Those that depend on the sun are called phototrophs. Those that depend on minerals are called chemolithotrophs. And there are some who have the ability to do both, called heterotrophs.

One of my favorite thermophiles has no common name and is referred to only by its Latin scientific genus name, *Sulfalobus*, and its species name, *acidocaldarious*. As the name suggests (and this might not be immediately obvious to everyone), these creatures have a very strict diet of sulfur, and sulfur is most commonly found in highly acidic hot springs—in other words, *Sulfalobus* only thrive in boiling sulfuric acid. You and I might only live a second or two in this same environment, but *Sulfalobus* not only thrive in it, they require it. They take on a chill and die in tap water.

In its unusual habitat, it might be tempting to conclude that *Sulfalobus* might have found its own nirvana, but alas, it's probably not the case. They live in an environment with many other competitive species that have also adapted to boiling sulfuric acid, so there may be competition for food or space. In addition to competitors, *Sulfalobus* also suffer from parasites and bacterial and viral diseases, and some of those agents have been scientifically identified.

We can conclude that *Sulfalobus* lives in a complex interactive ecosystem—just like we do, and all the ordinary creatures more familiar to us do—but unlike our ecosystem, its home is very rare on Earth, and of course very extreme.

The other lesson *Sulfalobus* might teach us also happens to be one of the big reasons why scientists study this species or other members of the hot-water crowd, and it has to do with genetics.

To develop this thought, let's use the human genome as our baseline to compare. In round numbers (rather than arguable numbers) it is said that the chimpanzee's (*Pan*) genome is around 99 percent similar to the human genome. Another way to state this is that 1 percent of the chimpanzee's genes are novel to chimps and are the genes that make the chimp look and act like a chimp, not a human. Similarly, it is said that the common house mouse (*Mus*) is around 60 percent like the human genome, and so about 40 percent are the genes that make the mouse the mouse. In *Sulfalobus*, 40 percent of its genes are the same as found in the human genome (yes, this number amazed me), and 60 percent are genes that are novel and make *Sulfalobus*, well, *Sulfalobus*. That means that the ability of this organism to eat sulfur and thrive in boiling sulfuric acid is found somewhere in the 60 percent of the creatures' novel genes, and so these are of great interest to scientists.

Many of the scientific holy grails are found in nonhuman, novel genes that allow life in extreme environments, such as boiling acid and sulfur. That is not to say that the 40 percent of the *Sulfalobus* genome that is like the human genome is not interesting and worthy of research too since, to give one example, the 40 percent of human-like genes may have changed *Sulfalobus*'s physiological pathways, and that could inform medicine about human problems.

LAKE YELLOWSTONE'S SECRETS

Many of you may have had the pleasure of sitting in the Sun Room of the Lake Yellowstone Hotel—the venerable hotel is 121 years new, as it was freshly remodeled for 2014. It may be better than ever, and you might enjoy your favorite beverage while gazing out at the remarkable body of water to which the hotel owes its name. What a beautiful sight it is: the lake, the background of surrounding wild mountains, and, of course, the big sky. Everything in this wonderful view-scape is protected within either Yellowstone or Grand Teton National Parks. So whether warranted or not, we get the feeling that this view is forever safe. It has been calculated that at the end of the southeast arm of the lake—which you can often see from the Sun Room—is the most distant you can get from a road in the lower forty-eight states. What could be more sublime?

Scientific inquiry has recently opened a whole new dimension to this scene. Understand that Yellowstone Lake has been studied by the scientific community for nearly one hundred fifty years, so what could possibly be new? Here is a sampler:

One University of Utah scientist tops the list. Dr. Robert B. Smith is a consummate geophysicist and earthquake expert, and because he has been studying Yellowstone Lake and the park since 1955, he could well be the dean of all of Yellowstone's many researchers. From his prolific work over the decades, I have learned that the lake, in addition to being largely a caldera lake—meaning it lies in an ancient volcanic cone—is crisscrossed with earthquake faults that are quite active. Based on temperature gradients of the floor of the lake and other geophysical data, that floor is like an old-fashioned hot plate, giving up heat to the 400-foot-deep lake waters that are mostly made up of cold snow melt. The surface of the lake is frozen for six months of the year, and I wonder if the ice would ever melt on the lake without that hot plate. But I think the hot plate is secure, because research tells us there is molten magma 1–3 kilometers below the bottom of the lake. We all know that molten magma is associated with volcanoes. Does this mean Yellowstone is a volcanic park? I know how Bob Smith would answer that question: "Of course it is." The evidence tells us that geysers, hot springs, and fumaroles occur between active volcanic periods. In fact, Dr. Smith has told us that it was volcanic eruptions that vaporized the large mountain range that once connected Montana's Madison Mountain Range with Wyoming's Teton Mountain Range. This resulted in the Yellowstone Plateau and formed the caldera within which the lake now lies. The vaporized mountains are now an identifiable layer of dust in the states surrounding Yellowstone and much of the Midwest. Bob's book on the Yellowstone, *Windows into the Earth*,[1] is a wonder by itself.

While it has long been known that there were geothermal areas in the lake's watershed, and a few hot springs around the perimeter of the lake, for most of its history the lake's waters were thought to be unaffected by geothermal heat and fluids. As a budding limnologist working on the lake in the 1970s, I could not find any effect of geothermal fluids on the pristine snowmelt that comprised the source of those waters. Later, I was with a visiting group of Russian scientists who thought it was important they swim in the lake, and they did. They thought it was unduly cold, and of course, Russians are experts in cold. I admit that I have been swimming in the lake several times, but I would quickly add that it was never my choice to do so. All of this "unaffected by geothermal" talk began to end in the late 1990s and early in the twenty-first century, with the work of Dr. Smith as well as Dr. Lisa Morgan and Dr. Pat Shanks of the United States Geological Survey, and Dave Lovalvo of Eastern Oceanics LLP.[2] Using the newest side-scanning radar/sonar techniques, these scientists constructed an extraordinary bathymetry of the bottom of the lake that redefined everyone's thinking. For the first time, they showed a heretofore unknown geothermal field on the bottom of the lake, perhaps the second or third largest in the entire park. They backed up their sonar data with video, temperature data, and water samples taken by Lovalvo's remotely operated vehicle (ROV). They found that in many ways the geothermal field on the bottom of the lake was much like what we would find in Yellowstone's terrestrial features, such as geysers and hot springs. One geyser has even been named the Trout Jacuzzi because when it erupts its current floats a lot of tasty food from the vent area and attracts a school of feeding cutthroat trout. In some cases, the name or category of the type of feature changes when underwater (e.g., terrestrial fumaroles become gas vents, and mudpots become smokers). Giant terrestrial hot pools such as Grand Prismatic Spring are not thought to exist because the lake's cold water and lively currents are quick to absorb geothermal heat and fluids. But around the vents of these features it was found that the frigid floor of the normal lake gives way to a mosaic of tropical patches, in some cases with monumental coral-like structures, some that are 20–30 feet high, complete with coral reef animals such as sponges, hydras, and giant worms.

But the work of Morgan, Shanks, and Lovalvo was largely limited to just physical and chemical data. Later, with the substantial help of Lovalvo and his ROV, our research group took on the problem of trying to figure out how to contrast the subalpine cold-water organisms with those that were collected in cold water but had geothermal origins, and of course the hot-water organisms themselves collected at the hot-water vents. It sounds simple but it is surprisingly difficult because so many of the organisms discovered were new to science and therefore their life histories, physiologies, and habitats were unknown. One part of our project was the Molecular All-Taxa Biological Inventory, or MATBI for short. Not all of our results have been published as yet but many are, and here is a glimpse. To begin with, we compiled a list of species that had been discovered in the Yellowstone Lake over the 130 years the lake had been studied by scientists. We end the older taxonomic work in 1990, which reasonably precedes the period of new PCR molecular science. The grand total of Yellowstone Lake species on the 130-year list numbered 236. All were from the domain *Eukaryota*, and there were no known representatives of the domains *Prokaryota* (i.e., bacteria) or *Archeota* (i.e., archaea). Our pilot effort, using molecular methods (PCR-TAQ), which lasted only three months, added 230 species for a total new species list of 496. A comparison between the old and new lists showed only two species were common to both, suggesting there was a heap of biodiversity we were missing. With the methods and techniques proven, we then geared up for full-scale research. This time the partners, in addition to the National Park Service, were the Gordon and Betty Moore Foundation, J. Craig Venter Institute, Montana State University, DOE Joint Genome Institute, and the US Geological Survey. In short, the species list had grown from 496 to an estimated 1,500 (some new eukaryotes have not been added and viruses are problematic). Projections estimate, from collector's curves and as a function of sequence identity set at 97 percent, the number of OTUs. These numbers suggest that if this work continues, the total biodiversity of Lake Yellowstone may turn out to exceed 4,500–5,000 species. But here is a surprise unrelated to the numbers game: our new friend, the great phototroph marine organism *Prochlorococcus marinus*, was discovered in Lake Yellowstone (for the first time unambiguously in a freshwater lake!). Another marine form was collected as well—an alphaproteobacteria, nearly identical to *Pelagibacter ubique*, a common oceanic heterotroph. The archaeal group included the abundant *picoplankter Nitrosopumilus maritimus* (at 98 percent sequence identity), also common in the oceans. In Lake Yellowstone it was identified not only from pelagic waters but also as a diet item sampled from the guts of the *diaphnids* and *copepods* (crustaceans) along with the cyanobacterium *Synechococcus*. This is more than suggestive evidence of a key link in the food chain. Another organism first discovered to be widespread and common in the oceans that we found for the first time in Lake Yellowstone was the microscopic eukaryote phototroph green algae *Ostreococcus*. It holds the current world record for being the smallest known member of the domain *Eukaryota*. To scientists who classify and add order to the evolutionary world of organisms, that's also the domain that includes you and me, plus apes, slime molds, cheat grass, rats, and a bunch of other things. So we are somewhat closely related to our new friend *Ostreococcus*, at least more so than any *Prokaryota* or *Archeota*. While its life and effects are not as well known as *Prochlorococcus*, and its sole known claim to fame is being "the smallest," I am pleased to introduce the eukaryote likely at or near the bottom of the food chain.

CONCLUSION

Many of us of a certain age grew up in biology learning concepts that twenty-first-century science now tells us are obsolete. The new science, which is tough and has a steep learning curve, is a worthwhile pursuit. If I can do it, surely you can too. The peculiarity and the beauty of science that many forget is that it's constantly correcting itself. Some people in fundamentalist religions or in the modern media might portray the old stuff as wrong, and then conclude that we can't trust the new stuff or that the new stuff is always right. Both views are unacceptable. The enlightened view is that ultimately truth will prevail.

When I first saw what science had done with the old animal and plant kingdoms when they were refashioned into three bizarre "domains," I had to fight off a feeling of betrayal. In school, I spent years studying to learn this stuff. But the more I learned about the three-domain system, the more it made sense. I am reminded there is a camp of scientists promoting a new five-domain system, and another promoting a new seven-domain system of classification. I think it is wonderful these folks are challenging today's truths because it makes tomorrow's truths far sturdier and more resilient.

When I was a college student a big deal was made about the barrier between saltwater and freshwater in determining the distribution of species. Freshwater species were never found in saltwater, and saltwater species were never found in freshwater. Finding so many species in Lake Yellowstone that had identical or nearly identical sequences with marine forms was surprising to me. But reason prevails when I remember that "the environment selects" the tenant. But how? Is it because the geothermal heat and geochemistry plus the many thermophile species add so much energy to an otherwise dilute snowmelt lake? Or perhaps it is simpler. Is the bottom part of the freshwater lake food chain so pitifully unknown that the marine forms we are just now finding in freshwater lakes is simply an extension of normal?

I hope we have learned here that there are a lot of inequities involved with measuring and counting biodiversity, and claims made in the popular media must be viewed with a critical eye. The evaluation of biodiversity richness can be fraught with errors, especially with sins of omission. Nonetheless, it is a worthy pursuit for many reasons and sometimes, as with the *Prochlorococcus* story, it can be rewarding, necessary, and even crucial.

We can learn much from the study of biodiversity, and it endlessly produces good stories, as I hope we have seen. But in the end, as *Sulfalobus*'s 40 percent sequence identity with the human genome teaches us, all life on Earth is related to all other life, and, as such, it should be properly respected.

* * *

As for men, God tests them so that they may see that they are like the
animals; Man's fate is like that of the animals; the same fate awaits
them both: As one dies, so does the other. All have the same breath;
Man has no advantage over the animal.... All go to the same place; all
come from the dust, and to dust all return; Who knows if the spirit of
man rises upward and the spirit of the animal goes down in the earth?

—Ecclesiastes 3:18–21

NOTES

1. Robert B. Smith and Lee J. Siegel, *Windows into the Earth: The Geo-
    logic Story of Yellowstone and Grand Teton National Parks* (New York:
    Oxford, 2000).
2. Lisa A. Morgan, Patrick Shanks, and David A. Lovalvo, "Exploration
    and Discovery in Yellowstone Lake," *Journal of Volcanology and Geo-
    thermal Research* 122, no. 3–4 (April 2003).

PART 2

Reimagine

Forging a New Ethic

Reimagining the American West

Building a North American West for the People Who Want to Stay

Harvey Locke

Harvey Locke examines the nineteenth-century grand narrative of the American West and looks at his own family's settlement on the frontier of Western Canada, and then takes us on a wide-ranging, descriptive tour along the boundaries—north, south, east, and west—of the American West. He concludes that it is time for us to "craft a new grand narrative of the North American West that will make the future worth living." Drawing from the model of the Yellowstone to Yukon Conservation Initiative, which he co-founded, Locke proposes similar initiatives on the Colorado Plateau and the Great Plains. The goal, as he sees it, is to start building a society where "all of us and all the species that belong here live together again, at home on the range."

Our vision for the West in the twenty-first century should be continental in scope and built on a healthy relationship with wild nature. We should adopt the Native American worldview in which we are one species among many, inextricably engaged in a life-giving and interdependent relationship with wild nature that is to be honored and celebrated. We should be building a North American West for the people who want to stay.

Not so long ago, borders in our part of the world were just ideas. The North American West was a vast, unbroken sea of grass that lapped up against white-capped mountains draped with tundra meadows and lined by forested valleys that shimmered with freshwater lakes. Rivers, the spinal column of the landscape, ran free and wild from the mountains across the plains and canyonlands, flooding and renewing their valleys on eternal annual cycles. Fires—some set by lightning, some set by native people to encourage grasslands—renewed the landscape by leaving a mosaic of different-aged habitats that nurtured a wide variety of species.

"When the land belonged to God" (as Charlie Russell entitled his masterpiece of a vast northern plains buffalo herd, dripping wet after crossing the Missouri River), there was no central, mountain, or Pacific time, only twenty-eight-day moons and four seasons, which were sometimes jumbled out of sequence by warm Chinook winds in winter and snows in summer. On the plains, vast herds of bison roamed among elk and pronghorn, and were hunted by grizzly bears, wolves, and people, and the spring air was filled with the song of western meadowlarks. There were no ribbons of steel, lines of asphalt roads, or airport runways. But there were people here who knew the way of the land.

It was like that when my mum's family came west. The steamboat they took from Bismarck, North Dakota, up the Missouri had to stop for seven hours to let a herd of buffalo (bison) cross the river. They disembarked at Fort Benton below the Great Falls, in the newly created Montana Territory. They then got on a horse-drawn Red River cart, whose wooden axles squealed and moaned across the 49th parallel to the Methodist Mission to the Stoneys (also known as Nakoda Sioux or Assiniboines) at Morleyville, on the banks of the Bow River. They came to establish an outpost of the British Empire in the newly created Northwest Territories of the young country of Canada, which only a few years before had been brought into being by the British North America Act. That was in the 1870s, and they were the first European settlers in southern Alberta. My ancestors carried the border in their minds. There was no other trace.

A few years later, still before the railway, my great-grandfather rode on horseback into tiny Morleyville, where he met his future wife. He had often ridden across the unbroken and wild Canadian prairie as a freighter of goods by packhorse between Edmonton and Winnipeg. He transported the first printing press to what would become Alberta and cut ties for the Canadian Pacific Railway as it was built across the Rockies, in what is now Banff National Park.

My great-grandparents on my father's side came by rail. They left the family homestead in Iowa to start a new homestead in central Alberta in the 1890s. Both my mum's and my dad's families found their way to the town in Banff National Park and worked in the tourism industry. I was born and raised downstream in Calgary because my dad was a dentist and Banff was too small. For us, the Calgary-Banff area is home, though Morleyville is now under a reservoir located halfway between the two. I am currently living in Banff National Park.

Before my ancestors' arrival and participation in the transformation of the western frontier, the North American West had a common history. Old Swan, a Blackfoot man encountered by Canadian fur trader Peter Fidler in 1801, drew a map by memory showing all the rivers draining the mountains from the Tetons in Wyoming up to the drainages of the Saskatchewan River System in central Alberta. Lewis and Clark used a map from Canadian fur trader David Thompson that showed the Roche Jaune River (French for "yellow stone") to guide them up the Missouri before they engaged local guides Sacagawea and her French Canadian husband, Toussaint Charbonneau, to help them find their way west from the edge of the map. Obsidian, a volcanic glass from the Yellowstone Plateau in present-day Wyoming, useful for its sharp edges that can be knapped into blades and arrowheads, was traded by early people in an exchange network that extended from Colorado to central Alberta.

In Colorado, north of the city of Pueblo and the Spanish land grants, place names reveal the shared history of the North American West. The Canadian and Cache la Poudre Rivers drain east from the Colorado Rockies. In Wyoming the name of the rugged Tetons bears witness to French Canadian fur traders' presence. In the 1840s both Canadian and American fur traders gathered with diverse Native Americans to party and do business at annual "rendezvous" in various valleys along the edge of the mountains of present-day Wyoming and Idaho.

The entire Columbia Basin was once known as the Oregon Territory. It was an area of joint sovereignty between Britain and the United States from 1818 to 1846—a strategy to avoid a war over territorial claims. The border was settled by drawing a straight line along the 49th parallel across the entire North American West. That line cuts the natural north–south flows of life in two. It is as arbitrary a border as any to be found on Earth. It became known to Native Americans as the Medicine Line. Though not physically apparent, its qualities were potent, for the whites behaved differently on either side of that invisible border.

The West is as much an idea as it is a place. In common with all ideas, it has fuzzy boundaries that rub up against the domains of others. Like color bands in a rainbow, the edges are indistinct but the heart is true. We know the West when we see it. We see that West not only in the United States but also in Western Canada. The border drawn in 1846 does not define it. It is still the North American West.

Where does this North American West begin? The eastern boundary is easy: it is "the ridge where the West commences" in Cole Porter's song "Don't Fence Me In." That mythical ridge is known to every Westerner, whether Canadian or American, who has felt out of place in the East. It is located somewhere near the 100th meridian, where the sky opens up, the clouds have definition, the light sharpens, and the horizon is far, far away.

How far west does the North American West go? It certainly includes the Rockies and the dry interior plateaux of the Columbia Basin, the Salt Lake Valley, the edge of the Great Basin Desert, and the Colorado Plateau. The West Coast, of course, is not the West. Novelist and newspaper publisher A. B. Guthrie got this paradox right when he wrote of his protagonist leaving the Willamette Valley of Oregon to go "west" to Montana. He also gave us the idea of "Big Sky" country, which beautifully describes the Great Plains of both countries.

The West's southern boundary is like a long tidal flat. It ebbs and flows across the landscape to the places where the character is more Mexican than Western, more pueblo than Big Sky, but a finger of it extends all the way across the bootheel of New Mexico to the Janos Prairie in northern Mexico. It is bounded on the north by the boreal forest that arcs across most of Manitoba, two-thirds of Saskatchewan, the top half of Alberta, and the northeast corner of British Columbia.

I am Canadian, from north of the Medicine Line. But I consider myself a Westerner, just as many Americans do. I am a Westerner of the North American variety and there are a lot of us. If you are a Mormon from Utah, you likely have family in southern Alberta. If you are a Blackfoot from Montana, the bulk of your nation lives in southern Alberta; if you are Kootenai or Salish, you have kinfolk in southern British Columbia. If you are a rodeo cowboy from Wyoming, you compete in the Calgary Stampede. If you are a resident of Colorado, your largest foreign trading partner is Canada. If you are a resident of Great Falls, you shop in Calgary, while Calgarians flock to recreate in Montana's Flathead Valley. Albertans and British Columbians watch cable TV that originates out of Spokane. And we have a common prophet: Wallace Stegner lived in and wrote about Saskatchewan, Montana, Utah, and Nevada.

The people who occupy the North American West have accumulated like sediment over time and they have lot in common. The bedrock is layers of varied aboriginal cultures, beginning with the pre-Folsom and coming forward through many language groups in an unbroken chain for at least twelve thousand years. These founding peoples are too often out of sight and out of mind but they are always present except where they were forcibly removed. Their first contact was with Canadian or American fur traders of European descent. A flood tide of American, Canadian, and European settlers followed them.

Of course, Canadian Westerners and American Westerners have significant cultural differences. We do not choose to live together in the same country. But we are cousins and we live in the same neighborhood. What one does affects the other. The joke is that people like me are unarmed Americans with health care. The difference runs deeper than that.

Our countries constructed different national narratives in the nineteenth century. America's is the Wild West and "cowboys and Indians" and the new Zion; ours is the land where the Mounties came first to make treaties and give us Peace, Order, and Good Government (though they were not invited to do so in British Columbia, with interesting consequences today). But apart from these matters of approach, the core motivations when it came to the North American West were quite similar.

American Western pioneers were driven by a shared vision, wonderfully depicted in the 1872 painting entitled *American Progress*, by John Gast. Commissioned and distributed by George Crofutt, who was the publisher of popular guides for Americans who wanted to settle the West, *American Progress* depicts a desired future in which farmers cultivate the prairie, miners extract the resources, and the trains bring settlers and civilization from the big cities of the East. The charming maiden Liberty carries the book of knowledge in one hand and a telegraph line in the other. Wildness is expelled before her guiding star: the bison are chased away and the Indians and wolves flee, looking over their shoulders, terrified.

This image would only need a few modifications to apply to the Canadian West. The treatment of indigenous people was less violent. Queen Victoria was less attractive. But the core vision was the same. Here are the words of Elizabeth Boyd McDougall, the first European woman in southern Alberta, about the motivation for the work she did with her missionary husband, John McDougall, at Morleyville: "The Indian missionary

American Progress. By John Gast, 1872.

pioneered the country, made peace, opened the way for settlement, prepared the way for Government and was the real foundation layer for
Empire."[1] This Canadian view of the pioneering enterprise was captured
in a giant mural by artist Don Frache that dominated the waiting area of
the Calgary Airport when I was a boy (a smaller copy now hangs in the
new terminal but in a less prominent location). It is a pioneer's vision of
a future metropolis (1950s prairie style). The light for that vision ema-
nates from the combined activity of Methodist missionary John McDougall standing beside Colonel Macleod of the Mounties. Chief Crowfoot
of the Blackfoot, who led his people to sign Treaty 7, is depicted shaking
hands with a representative of the queen. Catholic missionary Father
Lacombe rounds out the pantheon. They are accompanied by an anon-
ymous settler (also male). Thus was achieved the Peace, Order, and Good
Government that enabled the settlers to come and transform the plains.

These visions had an incredibly powerful and remarkably similar
impact on the land. The settlers spread out, most often one family at a
time. They converted the Great Plains from a wild Eden to utilitarian
domestication, one quarter-section at a time. The vast bison herds were
reduced from millions of animals to a few scattered stragglers, and the

Vision of Calgary. By Don Frache, 1960. Glenbow Archives.

wolves were eliminated. This achievement stands as both a great testament to individual initiative and one of the greatest ecological tragedies in the history of planet Earth.

Some other migrants went to the mountains, notably the loggers and miners. They extracted resources from public lands for private benefit in the declared public interest. Closely following the farmers, ranchers and resource workers were clusters of people who set up small towns to harvest the money generated by them. The first peoples, called "Indians," were removed, killed, or moved to reservations, depending on the area and country. Mormons collectively followed the vision of their own prophets and achieved similar results in the Salt Lake Valley. By the turn of the twentieth century, the nineteenth-century visions of "progress" had been largely realized, except in the northern Rocky Mountains, where something else happened.

The exploitive view of "progress" had a challenger in the nineteenth century: the counter-movement of Romanticism. Nature was seen as beautiful in its own right. Wild nature was seen as God's creation. The British Romantic poet William Wordsworth was widely read. American writer Ralph Waldo Emerson developed those ideas in the United States. In 1844 artist George Catlin called for a nation's park to preserve the wild buffalo herds and the lifestyle of the Native Americans. Romantic paintings brought the visual dreams of the North American West to national audiences. Eventually, in 1872, this powerful current of thought resulted in the creation of Yellowstone National Park, in Wyoming, Montana, and Idaho, soon followed by the creation of a national park at Banff in 1887.

There was also revulsion at the pioneers' indiscriminate slaughter of native animals, which pushed many species to the edge of extinction. There were different motivations: inconvenient "vermin," like wolves, were to be eliminated as "dangerous"; wild bison were competitors for range with domesticated cattle and their presence made the "Indians" hard to control; "game species," such as elk and pronghorn, were over-hunted as a food supply. Then writers such as Ernest Thompson Seton (who lived in both Canada and the US) helped our cultures to see wild animals as something of value in their own right by inventing the word "wildlife" and writing stories about the animals' lives. Wildlife refuges were created, such as the National Elk Refuge near Jackson, Wyoming, and Last Mountain Lake in Saskatchewan. Laws to control hunting were passed that applied on both public and private land. Perhaps most importantly, the wildlife sanctuary aspect of national parks was emphasized and enforced. Not long after came the protection of wilderness areas on public land, which protected more habitat.

Together, the two countries went further. Through government agencies we created the North American Waterfowl Management Plan, which has enabled the continued migration of ducks, swans, and geese up and down the great continental flyways. Through acts of Congress and Parliament we made the world's first International Peace Park, at Waterton-Glacier. Through civil society we built the Yellowstone to Yukon Conservation Initiative, to protect and connect habitat along the length of the Northern Rockies, which is known as the world's leading exemplar of large landscape conservation. These innovations for peace with nature and with each other were among the first ideas from the North American West to spread around the world. Thus was nature conservation pioneered hard up against the side of agrarian utilitarianism.

At first there were no big cities in the West, just bigger and smaller market towns. Living in isolation as a result of being widely dispersed across a vast landscape made us a friendly people, quick to invite strangers into our homes. At the same time we are united by a prickly attitude towards Easterners. We don't want Easterners telling us what to do or how to behave even when, and perhaps especially because, we descend from migrants who came from the East. We carry a colonial resentment toward our own countrymen because we were set up to be colonies of our national governments—not of any European power.[2]

In the late twentieth century a tide of people moved from the rural areas and from other parts of our countries to mix with new immigrants from all over the world in the big cities of Denver, Salt Lake City, Edmonton, and Calgary. Now these three look-alike metropolises dominate the region and are growing and spreading like active volcanoes. Amenity migrants sometimes replace the migrants of the rural exodus. Amenity migrants take advantage of the internet, the smartphone, and regional airports to move from the city to live a rural lifestyle based on recreation. Often, instead of living in the towns, these people subdivide and fragment the land so they can have their own piece of what should be a shared Eden. In general, this urban to rural migration has complicated the character of some rural areas more than the reverse has affected the character of cities. In summer a wave of tourists washes over any place with a national park or a clean freshwater lake nearby.

The North American Westerner is getting more diverse. Demand for oil has created a new transformative industry. The forces of globalization affect us. Yet the Westerner still embodies a strange mixture of unbridled optimism leavened by a measure of broken dreams from a legacy of boom and bust. When I was young, the abandoned homesteads of the Dust Bowl were a defining feature of the prairie landscape, and the Great Depression, a defining feature of the mental landscape. Both were haunting reminders of how horribly wrong we had gotten our relationship with nature in the driest part of the Great Plains. That tragedy was caused in part by the ridiculous belief that "rain follows the plow" into dry areas. Now we confront the equally stupid and destructive view that human-induced climate change and the extinction crisis are conspiracies perpetrated by those who "hate freedom." The facts are that we live in a world that is experiencing severe ecological stress that threatens destruction and human misery on the scale of a global Dust Bowl. Westerners, like all humans, must chart a new course. How well equipped are we do that?

Before I go further I must do explicit homage to Wallace Stegner. He challenged us Westerners to build a civilization worthy of the scenery. His writing about the West is so extensive and so insightful that it would be dangerous ignorance or extreme hubris to ignore it. He got so much right: "Deeply lived in places are the exception rather than the rule in the West. For one thing, all western places are new; for another, many of the people who established them came to pillage, or to work for pillagers, rather than to settle for life."³ So he began *Where the Bluebird Sings to the Lemonade Springs: Living and Writing in the West,* which serves as an essential reference to the character of a Westerner. And yet it is incomplete. Stegner's comment misses the first peoples of the West, for whom this is the only home they know and they are not leaving. They have something to teach us and a role to play in building the future of the North American West. So I view Stegner as analogous to an Old Testament prophet: you cannot understand Western civilization, religion, or culture without reference to Moses, but that is not the whole story.

A new story is needed but has yet to be written. It would be nice if a secular Angel Moroni could appear to reveal the book of the way forward to us. But I doubt that will happen. I think it will be up to us mere mortals to craft a new grand narrative of the North American West that will make the future worth living. It will be hard work of the pioneering kind. Strong winds of history and attitude blow against us, particularly on the plains, and the climate is literally changing under our feet. But we can know the essence of it already. It is time to build a North American West for the people who want to stay.

We need to acknowledge our starting point. North American Westerners live with a strange mix of wild mountains, transformed plains, economic prosperity, a few big cities, marginalized or removed aboriginal people, pride of place, optimism, resentment, and a confused future. We need a new vision of Western progress that builds on our past strengths in light of present conditions.

Stegner diagnosed an unlovely presence in us: the desire to get rich quick. But that spirit is juxtaposed with a Westerner's love of the outdoors and a love of nature. A Westerner who goes outside lives days that are so beautiful they can bring tears to the eyes. That naturally affects how we see the world. So how do we reconcile the love of the enduring with the lure of the quick buck? The answer is simple: we favor the people who want to stay over those who want to cash in and move on.

To make real progress in the twenty-first century we should embrace the traditional view of nature that was central to the first North American Westerners: the first nations or Native Americans, those people who were here when my pioneering family arrived. They knew we humans are one species among many, locked into an interdependent relationship with the natural world, and that we ought to celebrate and honor that relationship. Leroy Little Bear, a Blackfoot elder, likens the Native American worldview to Deep Ecology, which he describes as interrelationships between all animals, plants, humans, the earth, and so on, regardless of their value to humans: "In other words all beings have an inherent worth and all must be given an opportunity to 'be' and to 'exist.'"[4] In the traditional Native American worldview, there is a central belief in our kinship with all life. This can be seen in Lakota Sioux culture, which speaks of "elk people," "bear people," and "bird people." Joseph M. Marshall III points out this is not a form of anthropomorphism but rather a function of worldview reflected in language, "because in our language 'people' was not limited to humans, and animals are perceived as our relatives."[5]

This perception of other species as our relatives is not a quaint point of view. Recent work with DNA has shown that we humans do indeed have a strong genetic kinship with other species. But we also know our species is different and now dominant. The traditional aboriginal perspective provides a way to acknowledge this without losing perspective that we are part of the great scheme of life. Marshall describes it as knowing that "we are not the fastest or strongest of creatures, but we had the ability to reason and this enabled us to survive in the same way that the bear's strength, the antelope's speed or the eagle's keen eyesight sustained existence."[6]

The kinship-with-all-life perspective is common to many other indigenous cultures around the world. It is also linked to strong mythological or religious frameworks that explain how the world works. The French anthropologist Claude Lévi-Strauss described this holistic view of the world as "the totalitarian ambition of the savage mind." He notes Western civilization has an advantage because, through reductionism, we have a scientific approach that gives us the ability to control nature: "We are able, through scientific thinking, to achieve mastery over nature... while, of course, myth is unsuccessful in giving man more material power over the environment. However, it gives man, very importantly, the illusion that he can understand the universe.... It is, of course, only an illusion."[7] But we could apply this criticism of indigenous worldviews equally to the monotheistic religions followed by the people who first came west and which are still widely followed. A literal belief in the book of Genesis and the creation of the world in seven days does not square at all with the big bang theory, which is widely supported in physics, and the theory of evolution, on which all biological science is based. Yet we have a society that has profited from science and gone a far distance towards the illusory "mastery over nature."

Scientific criticism of religious frameworks does not prevent us from adopting the worldview that we are one species among many, bound together in an interdependent journey that demands the respect that flows from recognition of kinship with all life. We are capable of living with ambiguity, of rendering unto Caesar the things that are Caesar's and unto God the things that are God's. Lévi-Strauss noted that mythical thinking plays a similar role to conceptual thinking, and that the absolute gap between the findings of science and mythological thinking is narrowing, for the better.[8] This can be seen in a quote from Lakota Sioux Chief Luther Standing Bear that aligns in significant measure with current Western scientific thought on the origins of the universe: "From Wakan Tanka, the Great Spirit, there came a great unifying life force that flowed in and through all things—the flowers of the plains, blowing winds, rocks, trees, birds, animals—and was the same force that had been breathed into the first man. Thus all things were kindred, and were brought together by the same Great Mystery."[9] Lévi-Strauss suggested that considering traditional cultures' stories as a means of understanding the basic phenomena of life itself would make our civilization better: "[I]f we are led then to the feeling that there is not [an absolute] gap which is impossible to overcome between mankind on the one hand and all the other living beings—not only animals, but also plants—on the other, then perhaps we will reach much more wisdom."[10]

To be clear, the respect I have for the traditional Native American worldview of our relationship with nature is not a perspective I arrived at from romantic nostalgia based on a rose-colored view of "noble savages," disgust with my own cultural roots, or mistrust of science. Quite the contrary: I like my cultural roots. I am proud of my pioneer ancestors. I am an avid believer in the findings of science. I just don't like the cancer of environmental destruction that my species has set in motion since the Industrial Revolution. I think we ought to change, and I believe that the only way to make change is to change the story we live by. It is time for us to recognize that, as a philosophical underpinning for a healthy relationship with nature, the traditional Native American worldview has something to teach us that is wise.

Our dilemma is that in the pursuit of mastery over nature we have been clever but not wise. We can never be masters of the universe. We do have profound ability to manipulate and exploit natural systems and even transform them. But we do not know how to make a habitable planet, which is a function of interrelationships between plants, animals, and the nonliving elements of the world, and the earth's position in the cosmos. We do, however, have a good understanding of what is necessary to retain all the plants and animals.

Many scientific studies have been done in the West and elsewhere in the world that conclude that if we want to maintain all native species and natural processes, and allow species to be resilient to change, then we should protect in the range of half of any given landscape in an interconnected way.[11] We should certainly want to do that because native species and processes are necessary to keep the earth producing fresh water, clean air, and all the ecosystems that we depend on for life. Put another way, nature needs at least half to be managed for its purposes, not ours. We need to think of nature's needs because we are in a relationship with it. The first peoples of the North American West already knew this, albeit by different means.

The national parks, wildlife sanctuaries, and wilderness areas that Westerners pioneered are a wonderful starting point. They are the best tools known to humanity for protecting wild nature. But we have also learned that they cannot survive as "islands" in a transformed landscape. When they are isolated they tend to lose their species over time. They need to be connected to each other in a way that allows wildlife to move around the landscape to find mates. We know from the movements of animals as varied as grizzly bears, wolves, cougars, lynx, eagles, and swans that they travel north and south along the Rockies, without regard for the border. This is the reason that we started the Yellowstone to Yukon Conservation Initiative. Climate change now adds another reason to think big: as the landscape experiences warming, many species will have to adapt by moving to cooler areas across the landscape to the north or up-elevation.

In the southern portion of the Northern Rockies that runs from Yellowstone to Yukon we are close to achieving the needed level of protection of nature. The existing network of protected areas from the wilderness areas in the Wind River Mountains of Wyoming to the Willmore

Wilderness Park in Alberta, including the famous national parks along the Rockies between them, constitutes one of the world's largest collections of protected areas. We have also made good progress in this region by protecting nature on private lands in a way that is starting to stitch the protected areas together. There is significant work yet to be done to protect nature adequately in southern British Columbia but some promising progress is being made towards protecting places like the Flathead Valley, to fill in the missing piece of Waterton-Glacier International Peace Park and to connect it to Banff. Some paved roads and towns are starting to be properly planned, and their impact on the natural world mitigated in places like Banff National Park. Wolves are present again across the region. So are grizzly bears and native trout. Perhaps the greatest inspiration to get on with doing what else is needed is that the Northern Rockies today would be recognizable to my ancestors.

The Colorado Plateau, if it were unburdened by dams and aided by the removal of tamarisk and cheatgrass, would likely be recognizable to John Wesley Powell or to the Mormon pioneers. There is a strong network of national parks and national monuments already in place. It is not hard to imagine protecting at least half of the Colorado Plateau in an interconnected way.

The Colorado Rockies have some nice protected areas but are in need of a lot more conservation work, and big, inconvenient species ought to be restored to them. There are hopeful beginnings in places like Boulder County, where a mix of city, county, private, and federal lands has resulted in over half the county being protected in a prosperous community known for its quality of life. The reintroduction of lynx and moose is also a positive trend. But the landscape lacks the wild feeling so necessary to our psyches. The Colorado Rockies are beautiful in the way of a botanical garden. They need grizzly bears, wolves, buffalo, and native people to be whole.

The Great Plains are in very bad shape. They have been utterly transformed from an undulating ocean of wild grass and wild rivers that supported millions of wild animals to grids of cultivation or nonnative pastures that support cows watered by dugouts. Square patterns of land use dominate over more organic forms, and vast areas have been turned under and broken, though some isolated patches of native grasslands persist. Despite some ongoing noble efforts, we have protected and restored so little of the Great Plains that it is an embarrassment. Protecting nature at scale on the prairie seems very far off.

The uneasy truce we fashioned between "progress" and Romanticism in the nineteenth century has given us a schizophrenic attitude towards nature: we honor it in mountains and in canyonlands but have felt free to dominate it on the prairies. In our cities we turn our backs to the devastated plains while we face hopefully towards the mountains. Increasingly some see only the city itself; ignore nature altogether by treating it as an externality; or, blinded by postmodernism, think that nature is a human construct. The great floods of 2013 that ravaged developments on river floodplains in Boulder, Colorado, and Calgary, Alberta, proved the folly of those forms of ignorance.[12]

We should not live with a Janus face. The people of the prairie should not need to go to the mountains to know wild nature. I have seen wild plains in my lifetime. They are astonishing and inspiring. The Serengeti-Mara ecosystem, on the grassland savannah of Tanzania and Kenya, gives us a glimpse of what we have lost. It is time for a new beginning on the Great Plains.

We should engage in a great shared undertaking to bring back the wild buffalo ecosystem and the predators who once roamed the plains, to restore native grasses, to use fire to keep the land healthy, and to remove a lot of dams. We should back our urban developments out of the floodplains and let nature renew herself through flooding. I would like to see the Great Falls be great again.

Protecting in an interconnected way at least half of the Great Plains would support healthy human communities and still leave an enormous amount of land in agricultural production. Just as we pioneered the national park in our mountain environments, we can lead the world in the restoration of a big wild grassland ecosystem. I even have an idea of where to begin focusing our work to bring life back to the Great Plains. Some people are already working there, ahead of me, on the American Prairie Reserve project in Montana. They are the pioneers of the twenty-first century.

We need to right our relationship with wild nature on the Great Plains for another reason: our own psychological well-being. It is heartbreaking to consider that while our predecessors pioneered nature conservation in the Rockies, they saw fit to smash the prairie into dust. The colossal damage we have done to the Great Plains has also damaged our psyches. Eminent Jungian psychologist C. A. Meier pointed out that the wild aspect of human beings is held in check by the presence of wild nature. As our ability to dominate nature has grown, our respect for and fear of nature has declined. The wild forces of nature, which kept early humans "watchful and humble," when removed from the landscape around us will assert themselves in our psyche to the detriment of our mental health. Meier described the psychic cost to humans of the loss of wilderness: "[W]e find that we have lost something equilibrating, equalizing, healthy, sane and of value, a loss for which we have to pay. Thus, anxiety neurosis has become very widespread."[13] To Meier, the loss of wilderness turns our inner nature towards despair, or we turn the anxiety outward towards violence. Lakota Sioux Luther Standing Bear made a similar comment over one hundred years ago. He said, "The old Lakota was wise. He knew that a man's heart away from Nature becomes hard; he knew that lack of respect for growing, living things soon lead to a lack of respect for humans too."[14] When we yearn for a home where the buffalo roam and the deer and the antelope play, it is more than nostalgia.

The John A. Lomax version of the song "Home on the Range" laments, "The red man was pressed / from this part of the West / He's likely no more to return."[15] That is not right. Aboriginal people have been clustered in reservations, where they either try to rebuild from the ruins of a culture that was swept away when the wildness was destroyed, participate in the new way, or migrate to cities. Too often they live in a downward spiral of despair. We turn our backs on them. But we do not escape. The first inhabitants of the North American West, both human and wild, haunt our memory.

Haida Canadian artist Bill Reid wrote of the anger and despairing rage that First Peoples (Native Americans) feel as result of the loss of the world they knew and how that anger turns either inward in self-destructive ways or outward to be destructive to what is near at hand. He suggested honoring the artistic traditions of those first cultures as a way forward: "Perhaps by doing so we may all move a little bit along the way to becoming, at last or again, true North Americans—neither displaced aborigines nor immigrant settlers."[16] I would extend his words to include honoring the First Nations' perspective on our relationship with the natural world.

We humans must learn to live with all of nature for our own good. Nature is not always convenient. We need processes that we do not control. We need floods and fires. We need undammed rivers. We need carnivores and undomesticated grazers—such as grizzly bears, wolves, and wild bison—that perform key roles in the structure of ecosystems. We need humility. We need to treat our home with love.

The land and our common history make us North American Westerners. Together we should start building the West for the people who want to stay. We can do this with due regard for our own national traditions. We can restore equilibrium to our psyches and return at least half the land to a condition that would be recognizable to its first inhabitants. Then a bright future would lie ahead. Of course we must also educate our young, ensure access to health care, farm with the earth in mind, build beautiful towns and cities, have a vibrant cultural life, and create an economy that serves our needs. But those challenges apply everywhere. The essential work for us North American Westerners to do is to right the wrongs done to nature, to native people, and to ourselves in the place that we call home.

When we begin building the West for the people who want to stay, we will be on our way to fulfilling Wallace Stegner's prophecy of a society worthy of the scenery. For a civilization that embraces wildness, beauty, and difference will be healthier, happier, and more resilient than one that attempts to suppress them. We will know when we have arrived— that day when all of us and all the species that belong here live together again, at home on the range of the North American West.

NOTES

1. Elizabeth Boyd McDougall, "Just a Few Sentences About the Indian...," in *McDougall Reflections: The Future of the Indians of Canada,* eds. G. Hutchinson and S. Wilks, Historical Booklet no. 1, (Calgary: McDougall Mission Society, 1996), 17.
2. Harvey Locke, "The Two Albertas," *Literary Review of Canada* 22, no. 23(2) (April 2014).
3. Wallace Stegner, *Where the Bluebird Sings to the Lemonade Springs: Living and Writing in the West* (New York: Random House), xvi.
4. Leroy Little Bear, personal communication with the author, 2014.
5. Joseph M. Marshall III, *The Lakota Way: Stories and Lessons for Living* (New York: Penguin Compass, 2001), 211.

6. Ibid.
7. Claude Lévi-Strauss, *Myth and Meaning,* http://www.cbc.ca/radio /ideas/the-1977-cbc-massey-lectures-myth-and-meaning-1.2946825.
8. Lévi-Strauss, *Myth and Meaning.*
9. Luther Standing Bear, "Luther Standing Bear: Chief of the Oglala Lakota (1905 to 1939)," Indigenous Peoples Literature, compiled by Glenn Welker, accessed April 16, 2017, http://www.indigenouspeople .net/standbea.htm.
10. Lévi-Strauss, *Myth and Meaning.*
11. Harvey Locke, "Nature Needs Half: A Necessary and Hopeful New Agenda for Protected Areas in North America and Around the World," *The George Wright Forum* 31, no. 3 (2014): 359–371.
12. Harvey Locke, "Nature Answers Man," *Policy Options,* September 19, 2013, http://policyoptions.irpp.org/magazines/the-age-of-man/locke.
13. C. A. Meier, "Wilderness and the Search for the Soul of Modern Man," in *A Testament to the Wilderness* (Santa Monica: The Lapis Press, 1985), 6.
14. Luther Standing Bear, "Luther Standing Bear."
15. John A. Lomax, "Home on the Range," accessed April 16, 2017, Library of Congress, https://www.loc.gov/item/ihas.200196571/#ref1, and Wikipedia, https://en.wikipedia.org/wiki/Home_on_the_Range #Major_versions_compared.
16. Bill Reid, *Solitary Raven: The Essential Writings of Bill Reid* (Vancouver: Douglas and McIntyre, 2000), 161.

Reimagining Wild Life on the Northern Plains

Lessons from the Little Bighorn

Gregory E. Smoak

In the previous essay, Harvey Locke laments the disappearance of the grasslands of middle America; now Gregory Smoak focuses on the Great Plains—and the Little Bighorn Battlefield National Monument in particular—as a "testing ground" for negotiating a place for "wild life," a negotiation profoundly grounded in the relationship of human and nonhuman nature. He describes the fascinating and complex ecological web binding prairie dogs, black-footed ferrets, burrowing owls, and mountain plovers, along with countless insects and arachnids—all who depend on the health of the plains. He recounts the competing interests between the Plains Indians and their horse herds and the bison, and later, between the Euro-Americans and their cattle and railroads. By understanding the "complex and dynamic" story of the Little Bighorn, Smoak thinks, "we might better reimagine the future of the Great Plains."

Historians are notoriously poor prophets, and those with at least a lick of sense shy away from predicting the future. Imagining is another thing entirely. History without imagination is pretty dull, and only by considering the possibilities that historical actors faced can a historian hope to make sense of the choices they made. So what I will attempt here is to imagine how the environmental history of one specific place might facilitate a larger reimagining of the Great Plains. Environmental history is well suited to this task. It takes as its subject human interactions with nonhuman nature and the reciprocal effects of that engagement. It is grounded in the material realities of the natural world but is equally concerned with historically and culturally derived perceptions of nature and what constitutes a proper relationship with that world.

The place that I imagine might serve as a testing ground for negotiating a place for "wild life" on the northern plains will probably come as a surprise—Little Bighorn Battlefield National Monument (LIBI).[1] Around three hundred thousand people come to the park every summer to experience the place where Lt. Col. George Armstrong Custer made his "last stand" against Lakota and Cheyenne warriors, led by Sitting Bull, Crazy Horse, and Gall. These visitors do not come seeking a natural experience. It is one of the many historic sites that the late Edward Abbey derisively called "cannonball parks," to set them apart from the big natural (read: "real") parks.

So what promise does a place like LIBI hold for reimagining the plains? Nearly thirty years ago Deborah and Frank Popper reimagined the future of the northern plains on a grand scale. They proposed the "world's largest historic preservation project" and suggested turning much of the area into a "buffalo commons" as a means of addressing the problems of rural poverty, depopulation, and unsustainable agriculture that plagued the region.[2] A park as small and fragmented as LIBI (eight hundred acres divided between two units separated by four miles of tribally and privately owned lands) cannot realistically become a refuge for threatened and endangered species. It is simply not a viable "island" of biodiversity. Rather, what I will suggest here is that the unique combination of the park's physical location and the intense public interest in the place offers real opportunities to learn about the historic and current ecological relationships that make up the northern plains and to apply those lessons in other places.

To begin reimagining a place for "wild life" at LIBI, and by extension in the northern plains, we must understand the complex and changing relationships between grasslands, wildlife, domesticated animals, and human beings that produced both historic and current landscapes.

As the glaciers receded at the end of the Pleistocene, the North American grasslands expanded and the bison became the most populous large grazing mammal to ever exist on the continent.[3] Historic estimates of peak populations—up to one hundred million—were wildly inflated guesses.[4] Current estimates take into account complex environmental factors and suggest that the total bison population for all of the Great Plains before the introduction of horses was perhaps twenty-eight to thirty million.[5] Still, as the most numerous grazer, the bison's life cycle and behavior were undeniable forces in shaping the North American grasslands. Bison graze intensively on dominant grasses, reducing their relative abundance, while the bison's wallowing and pawing creates micro-environmental heterogeneity and contributes to species diversity. Bison migrated within "home ranges," where they habitually returned to sites offering forage, water, and shelter. These familiar areas could be substantial but they were not continental (a popular nineteenth-century myth). Nor were they static. Rainfall and range fires impacted the availability of forage and could shift migration patterns. Cycles of drought and fire may also have "imposed a deferred rotation" that prevented migratory bison herds from grazing the same land year after year and promoted "vegetation-herbivore stability in the Great Plains grasslands."[6]

Within a home range, bison populations aggregated and dispersed with the seasons. Bison spent fall through late spring in smaller, sexually segregated herds. The calving season began in April, just as the growth of cool season grasses (species that actively grow and bloom in fall and spring) offered a renewed food source. Much larger herds congregated several months later, during the summer breeding season, or rut, which peaked in July and August. Warm season grasses provided the bulk of the bison diet at this time. As summer turned to fall and warm season grasses went dormant the great herds again split up into cow-calf and bull herds. These smaller groups moved into more sheltered broken topography, where they again consumed cool season grasses, now in their secondary growth phase. As winter set in, the nutritional value of the grasses steadily declined to the point that the animals could not maintain their body weight. By the end of March each year the available nutrition as well as the bison population reached its absolute nadir just as a new season was to begin.[7]

While the northeastern plains produced the most abundant forage, the higher, drier northwestern plains, including the Little Bighorn Valley, produced superior forage during the critical months of late winter and early spring. This was because much of eastern Montana was not a true shortgrass prairie like those found farther south, where warm season species predominated. Instead, this northern mixed prairie contained a much higher proportion of cool season grasses. Because grasses are the most nutritious during their active growth phase, mixed prairies provide better year-round forage for grazers. Moreover, relatively greater precipitation, rougher topography that made for sheltered valleys, and the phenomenon of foehn winds (also known as Chinooks or "snow-eating" winds) that cured the grasses and kept them exposed throughout the winter all made the northern mixed prairies a vital bison range.[8]

The ecosystems of the Great Plains were not just the product of grasses and large grazers; smaller species also exerted important influence. The prairie dog town was certainly the most visible and iconic western landscape shaped by small mammals.[9] Historic prairie dog towns could be immense. Massive colonies as well as complexes of smaller towns probably characterized prairie dog distribution before Euro-American conquest. Nineteenth-century reports suggest that very large colonies, some stretching for nearly forty miles across the plains, marked the Montana plains.[10] (Today, a small colony currently exists just outside the northern boundary of the park.) Prairie dogs eat native perennial grasses and forbs, making for substantial dietary overlap with native ungulates, such as bison and pronghorn, as well as introduced domestic livestock.[11]

Prairie dogs are a keystone species indicating the health of native grassland ecosystems. Biodiversity is greater in proximity to their colonies. Their burrowing mixes soil layers and improves the distribution of nutrients and retention of moisture. Bison benefit from the foraging on the edges of prairie dog towns, and numerous other vertebrate and invertebrate species thrive in the ecosystem, including a range of insects and arachnids. Burrowing owls commonly make their home in colonies where prairie dog burrows provide nesting space and short vegetation allows them to more easily spot predators. Likewise, the mountain plover finds welcoming habitat in the short vegetation and bare ground within prairie dog colonies. Over the course of the twentieth century, as prairie dog habitat was destroyed and the animals extirpated, the once-common mountain plover became increasingly rare in the plains.[12] But no obligate species is more dependent upon prairie dogs than the black-footed ferret. A dangerously specialized predator, a single ferret requires a relatively large prairie dog colony (between forty and sixty hectares) to survive. Few accounts of the animal appear in the historic record, and they were not scientifically described until 1851. Still, the great expanse of prairie dog ecosystems suggests that relatively large ferret populations existed before intensive Euro-American settlement. Using population densities observed in the early 1980s as a model, it is possible that 150,000 ferrets could have occupied southeastern Montana at the turn of the twentieth century.[13]

The acquisition of horses by native peoples was one of the greatest catalysts for cultural and environmental change on the plains. The ancestors of modern horses evolved in North America but all were extinct by the end of the Pleistocene. In the sixteenth century Spanish conquistadors brought horses, as well as an Iberian horse culture, to the Americas. In the wake of the Pueblo Revolt of 1680, thousands of horses poured out of New Mexico, where they moved through preexisting native trade routes on both sides of the Rocky Mountains and reached as far north as Canada by the mid-eighteenth century.[14]

Horses revolutionized the ecological relationships between native peoples, bison, and the grasslands. Before the acquisition of horses, dogs were the only domesticated animals that the pedestrian hunters of the plains possessed. In many ways horses replaced canines, yet they were much more than simply "big dogs" (the literal translation of the Blackfeet word for "horse"). Horses entailed a fundamentally different trophic relationship with the plains. Grasses converted the energy of the sun into protein and carbohydrates. That energy, however, was essentially locked away from human beings—and their dogs—in a largely inedible form. To get at that stored energy, hunting peoples had to eat the grazing species that could digest the grass. Horses, on the other hand, were commensal with bison and could tap into the energy reserves of the plains. The size, speed, and endurance of horses greatly exceeded that of dogs for this reason. "The crucial relationship, in short, is not so much between people and their animals," writes historian Elliott West, "it is between people and the things their animals eat."[15] Horses allowed plains people to pursue the bison as specialized hunters, a possibility that their pedestrian ancestors could not imagine. Horses revolutionized the hunt in other ways. Taking bison from horseback increasingly replaced older communal methods, such as arroyo traps and corrals. At approximately the same time that horses reached the plains from the southwest, guns were coming from the northeast. The combination of horses and guns led to the development of distinct warrior cultures across the Great Plains.[16]

Yet with every opportunity there is also a cost. The new horse-bison economy demanded strict adherence to seasonal rules. First, and most obviously, dedicated bison hunting demanded great mobility. While bison generally stayed within a home range, their movements were irregular and finding the herds meant moving constantly.[17] Moreover, since horses and bison are commensals, they came into direct competition for both forage and water. Keeping large horse herds meant constantly searching for fresh pasture. For much of the year then, a Plains Indian village could only remain in one place for a few days.[18] The second rule of life for equestrian peoples seemingly contradicted the first; they had to remain relatively sedentary and in control of vital resource areas during the winter. Liebig's law of the minimum states that the success of any organism is not governed by the total amount of resources available, but rather the minimum amount available at any one time. Both the bison and the people who depended on their meat had to confront this reality. Through the long plains winter, the amount of energy available in forage inexorably declined. Extended camps in riparian areas that offered forage, water, timber, and shelter replaced the mobility of summer. Of course, these same bottomlands were also the refuge of the smaller, sexually segregated winter bison herds, meaning the competition between horses and bison for forage continued year round.[19]

The Northern Cheyenne warrior Wooden Leg recalled his people's annual cycle, and his account illustrates the rules of mobility and strategic security that plains people were bound to live by. In 1874, his people undertook a lengthy hunting trip through the Powder, Tongue, and Little Bighorn Valleys. "Many thousands of buffalo, deer, antelope," Wooden Leg recalled, "many skins, much meat, everybody prosperous and in health." Before the large camp divided, the united Cheyenne held their Sun Dance on the Little Bighorn. With the end of the rutting season the buffalo broke into smaller groups and so too did their hunters. Moreover, mobility was traded for the security of sheltered riparian areas. "An early autumn snowstorm...put a check on our great summer movements," he remembered. "Separations came again." Wooden Leg's band moved to the upper Tongue River, where they spent the entire winter amongst herds of buffalo. His fond recollections of that winter camp neatly summarized how plains peoples ideally made it through the often brutal winters: "We had but to kill and eat.... That is all anybody actually needs—a good shelter, plenty of food, plenty of fuel, plenty of good water."[20]

Through the course of the nineteenth century, the horse-bison economy of Plains Indians reached its peak and then declined as the numbers of the animals on which it depended spiraled downward. The

Landscape with Buffalo on the Upper Missouri. By Karl Bodmer, 1833. Watercolor.

decline did not occur evenly across the plains. It was felt first in the east and then the south. Other areas, however, saw bison numbers remain more stable well into the century. Eastern Montana, including the Little Bighorn Valley, was one of those areas. The ecology of the Northern Mixed Grasslands was certainly part of the equation. But so were historical factors, most notably intertribal conflict, which created a dangerous borderland.

Across North America one of the most important ecological consequences of the chronic intertribal warfare was the maintenance of what historians and anthropologists have variously called "debatable zones" or "borderlands," where "hunters entered only when prepared for war."[21] When warfare persisted and no group could control an area outright, game was not depleted. In the 1820s and 1830s the area between the Platte and Arkansas Rivers was such a neutral zone. But after the great peace of 1840 ended chronic warfare between the Comanche, Kiowa, Cheyenne, and Arapahos, the pace of hunting increased and bison numbers began to fall.[22] No great victory or peace, however, had changed the military-political situation in the Little Bighorn Valley.

Eastern Montana had, in fact, long been a contested borderland and erstwhile game preserve. On their outbound trip the Lewis and Clark expedition encountered few native people between the Mandan villages and the Forks of the Missouri. They did, however, encounter an abundance of wildlife.[23] Some scholars have argued that the abundance of game reported by Lewis and Clark along the upper Missouri and Yellowstone drainages was not a reflection of the rich environment, but rather of the contested nature of the area.[24] The decades after Lewis and Clark's visit saw a growing conflict between the Crow people and the expanding Lakota and Cheyenne, who fought them for control of the rich bison ranges. The drainages of the Powder and Tongue Rivers, straddling the modern states of Wyoming and Montana, became the most hotly contested ground. The Fort Laramie Treaty of 1851, the supposed grand solution to native warfare on the plains, recognized the Little Bighorn Valley as well as the contested Powder River country as Crow territory.[25] The next two and a half decades, however, only witnessed increased intertribal competition. Although great changes had taken place by the mid-1850s, fur trader Edwin Denig could still call the valleys of the Yellowstone and its tributaries east of the mountains "perhaps the best game country in the world."[26]

Euro-American encroachment further complicated the situation. The discovery of gold in western Montana led to the establishment of the Bozeman Trail, which cut directly through the Powder River country and crossed the Little Bighorn River near the modern Wyoming-Montana border. The resulting conflict between the United States and the Lakota-Cheyenne alliance, known as Red Cloud's War, ended with the closing of the trail and the three forts that had been built along it. In 1867 and 1868 a series of new treaties was negotiated at Fort Laramie. The Crow treaty set the Little Bighorn Valley as part of their reservation. The Lakota Fort Laramie Treaty of 1868 created the Great Sioux Reservation out of the western half of Dakota Territory and guaranteed that the "country north of the North Platte river and east of the summits of the Big Horn mountains shall be held and considered to be unceded."[27] And so the Powder River country remained the epicenter of intertribal conflict into the mid-1870s. There, the bison herds could still sustain native peoples, but could only be accessed by small, daring groups of hunters, or by much larger villages always prepared for the possibility of war.[28]

The struggle to control the plains was as much environmental as it was military and political. The "unbendable" rules of Plains Indian life not only put them and their horse herds into direct competition with the bison herds, but also with Euro-Americans who coveted the same areas.[29] Between 1868 and 1876 the United States exerted increased pressure on native peoples to remain permanently on the reservations. While many Lakota began the adjustment to reservation life, others sought to continue their customary lifeways based on pursuit of the bison. This entailed spending most of their time in the Powder River country, where viable bison herds remained. The Hunkpapa leader Sitting Bull was the most influential and respected leader of this group, although the Hunkpapa Gall and Crazy Horse of the Oglalas also emerged as leaders of the off-reservation peoples. While they have been deemed "hostiles" or "militants" in older literature, their desire was not to go to war with Euro-Americans, but rather to pursue their customary ways free of the whites and the reservations. Still, their stance that Euro-Americans must stay out of the Powder River country inevitably led to conflict. The Battle of the Little Bighorn, known to the Lakota as the Battle of the Greasy Grass and romantically to the American public as "Custer's Last Stand," was the greatest engagement of the resulting "Great Sioux War." And although native warriors won a stunning victory that June day in 1876, within a year the mighty, industrial United States crushed their resistance.

In the decade following the battle, eastern Montana began a far-reaching and seemingly irreversible transformation. It began with the annihilation of the bison. Market hunting by both native peoples and Euro-Americans had already taken its toll when the insatiable demands of industrializing America pushed the herds over the brink. A new tanning process developed in 1870 allowed the production of industrial-grade leather from previously unusable bison hides. Quickly, unprocessed hides supplanted native-processed robes in the bison trade. The extension of railroads and widespread availability of accurate big bore rifles facilitated the slaughter.[30] Eastern Montana's status as a contested native borderland had only delayed the process. The herds were already weakened when the end of native resistance and the extension of the Northern Pacific's tracks into the Yellowstone Valley set the stage for commercial hunting. The first big wave of hide hunters arrived in 1880. Soon, thousands of hunting outfits fanned out across the territory. By the spring of

1884, what was once the most abundant large mammal to ever roam the North American continent was all but extinct.

Domestic cattle filled the niche left by the bison. When the commercial hunting outfits had descended on the Bighorn, Rosebud, Powder, and Tongue Valleys, nearly all of Montana's domestic livestock still grazed in the western reaches of the territory. As soon as those valleys were hunted out, large cattle concerns drove tens of thousands of head onto the range.[31] Granville Stuart, himself a founder of the Montana Stockgrowers Association, recalled the enormity of the change:

> It would be impossible to make persons not present on the Montana cattle ranges realize the rapid change that took place on those ranges in two years. In 1880 the country was practically uninhabited.... Thousands of buffalo darkened the rolling plains. There were deer, antelope, elk, wolves, and coyotes on every hill and in every ravine and thicket. In the whole territory of Montana there were but 250,000 head of cattle.... In the fall of 1883 there was not one buffalo remaining on the range and the antelope, elk, and deer were indeed scarce. In 1880 no one had heard tell of a cowboy in "this niche of the woods" and Charlie Russell had made no pictures of them; but in the fall of 1883 there were 600,000 head of cattle on the range.[32]

Both the grazing habits of cattle and the management systems that the stockmen employed contributed to environmental changes. While cattle and bison are in many ways analogous grazers, there also are important differences. Cattle seek out higher-quality forbs and woody species and consequently reduce the diversity of forage species. The generalized ecological impact of cattle grazing on shortgrass prairies, then, was an increase in the relative cover of dominant grasses and succulents, like prickly pear, at the expense of forbs and shrubs, and an overall decrease in plant cover and species diversity.[33] Management techniques led to even more profound change. Cattle do not naturally exhibit the same seasonal migratory patterns as bison. Ranchers moved their herds according to forage conditions, ownership considerations, and the market, not ecological concerns. Fences reoriented plant-animal relationships in spatial and temporal terms, while artificial watering points led to the habitual congregation of cattle and ultimately defoliation, feces accumulation,

soil compaction, and the disturbed bare earth necessary for the colonization of weeds.[34]

And so on the heels of the cattleman's invasion came a weed invasion. Weeds are opportunistic plants that thrive in bare or disturbed soils.
They out-compete native vegetation as well as economically desirable cultivated species through rapid growth, the ability to regenerate from root
fragments, wide-spreading leaves and low branches that crowd out other
plants, and high, sustained seed output. Weeds traveled via three princi-
pal natural mechanisms. Some, such as dandelions and the Russian thistle,
depended upon the wind. Water was the second means of weed distribution.
With light, waterproof coverings that allowed seeds to float long distances,
nearly all weeds could be spread via flowing water. Animals provided the
third means of transportation. Some weeds produce seeds with impervi-
ous coverings, enabling them to survive the passage through an animal's
digestive track, while others have barbed or sticky seeds that attach themselves to feet or fur of passing hosts.[35] In addition to these natural mechanisms of transmission, some weeds were purposely introduced as forage
crops, wind breaks, or ornamentals. Weeds first appeared along watercourses, trails, roads, and railroad lines. Railroad construction crews created an ideal weed habitat while the trains that followed carried weed seed
with them in their cars and in and on the livestock they moved. The development of irrigation canals added hundreds, even thousands, of miles of
new avenues to the region's natural watercourses. Moreover, they deliv-
ered that water to newly cleared lands where weeds could thrive.[36] Of the
thirty-eight invasive species found at Little Bighorn Battlefield National
Monument in 2006, fifteen were weed species that first appeared in Montana before 1900, largely as a result of grazing.

While the Little Bighorn Valley had long been Crow territory, divisions within the tribe, federal policy, and the longstanding conflict with
the powerful Lakota-Cheyenne alliance meant that permanent Crow
settlement in the area did not occur until the 1880s.[37] The federal government moved the agency to its current location at Crow Agency, Montana, just three miles from the Little Bighorn battlefield in 1884. From
that time on the valley experienced constant human occupation as well
as agricultural development and commercial grazing. The construction of
some of the earliest irrigation canals in the region was one consequence
of the agency relocation. These early works were crudely engineered, and
while they did not substantially diminish the flow of the river or turn the

Crow people into Jeffersonian yeoman farmers (as Indian Bureau officials hoped), they proved to be perfect avenues for the advance of weeds.[38]

A homesteading boom after the turn of the twentieth century accelerated and magnified the environmental changes taking place in Montana. The Enlarged Homestead Act of 1909 provided for 320-acre claims,
double the size of the original law. Between 1909 and 1923, homesteaders
filed 114,620 claims on twenty-five million acres in the eastern part of the
state. During this same period, the Northern Pacific Railroad, the ben-
eficiary of the largest land grant in the nation's history, sold off over ten
million acres of its remaining Montana lands.[39] But available land alone
was not enough. The homesteaders also had to believe that agriculture
could actually prosper on the semiarid high plains. Irrigation held great
promise, but water projects proved too expensive for most farmers. The
majority turned to a vaunted new method of dry farming. The "Campbell system" relied solely on preparation of the soil to retain natural moisture and enjoyed great popularity throughout the West between 1902 and
1914.[40] Railroad promotions, Montana officials, and local boosters all
touted the quality of Montana farmlands and the efficacy of the Campbell system. Above-average rainfall between 1910 and 1917 and booming
commodity prices seemed to confirm the inflated claims.[41]

The homestead boom collapsed as quickly as it began, falling vic-
tim to the environmental realities of the high plains and the economic
uncertainties of a world market. Drought set in by 1918, and the war's
end brought a free fall for commodity markets. As farm bankruptcy
skyrocketed the exodus from the eastern plains began. The population plunged about 75 percent. Over eleven thousand farms were abandoned to nature.[42] The bust brought environmental impacts that proved
as consequential as the boom's. Millions of acres lay abandoned across
eastern Montana. Stripped of their native sod, these lands became the
source of massive dust storms as well as the perfect breeding ground for
weeds. Numerous introduced/invasive species were first noted in Montana after the turn of the twentieth century and spread rapidly because
of the homestead boom and bust.[43]

If the destruction of the bison paved the way for the agricultural
transformation of southeastern Montana, the changes it wrought proved
disastrous for the black-tailed prairie dog and the black-footed ferret.
The expansion of cropland came at the expense of prairie dog towns. At
the same time, ranchers perceived the small rodents as a direct threat to

their livelihood. The extirpation of prairie dog colonies began in some areas as early as the 1880s, but it was with the homestead boom that the campaign to eradicate prairie dogs began in earnest. Shooting, plowing, and drowning were all used. The most pervasive and effective control measure was poisoning. Private ranchers spread strychnine-laced grain across colonies. Arsenic and potassium cyanide were also widely used, while toxic fumigants such as carbon bisulfide were pumped into burrows. Individual poisoning campaigns soon gained government sanction and support. The federal Bureau of Biological Survey first began demonstrating poison control techniques in 1905, and after 1915 became directly involved in eradication efforts in partnership with western states. Between 1915 and 1965 a total of 3.4 million hectares (8.4 million acres) of prairie dogs were poisoned in Montana. In 1920 alone 2.8 million hectares were treated with poisoned bait.[44]

The spread of sylvatic plague also led to prairie dog decline. Caused by the same bacteria—*Yersinia pestis*—responsible for the bubonic plague, the disease was introduced into North America in the early twentieth century. Because they evolved without exposure to the bacteria, prairie dogs had little innate or adaptive immunity. Mortality rates during outbreaks can top 90 percent.[45] The combined effects of plague and poison decimated prairie dog populations across their historic range. By the mid-1980s it is likely that the number of prairie dogs in eastern Montana was less than 10 percent of its historic level.[46] Black-footed ferret populations suffered even worse decline. The destruction of prairie dog colonies eliminated ferret habitat, while the consumption of poisoned prairie dogs killed countless ferrets. To make matters worse, black-footed ferrets are also highly susceptible to sylvatic plague. The fractured prairie dog ecosystems that characterized the Great Plains by the mid-twentieth century simply could not sustain viable self-sustaining ferret populations. Ferret numbers continued to spiral downward until the animal was believed extinct by the end of the 1970s.[47]

With this general history of environmental change in mind we can now turn to the specific history of LIBI to understand the ways in which it followed or diverged from these patterns and why it might serve as a means of reimagining "wild life" on the northern plains.

In the wake of Custer's shocking defeat the army moved to memorialize the soldiers and protect their graves. A reburial party visited the battlefield in 1877, and that same year Fort Custer was established at the confluence of the Bighorn and Little Bighorn Rivers. For the next fifteen years the post commander there served as the de facto superintendent of the battlefield. In 1881 the soldiers' remains were reinterred in a mass grave beneath the granite obelisk installed atop Last Stand Hill. Although a War Department order had authorized Custer Battlefield National Cemetery in 1879, it was not until 1886 that the land was officially taken from the Crow Reservation. The initial plan had called for the withdrawal of eighteen square miles, but the Crows were loath to lose any more of their reservation, and the Bureau of Indian Affairs did not want to cede valuable agricultural lands that might further their assimilation program. Instead, the federal government took a single section— one square mile, 640 acres. It was not for another four decades that the 160-acre Reno-Benteen Defense Site, four miles south of the main battlefield, was acquired from the Crow Nation.

From the 1880s until 1941 the War Department administered the site as a national cemetery. And while preserving "wild life" never factored into the army's policies, it nevertheless set the battlefield lands off on a divergent course. The small cemetery itself—not to be confused with the larger cemetery reservation, with its scattered white granite markers— was eventually landscaped in a traditional style replete with a bluegrass lawn, spruce-lined walks, and an introduced honeysuckle hedge. The rest of the parcel, however, was essentially left alone.

Among the army's earliest, and most consequential, management decisions was to fence the cemetery and prohibit grazing. By 1890 a barbed-wire fence enclosed most of the Custer Battlefield section of the modern monument. (Due to the difficulties posed by "deep arroyos," the riparian bottomlands largely remained open.) The army was not concerned with the ecological impact of the grazing but with the threat of damage that livestock posed to the gravesites and headstones.[48] In agricultural production, fences were meant to separate and organize plants and animals, while for the monument, the fence was intended to restrict the use of a memorialized space. Regardless of the intended purpose, the fence could only restrict the travel of some organisms. It could not completely control the effects of the greater changes that surrounded the cemetery. Rather, the fence served as a "biological sieve" that restricted the passage of large, mostly domesticated, animals, but posed no obstacle to life forms ranging from native birds and small mammals to the airborne seeds of invasive dandelions. Still, the relative absence of large grazers from the cemetery reservation was a critical factor that affected the composition of plant communities and fire regimes in the decades that followed.[49] In later reports and planning documents, National Park Service (NPS) officials cited the fence as the key factor in preserving the dominance of native grasses and maintaining the historic "natural" landscape at the park.[50]

Yet a completely ungrazed landscape in the Little Bighorn Valley was as "man-made" as one marked by overgrazing. The battlefield in 1876 was the product of grazing by bison and other native species as well as Indian ponies. This grazing was never as intensive and sustained as that associated with commercial stock growing, but it did shape the vegetation and landscape. A 1964 NPS document acknowledged that "the area was long grazed by buffalo and other ruminants so the present growth of ground cover may be somewhat different from that of 1876."[51] This insight, while not completely lost, was largely set aside in favor of less critical evaluations that characterized the park's grasslands as "pristine" or "virgin."

In 1940 management of Custer Battlefield (the name change to Little Bighorn Battlefield National Monument took place in 1991) was transferred to the National Park Service. While preservation was central to the agency's mission, it would be wrong to assume that this meant an immediate focus on "wild life." For example, most wildlife was simply not integral to NPS management policies during the agency's first half century of existence. Well into the 1960s the park service generally treated species in a dichotomous manner, ignoring some while over-manipulating others. Birds, small mammals, reptiles, and insects (unless they threatened resources) could be and were usually ignored. Large iconic wildlife—bison, elk, grizzly bear, or wolves—became the subject of intense management programs, either to ensure viewing opportunities for visitors or to be controlled when deemed a threat.[52] Broader park service policies underwent significant change from the mid-1960s through the early 1980s but at a unit as small and historically oriented as Custer Battlefield, wildlife management was simply not a priority. With a few exceptions (a prohibition on hunting and the removal of stray animals) the "protection" offered to wildlife at Little Bighorn was essentially passive.[53] Into the 1970s there were no active efforts to manage habitat with wildlife values in mind. One resource management plan from late that decade concluded that the small size of the monument, under eight hundred total acres, "would seem to have little or no control over a wildlife management program due to outside forces," and thus recommended: "Continue doing nothing."[54] But then the park burned down.

On August 10, 1983, high winds whipped up a smoldering human-caused fire at Little Bighorn Battlefield National Monument. Within ninety minutes approximately six hundred acres—over 90 percent—of the Custer Battlefield section of the park burned. Miraculously no one was injured and there was no damage to the park's visitor facilities or to the National Cemetery. But with nearly all grasses, forbs, and shrubs burned to the ground, thousands of battle-related artifacts, as well as human remains that had lain on or near the surface since 1876, were exposed. The archaeological surveys of the battlefield that followed reshaped the public interpretation of the fight, largely corroborating native accounts that had been ignored or dismissed. It was not just archaeologists who saw a research opportunity in the blaze's aftermath. Numerous scientists came to LIBI to study the fire's effects on the area's plant and animal communities. As a result of decades of study, scientists (such as Jane and Carl Bock of the University of Colorado, who conducted some of the most important research between 1984 and 2006) have come to a more nuanced understanding of plains ecology, and LIBI offers a unique opportunity to interpret those discoveries.[55] Perhaps the most important insight is that Little Bighorn Battlefield National Monument is an ecotone, a transition area between two ecosystems. Located at the intersection of the Northern Mixed Grassland and the sagebrush steppe that characterizes much of the intermountain West, the landscape at Little Bighorn can shift in relation to historic environmental factors.

The most "dramatic" consequence of the 1983 fire was the complete destruction and long-term absence of big sagebrush from the burn area. *Artemisia tridentata* is notoriously vulnerable to fire. The 100 percent mortality of the shrub was characteristic of the effect of intense fires on big sagebrush throughout the West. Moreover, the recovery period for big sagebrush is substantial, taking at least a century under optimal conditions. Three decades after the fire, big sagebrush is still largely absent from the burn area. The prohibition on grazing within the monument likely contributed to the fire's intensity, the mortality of the big sagebrush, and the plant's negligible recovery. The fire burned mostly on park service lands rather than on surrounding ranges. Studies suggest that fencing the park off from livestock allowed a heavy fuel load to build within park boundaries. Indeed, fires in sagebrush-grassland habitats are often "patchy" due to the lack of a sufficient fuel load. The Little Bighorn fire, by comparison, was broad and intense. There is also the possibility that the "relatively lush" groundcover at Little Bighorn then "reduced opportunities for recruitment of big sagebrush seedlings after the fire."[56]

Big sagebrush is an iconic yet often misunderstood and sometimes maligned plant. Sustained overgrazing can result in the expansion of sagebrush into grasslands. Drawing a direct correlation between overgrazing and the expansion of big sagebrush in the Little Bighorn Valley, Jane and Carl Bock linked the grazing of bison and horses to "the invasion of this Northern Mixed Grass Prairie by big sagebrush." They believed that the 1983 fire offered an "opportunity to study patterns of *Artemisia tridentata* invasion in the absence of large domestic or native grazing animals."[57] Fires kept sagebrush in check, but as the Bocks noted for Little Bighorn: "Fire frequency has been episodic in this region historically and prehistorically, related to climatic cycles and probably fuel reductions caused by ungulate grazing. Therefore, ecological opportunities have long existed across the northern Great Plains for plants that are intolerant of fire, as well as for those dependent upon or unaffected by it." At Little Bighorn, however, this general trend had been reversed. Fencing had prevented overgrazing and allowed relatively lush stands of native grasses to survive intermixed with big sagebrush.[58]

What was catastrophic for big sagebrush was beneficial for the other native flora of the park, especially the grasses. More importantly, native grasses, such as bluebunch wheatgrass, grama grasses, junegrass, needle and thread, alkali bluegrass, and green needlegrass, all "showed significant increases during at least one post-fire growing season." Compared to the grasses and forbs, shrubs did not benefit as clearly from the fire, although many returned to "pre-burn densities or higher by the second year." Chokecherry and wild rose had recovered well and were especially abundant in the ravines, where the Bocks found "little or no long-term negative effects of the 1983 fire." While big sagebrush was absent, silver sage was more common in all habitats. The Bocks felt that the prevalence of silver sage contributed to the historic character of the battlefield, as it presented the "same general aspect" of its larger relative.[59]

While the 1983 fire seemed beneficial for native grasses, its effects were not uniformly advantageous for all life forms. In their mid-1980s survey, the Bocks compared the burned portions of the battlefield with the surviving sagebrush-grassland habitat at the Reno-Benteen site. Many

previously common breeding birds, such as lark buntings, lark sparrows, and Brewer's sparrow, that relied on the sage canopy completely,
avoided the burned area and no species was found to prefer the burned
plots. Only the western meadowlark, "perhaps the most adaptable of all
North American grassland birds," could be found in the burn area in
the years immediately following the fire.[60] The Bocks' follow-up study
reinforced the effects of fire on sagebrush-dependent birds. Many species had returned to the 1983 burn area, where they found refuge in the
recovered shrub populations of chokecherry and skunkbush. Meanwhile, an August 1991 fire swept the Reno-Benteen site, killing all of the
big sagebrush and leading to an absence of "shrub dependent bird species." The Bocks concluded, "From an avian perspective, loss of big sage
from fires at LIBI has had a negative impact on its biological diversity."[61]

The evolution of the Bocks' thinking reflected a more complex and
dynamic picture of the ecology of LIBI that took shape over the years.
In 1987 the Bocks identified the habitat at Little Bighorn as a "Northern
Mixed Grass Prairie," eschewing earlier characterizations of the place as a
transitional zone between true grasslands and sagebrush steppe. In doing
so they effectively marked grasslands as the preferred, or more "pristine,"
ecosystem at the park. Indeed, they characterized the expansion of big
sagebrush as an "invasion."[62] This view was consistent with the perception of sagebrush as a "pest" that marked overgrazing. In their ongoing
studies, however, the Bocks came to a more nuanced understanding of
the fire's impact as well as the importance of sagebrush to the local ecosystem. The change in perspective was due to both the impacts on avian
life they witnessed and the growing body of research that illustrated what
the eradication of big sagebrush meant to obligate species. In 1983 the
Bocks wrote, "Fire is a natural and non-destructive feature of the western American grasslands." Two decades later they still viewed fire as a
natural feature of the ecosystem but they also recognized that it was not
a simple answer to restore a "pristine" grasslands ecosystem, and they
argued against prescribed burns at LIBI unless there was "some recovery
of big sagebrush in areas that could be exempted from fire."[63]

In the three decades since the fire, the management of the park's
"wild life" has become increasingly important. The presence or reintroduction of endangered species has even become part of the conversation.
The large cottonwoods along the course of the Little Bighorn River offer
potential nesting sites for bald eagles, although none currently nest there.

The same riparian areas provide whooping cranes possible stopover sites during their migration.[64] Black-footed ferrets are one listed species with the potential for reintroduction at or near LIBI. Considered extinct in 1981, when a small population was discovered in northwest Wyoming, all of the known ferret populations today are the result of reintroductions using animals bred in captivity. The decline of the ferrets as well as their potential survival is of course directly linked to the presence of black-tailed prairie dogs. This species was itself in rapid decline but population rebounds led to its removal from the list of candidate species in 2004. In the 1960s the expansion of prairie dog colonies reportedly was considered a threat to the monument's resources. By the early 2000s a small colony had established itself near the north boundary of the park. This colony, however, covers only a few acres, and since a single ferret needs a colony of between one hundred and one hundred fifty acres to survive, it is far too small to warrant the reintroduction of the species.[65]

Of course, it is highly unlikely that LIBI could ever become a functioning refuge. The large species most responsible for shaping the landscape at the time of the battle are the ones notably absent from the park today. The last chief historian of the park, John Doerner, who retired in 2011, lamented to me on several occasions that he wished we could "bring back the buffalo." He knew full well that agricultural development, fences, and the patchwork of land ownership and jurisdictions pose insurmountable obstacles for the restoration of historic grazing patterns. Short of a radical and seemingly impossible move, such as creating the Poppers' "buffalo commons," Doerner's wish must remain just that.

On the other hand, we might envision another role for LIBI. It is situated at a critical junction, an ecotone between two of the most widespread ecosystems in the American West. Moreover, people care about LIBI. The bloody fight that took place there over two June days nearly a century and a half ago makes it the subject of intense public fascination. LIBI, then, offers a unique opportunity to study the complexity and dynamism of the Great Plains and to interpret that story for visitors. As environmental historian William Cronon so famously pointed out, one of the "troubles" with wilderness is that it oftentimes leads us to ignore the "wildness" of the nature and the beauty and the lessons found in more subtle landscapes.[66] There are no lofty peaks or spectacular canyons or towering redwoods at Little Bighorn, but there is a complex and dynamic Great Plains ecosystem that is both natural and cultural. By understanding that story we might better reimagine the future of the Great Plains.

NOTES

1. Within the National Park Service, each unit goes by its four-letter acronym. The code LIBI is especially fitting for Little Bighorn as Elizabeth Bacon Custer—"Libby" Custer—was largely responsible for preserving and enhancing her late husband's memory and reputation until her own death, in 1933.

2. Deborah Epstein Popper and Frank J. Popper, "The Great Plains: From Dust to Dust," *Planning* (December 1987).

3. The mass extinctions at the end of the Pleistocene left only five grazing and browsing species on the Great Plains: bison, pronghorn, mule deer, whitetail deer, and elk. Today, two subspecies of bison exist: the Plains bison (*B. bison bison*) and the slightly larger wood bison (*B. bison athabascae*) found on the northeastern plains of Canada. D. C. Hartnett, A. A. Steuter, and K. R. Hickman, "Comparative Ecology of Native and Introduced Ungulates," in *Ecology and Conservation of Great Plains Vertebrates*, eds. Fritz B. Knopf and Fred B. Samson (New York: Springer, 1997), 72–101. See also Jerry N. McDonald, *North American Bison: Their Classification and Evolution* (Berkeley: University of California Press, 1981); R. D. Guthrie, "Bison Evolution and Zoogeography in North America During the Pleistocene," *The Quarterly Journal of Biology* 45 (March 1970): 1–15; Björn Kurtén and Elaine Anderson, *Pleistocene Mammals of North America* (New York: Columbia University Press, 1980), 335–38; Francis Haines, *The Buffalo: The Story of the American Bison and Their Hunters from Prehistoric Times to the Present* (reprint ed., Norman: University of Oklahoma Press, 1995), 7–15.

4. William Temple Hornaday, *The Extermination of the American Bison*, in the *Annual Report of the Board of Regents of the Smithsonian Institution*, 1889 (reprint ed., Washington, DC: The Smithsonian Institution, 2002), 387; Frank Gilbert Roe, *The North American Buffalo: A Critical Study of the Species in Its Wild State* (Toronto: University of Toronto Press, 1951).

5. Dan Flores, "Bison Ecology and Bison Diplomacy: The Southern Plains from 1800 to 1850," *Journal of American History* 78 (September 1991); Andrew C. Isenberg, *The Destruction of the Bison* (New York: Cambridge University Press, 2000), 23–25.

6. Douglas B. Bamforth, *Ecology and Human Organization on the Great Plains* (New York: Plenum Press, 1988), 45–48.

7. Bamforth, *Ecology and Human Organization*, 80–82; Isenberg, *The Destruction of the Bison*, 66–68; Theodore Binnema, *Common and Contested Ground: A Human and Environmental History of the Northwestern Plains* (Norman: University of Oklahoma Press, 2001), 40–43; Elliott West, *Way to the West: Essays on the Central Plains* (Albuquerque: University of New Mexico Press, 1995), 72–79.

8. Binnema, *Common and Contested Ground*, 20, 27–28, 31.

9. John L. Hoogland, *The Black-Tailed Prairie Dog: Social Life of a Burrowing Mammal* (Chicago: University of Chicago Press, 1995); John L. Hoogland, ed., *Conservation of the Black-Tailed Prairie Dog* (Washington, DC: Island Press, 2006); C. N. Slobodchikoff, Bianca S. Perla, and Jennifer L. Verdolin, *Prairie Dogs: Communication and Community in an Animal Society* (Cambridge, MA: Harvard University Press, 2009). Of the five species of prairie dog that inhabit North America, the black-tailed prairie dog was the most widespread.

10. Craig Knowles, Jonathan Proctor, and Steven Forest, "Black-Tailed Prairie Dog Abundance and Distribution in the Great Plains Based on Historic and Contemporary Information," *Great Plains Research: A Journal of Natural and Social Sciences* 12 (Fall 2002): 227–28; Dennis L. Flath and Tim W. Clark, "Historic Status of Black-Footed Ferret Habitat in Montana," *Great Basin Naturalist Memoirs* 8 (1986): 65, 68.

11. James K. Dettling, "Do Prairie Dogs Compete with Livestock?," in *Conservation of the Black-Tailed Prairie Dog*, ed. Hoogland, 74.

12. Natasha B. Kotiliar, Brian J. Miller, Richard P. Reading, and Timothy W. Clark, "The Prairie Dog as Keystone Species," in *Conservation of the Black-Tailed Prairie Dog*, ed. Hoogland; Kirsten Krueger, "Feeding Relationships Among Bison, Pronghorn, and Prairie Dogs: An Experimental Analysis," *Ecology* 67 (1986): 760–70; Knowles et al., "Black-Tailed Prairie Dog Abundance," 244–45, 254–60.

13. Flath and Clark, "Historic Status," 69; Dean E. Biggins and Max H. Schroeder, "Historical and Present Status of the Black-Footed Ferret," *Great Plains Wildlife Damage Control Workshop Proceedings*, Paper 50 (1987), http://digitalcommons.unl.edu/gpwdcwp/50.

14. Francis Haines, "Where Did the Plains Indians Get Their Horses?," *American Anthropologist* 40 (1938): 112–17; Francis Haines, "The Northward Spread of Horses Among the Plains Indians," *American Anthropologist* 40 (1938): 429–37.

15. William R. Swagerty, "History of the United States Plains Until 1850," in *Handbook of North American Indians, Volume 13: Plains, Part 1*, ed. Raymond J. DeMallie (Washington, DC: Smithsonian Institution, 2001), 258–260; Elliott West, *The Contested Plains: Indians, Goldseekers, and the Rush to Colorado* (Lawrence: University Press of Kansas, 1998), 51; Alan T. Osburn, "Ecological Aspects of Equestrian

Adaptations in Aboriginal North America," *American Anthropologist* 85 (September 1983): 563–91.

16. West, *The Contested Plains*, 50–51; Preston Holder, *The Hoe and the Horse on the Plains: A Study of Cultural Development Among North American Indians* (Lincoln: University of Nebraska Press, 1970); Frank Raymond Secoy, *Changing Military Patterns of the Great Plains Indians* (Seattle: University of Washington Press, 1953; reprint ed., Lincoln: University of Nebraska Press, 1992); Pekka Hämäläinen, "The Rise and Fall of Plains Indian Horse Cultures," *Journal of American History* 90 (December 2003): 833–62.

17. Bamforth, *Ecology and Human Organization*, 41–52, 67–84.

18. West, *The Contested Plains*; James E. Sherow, *The Grasslands of the United States: An Environmental History* (Santa Barbara: ABC-CLIO, 2007), 43–45.

19. Bamforth, *Ecology and Human Organization*; Binnema, *Common and Contested Ground*, 18–20; West, *The Way to the West*, 24–26.

20. Thomas B. Marquis, interpreter, *Wooden Leg: A Warrior Who Fought Custer* (Minneapolis: The Midwest Company, 1931; reprint, Lincoln: University of Nebraska Press, 2003), 25, 33, 35.

21. Harold Hickerson, "The Virginia Deer and Intertribal Buffer Zones in the Upper Mississippi Valley," in *Man, Culture, and Animals: The Role of Animals in Human Ecological Adjustments*, eds. Anthony Leeds and Andrew P. Vayda (Washington, DC: American Association of the Advancement of Science, 1965), 43–66; Harold Hickerson, *The Chippewa and Their Neighbors: A Study in Ethnohistory* (New York: Irvington Publishers, 1970), 96–98; Richard White, *The Roots of Dependency: Subsistence, Environment, and Social Change Among the Choctaws, Pawnees, and Navajos* (Lincoln: University of Nebraska Press, 1984), 8–10; West, *The Way to the West*, 61–63.

22. West, *The Way to the West*, 61–66; Flores, "Bison Ecology and Bison Diplomacy."

23. John L. Allen, "Landscape Change at the Confluence: From Lewis and Clark to the Present," *North Dakota History* 69 (2002): 2–23.

24. Gary E. Moulton, ed., *The Definitive Journals of Lewis & Clark, Vol. 7: From Fort Mandan to Three Forks* (Lincoln: University of Nebraska Press, 1987), 81–87; Paul S. Martin and Christine R. Szuter, "War Zones and Game Sinks in Lewis and Clark's West," *Conservation Biology* 13 (February 1999): 36–45.

25. Treaty of Fort Laramie, September 17, 1851, 11 Stat. 749.

26. Edwin Thompson Denig, *Five Indian Tribes of the Upper Missouri*, ed. John C. Ewers (Norman: University of Oklahoma Press, 1961), quote at 139, 144–47, 184–85, 201.

27. Transcript of Treaty of Fort Laramie with the Crows, 1868, https://www.ourdocuments.gov/doc.php? flash=false&doc= 42&page=transcript.

28. For overviews of the northern plains wars, see Robert M. Utley, *The Indian Frontier of the American West 1846–1890* (Albuquerque: University of New Mexico Press, 1983), and Jeffrey Ostler, *The Plains Sioux and U.S. Colonialism from Lewis and Clark to Wounded Knee* (Cambridge: Cambridge University Press, 2004). Treaty with the Sioux—Brule, Oglala, Miniconjou, Yanktonai, Hunkpapa, Blackfeet, Cuthead, Two Kettle, San Arcs, and Santee—and Arapaho, April 29, 1868, 15 Stat. 635; Treaty of Fort Laramie with the Crows, May 7, 1868, 15 Stat. 649.

29. For bison decline see Dan Flores, "Wars Over Buffalo: Stories versus Stories on the Northern Plains," in *Native Americans and the Environment: Perspectives on the Ecological Indian*, eds. Michael E. Harkin and David Rich Lewis (Lincoln: University of Nebraska Press, 2007), 153–70; Jeffrey Ostler, "'They Regard Their Passing as Wakan': Interpreting Western Sioux Explanations for the Bison's Decline," *Western Historical Quarterly* 30 (1999): 475–97.

30. West, *The Contested Plains*.

31. Isenberg, *The Destruction of the Bison*, 130–32; Francis Haines, *The Buffalo: The Story of the American Bison and Their Hunters from Prehistoric Times to the Present* (Norman: University of Oklahoma Press, 1970), 189–90, 196.

32. Haines, *The Buffalo*, 203–5.

33. Michael P. Malone and Richard B. Roeder, "Agriculture: 1876 in Field and Pasture," *Montana: The Magazine of Western History* 25 (Spring 1975): 28–35.

34. Granville Stuart, *Forty Years on the Frontier: As Seen in the Journals and Reminiscences of Granville Stuart* (Cleveland: The Arthur H. Clark Company, 1925), 187–88.

35. Hartnett et al., "Comparative Ecology," 77–80, 83–85.

36. Ibid., 81–82, 90–91.

37. Joseph William Blankinship, *Weeds of Montana*, Montana Agricultural Experiment Station of the Montana College of Agriculture, Bulletin No. 30 (Bozeman, MT: Avant Courier, 1901), 7–9; Mark Fiege, "The Weedy West: Mobile Nature, Boundaries, and Common Space in the Montana Landscape," *Western Historical Quarterly* 36 (Spring 2005): 22–47.

38. Fiege, "The Weedy West," 29.

39. For an ethnographic summary of the Crows, see Fred W. Voget, "Crow," in *Handbook of North American Indians*, ed. DeMallie, 695–717. Treaty of Fort Laramie, 1851, 11 Stat. 749. See also, Frederick E. Hoxie, *Parading Through History: The Making of the Crow Nation in America 1805–1935* (New York: Cambridge University Press, 1995).

40. Megan Benson, "The Fight for Crow Water, Part 1: The Early Reservation Years Through the Indian New Deal," *Montana: The Magazine of Western History* 57 (Winter 2007): 27; Hoxie, *Parading Through*

History, 274; Annual Report of the Commissioner of Indian Affairs, 1894, 166–67.

41. Malone et al., "Agriculture," 232–38; K. Ross Toole, *Twentieth-Century Montana: A State of Extremes* (Norman: University of Oklahoma Press, 1972), 32–38; Paul W. Gates, "Homesteading in the High Plains," *Agricultural History* 51 (January 1977): 125.

42. Malone et al., "Agriculture," 236–37; Toole, *Twentieth-Century Montana*, 39–41; Hardy W. Campbell, *Campbell's 1907 Soil Culture Manual: A Complete Guide to Scientific Agriculture as Adapted to the Semi-Arid Regions* (Lincoln, NE: The Campbell Soil Culture Company, 1907).

43. Malone et al., "Agriculture," 238–44; Toole, *Twentieth-Century Montana*, 45–51.

44. Malone et al., "Agriculture," 283; Toole, *Twentieth-Century Montana*, 70–96.

45. Jane H. Bock and Carl E. Bock, "A Survey of the Vascular Plants and Birds of Little Bighorn National Battlefield," CESU Task Agreement CA-1200-99-007, July 2006; Blankinship, "Weeds of Montana." The species likely fitting this profile found on the Little Bighorn battlefield include Russian knapweed (*Centauria repens*), alyssum (*Alyssum allyssoides* and *A. desertorum*), tansy mustard (*Descurania sophia*), leafy spurge (*Euphorbia escula*), St. John's wort (*Hypericum perforatum*), quackgrass (*Agropyron repens*), several species of brome grasses (*Bromus hordeaceus, B. inermis, B. japonicas*), and butter-and-eggs, a.k.a. toadflax (*Linaria dalmatica*). The lists provided in these two sources were compared in order to estimate the date that introduced species first appeared at Little Bighorn.

46. Knowles et al., "Black-Tailed Prairie Dog Abundance," 227–28; Steve C. Forrest and James C. Luchsinger, "Past and Current Chemical Control of Prairie Dogs," in *Conservation of the Black-Tailed Prairie Dog*, ed. Hoogland, 115–28.

47. "Protecting Black-Footed Ferrets and Prairie Dogs Against Sylvatic Plague," U.S. Geological Survey, Fact Sheet 2008-3087, May 2011.

48. Flath and Clark, "Historic Status," 63, 68.

49. Carl B. Koford, "Prairie Dogs, White Faces and Blue Grama," *Wildlife Monographs* 3 (1958): 1–78.

50. W. H. Owen to Quartermaster General, 3 August 1893, copy in LIBI White Swan Library; Jerome Greene, *Stricken Field: The Little Bighorn Since 1876* (Norman: University of Oklahoma Press, 2008), 39, 41–42.

51. Fiege, "The Weedy West," 25.

52. Master Plan Narrative, Volumes I & III, Custer Battlefield National Monument, Montana, 20 July 1964, Denver TIC, Chapter 1, 8; Master

Plan Narrative, Chapter 3 Management Programs, 28 June 1965, Denver TIC.

53. Master Plan Narrative, Ch. 3.

54. Richard West Sellars, *Preserving Nature in the National Parks*, Annual Reports of Superintendent, CBNC, 1 October 1942; 22 August 1943; 1 July 1944; 30 June 1945, NARA KC Bx 166, Fld. 207 Reports; Luce to NPS Director, 30 September 1945, NARA KC Bx 168, Fld. 715 Mammals; Master Plan Narrative, Ch. 1, 9.

55. Resource Management Plan National Park Service, Denver Technical Information Center, n.d. (c. 1970s), 9–11.

56. Jane H. Bock and Carl E. Bock, "The Effects of Fire on Virgin Northern Mixed Grassland at Custer Battlefield National Monument: Final Report," NPS Contract No. CX-1200-4-A034, May 1987; Bock and Bock, "A Survey"; Steven V. Cooper, Peter Lesica, and Greg M. Kudray, "Post-Fire Recovery of Wyoming Big Sagebrush Steppe in Central and Southeast Montana," *Natural Resources and Environmental Issues* 16(1): Article 12 (January 2011), http://digitalcommons .usu.ed/nrei/vol16/iss1/12; Steven V. Cooper, Peter Lesica, and Greg M. Kudray, "Post-Fire Recovery of Wyoming Big Sagebrush Steppe in Central and Southeast Montana," report prepared for the Bureau of Land Management, Agreement Number ESA010009 Task Order #29, Montana Natural Heritage Program, 2007; William L. Baker, "Fire Restoration of Sagebrush Ecosystems," *Wildlife Society Bulletin* 34 (2007): 177–85.

57. Bock and Bock, "The Effects of Fire," ii; Baker, "Fire Restoration," 177; Cooper et al., "Post-Fire Recovery" (2011), 4–5; Bock and Bock, "A Survey," 23, 26.

58. Bock and Bock, "The Effects of Fire," 12–13.

59. Bock and Bock, "A Survey," 27.

60. Bock and Bock, "The Effects of Fire," 9, 13–14; Bock and Bock, "A Survey," 23, 26–27, 29.

61. Bock and Bock, "The Effects of Fire," part II, 2, 4, 7–8.

62. Bock and Bock, "A Survey," 13.

63. Bock and Bock, "The Effects of Fire," 11, 12–13.

64. Bock and Bock, "The Effects of Fire," 15; Bock and Bock, "A Survey," 28.

65. Little Bighorn Battlefield National Monument Rehabilitate Route 10 Environmental Assessment, Biological Report, David Evans and Associates, November 2004, 6, 7–9.

66. William Cronon, "The Trouble with Wilderness; or, Getting Back to the Wrong Nature," in *Uncommon Ground: Rethinking the Human Place in Nature*, ed. William Cronon (New York: W.W. Norton & Co., 1996), 69–90.

Snowy Owl (detail). By John James Audubon, 1831–1834. The engraving shows a detail of an owl's foot. Wikimedia Commons, from Archives and Collections, University of Pittsburgh Library System, Digital Collections, the Darlington Collection, *The Birds of America*.

Beauty as a Foundation for Conservation Ethics

Kirk C. Robinson

Kirk Robinson relates a childhood encounter with the wild, which he describes as his "Aldo Leopold moment," and moves to consider two logically distinct definitions of intrinsic value relating to things of beauty; he suggests that we may value something for its own sake, "like a sunset or dancing," but that something might possess intrinsic value "by virtue of its existence," quite apart from our valuing it. Robinson leads us on an exploration of the meaning and significance of intrinsic value as he argues that a thing of beauty has intrinsic value not simply because we like it but by virtue of its very existence. He concludes that beauty "is a real feature of the natural world" and aligning our sentiments with this reality forms the underpinning of a compassionate conservation ethic.

Dedicated to David Richard Keller, a.k.a. the Freakin' Deacon

This whole is in all its parts so beautiful, and is felt by me to be so intensely in earnest, that I am compelled to love it.

—Robinson Jeffers, 1934

The summer I was sixteen I worked alongside my grandfather on his ranch. I learned to drive a tractor, buck hay, saddle a horse, round up calves and brand them. The days were long and the work hard. After dinner, I had time to myself. One evening I went for a walk with my Winchester .22

rifle, on the lookout for something to shoot. In those days, it was a rite of passage for western boys to get a "varmint" rifle at about age fourteen.

While walking a path along the edge of an alfalfa field, I espied a large bird with a whitish breast standing in the middle of the field about one hundred yards away. I wasn't sure it was a varmint but it was a sitting duck, so to speak. So, pointing my rifle in the direction of the bird and raising it slightly to allow for distance, I pulled the trigger. Instantly the bird fell over. Excitedly, I climbed over the fence and ran over to it. It was a barn owl, though I didn't know it at the time. It was stone dead, its dark eyes wide open. I wondered what to do with it. Taxidermy wasn't an option, but just leaving it seemed terribly wasteful, so I plucked out a few tail feathers and sawed off its talons with my pocket knife. Stowing my trophies in a shirt pocket, I carried the dead bird to the edge of the field and threw it into the sagebrush. Then I began walking back to the ranch house in the waning light.

As I walked along, feeling remorseful for what I'd done, another owl just like the one I'd killed appeared and began to fly silent circles a few feet above my head. It occurred to me that it was probably the mate of the dead owl, and that it might attack me out of revenge, so I stopped. When I did, it lit on the nearest fence post a few feet away and stared straight into my face with its big dark eyes. Spooky! What was it doing? I thought of shooting it too, but hated to do it. Instead, I tried shooting at the post beneath it, hoping to scare it off, but it didn't as much as move a feather. I resumed walking again, and it resumed circling me on its silent wings. I stopped again and it stopped too, lighting on the nearest fence post and silently staring straight into my face. I shot at the post. It did not move. This was repeated several times, the owl following me all the way back to the ranch house, each time silently looking me in the face with its big dark eyes. I don't know what became of my trophies, but the memory of that experience has remained with me for fifty years. It was my Aldo Leopold moment.

A FIERCE GREEN FIRE

In the foreword to *A Sand County Almanac*, Leopold says, "There are some who can live without wild things, and some who cannot. These essays are the delights and dilemmas of one who cannot."[1] Leopold's remark suggests that his chief interest in the essays was wilderness preservation and wildlife conservation. But he didn't start out with these concerns. He was educated at the Yale Forest School in the first decade of the twentieth century, where the guiding principle was the strictly utilitarian one of sustainable use, as set forth by Gifford Pinchot, first chief of the US Forest Service. Leopold's first job, at age twenty-two, was forest assistant in the Apache National Forest in the Arizona Territory.

In his essay "Thinking Like a Mountain," Leopold recounts an experience from the time he was a young forest assistant, when he participated in killing a Mexican wolf (a.k.a. *lobo*) and her pups. (Today the Mexican wolf [*Canis lupus baileyi*] is on the brink of extinction, with just over one hundred lobos living in the wild in the United States and Mexico, all of them descended from the last seven lobos on Earth.) After raining a fusillade of bullets on some wolves they espied in a gorge, Leopold and his companion climbed down to where the wolves lay bleeding, arriving in time for him to "watch a fierce green fire dying in her eyes." He goes on to say, "I realized then, and have known ever since, that there was something new to me in those eyes—something known only to her and to the mountain."[2] Leopold saw something in the eyes of the old wolf that suggested an ancient connection between it and the mountain. I don't think we will go wrong if we understand the wolf to represent *wildness*— the ultimate otherness, the antipode of the human-dominated world— and the mountain to represent wilderness, the place of *wildness*.

Leopold's account doesn't read as though he experienced a sudden and dramatic change of aspect, as happens with ambiguous figures like the old woman–young woman and the duck-rabbit drawings, which can be seen now one way, now another, but there is no doubt that he was profoundly affected by his experience. He had the uncanny sense that he was seeing something new, but didn't grasp what it was. Like my experience with the barn owls, Leopold's experience with the wolf must have initially affected him emotionally more than it did intellectually, but over time its intellectual import dawned on him, ultimately changing the way he looked at nature and his own place in nature. He came to view nature more deeply in terms of relationships, such as the predator-prey relationship, and the complex roles of living things in the larger biotic community. He began to understand and appreciate untrammeled nature more fully as a complex, self-organizing, and evolving whole. He came to view nature from an entirely new perspective—a change in perspective that entailed no longer seeing himself as a "land conqueror" but as a "plain citizen" and member of the whole community of life. Many years later he wrote, "I do not imply that this philosophy of land was always clear to me. It is rather the end result of a life-journey, in the course of which I have felt sorrow, anger, puzzlement or confusion over the inability of conservation to halt the juggernaut of land abuse."[3]

Near the end of his life, Leopold formulated his famous "Land Ethic": "A thing is *right* when it tends to preserve the integrity, stability, and *beauty* of the biotic community. It is *wrong* when it tends otherwise"(emphasis mine).[4] This famous passage is frequently quoted, but to my knowledge has never received the kind of attention I believe it deserves. Notice the words "right," "wrong," and "beauty." These are value terms, whereas "integrity" and "stability" are scientific terms that apply to facts. This stark contrast invites reflection. According to common opinion, the difference is that the facts investigated by the natural sciences are objective features of the material world and obtain independently of what people happen to believe, whereas value is a mental attitude towards something and is therefore subjective, i.e., dependent upon a *mind* (whatever that is).

FACTS AND VALUES: THE COMMON VIEW

It is well known that you cannot logically derive a value statement from a set of factual statements. In other words, statements about publicly observable facts never logically entail statements that appraise the quality of those facts (as beautiful or ugly, good or bad). To think otherwise is to commit what has been dubbed "the naturalistic fallacy."[5] This means that it is possible for all the factual statements to be true and the value statement false, this possibility rendering the inference from the one to the other fallacious. Compare these two inferences to see the point: "This instrument is a violin, therefore it is a musical instrument" and "This violin is a Stradivarius, therefore it will have a beautiful tone." In the first example, the conclusion has to be true if the premise is true because the first concept, "violin," is included in the second one, "musical instrument." Not so in the second example. It doesn't follow as a matter of logic that a given violin will produce a beautiful tone just because it is a Stradivarius. It is conceivable that the tone will be ordinary or subpar. Accordingly, the first is an example of logical entailment, the second a lack thereof. The violin in question might have a beautiful tone nonetheless, and it might be reasonable to expect that it will, but that is beside the point. The point is that there is a philosophical puzzle as to whether beauty (a value) can be a real objective feature of things, or whether it is strictly subjective—something "in the eye of the beholder," as it were. If we can't logically deduce that something is beautiful from a complete factual description of it, then what basis is there for ascribing beauty to it? Wouldn't it be more accurate to simply say, "I like it"?

Leopold was certainly aware of a deep difference between fact terms and value terms, and no doubt deliberately meant to imply that, despite this difference, facts can be bearers of value—value in "the philosophical sense," as he put it,[6] or what is more commonly referred to as intrinsic value—and that this value is not dependent upon a mind but is just as real and just as much a part of the material world as those facts. I suspect this conviction was planted in his mind decades earlier by the incident with the wolf, though he would not have understood it in these terms at the time.

We have here two quite different views of the relation between facts and values. On the common view, the facts that make up the natural world are "objective" and value-free (neither good nor bad), while values are "subjective" mental attitudes that can shift even while the facts of the world remain the same. According to this view, people project their personal values onto a reality that in itself is value-free or value-neutral. This is a more general version of the popular idea that beauty, which is a kind of value, is strictly in the eye of the beholder. Indeed, this is supposed to be a truism. And no doubt there is truth in it. People do often make different aesthetic (and ethical) evaluations concerning the same matters of fact. However, it may not be the whole truth. Value can still be more than private sentiment. Maybe some things really do have intrinsic value in the sense of being beautiful, although not everyone is capable of experiencing or appreciating their beauty.

Science reinforces the common view of facts and values by training us to think of the natural world as consisting exclusively of assemblages of mind-independent physical facts that are in principle susceptible of exhaustive description in quantitative terms, such as mass and momentum, representable in precise mathematical formulae à la Newton's three laws of motion. This view receives strong reinforcement from the dominant economic paradigm of our time, which treats all things as human resources having only extrinsic value—as commodities to be sold and used at will. This "resourcism" is even reflected in the names of wildlife management agencies and institutions, such as the Utah Division of Wildlife Resources and the somewhat oxymoronic Utah State University Department of *Wildland Resources.*

FACTS AND VALUES: A COMPETING VIEW

A competing view of facts and values is that facts are not always value-neutral, but are sometimes bearers of value, and that appreciation of this value is required for sound moral judgment and appropriate action. This value is supposed to be intrinsic to things. It is value that things are believed to have independently of human valuing—a kind of value that a thing possesses just by virtue of its very being but that isn't captured by scientific theories and isn't commensurable with economic value, and which therefore cannot be represented in a cost-benefit analysis. On this view, Leopold's experience of the fierce green fire might have been a glimpse of the intrinsic value of the wolf and of wildness. Something similar will have been true of me and my experience with the owl.

It is probably a mistake to try to get too technical about this "bearer of" relationship between facts and values, but the idea is that things can possess value simply by virtue of the facts that comprise them. This is important, for if facts can be bearers of value they can also have implications for how we *ought* to treat things despite the naturalistic fallacy. If something has intrinsic value, this value is a reason for us to respect it and to exercise appropriate restraint in our treatment of it. We can put it this way: to possess intrinsic value is to possess a kind of inherent goodness, and what possesses inherent goodness we should not harm without good reason. I take this conjunction of propositions to state a necessary truth as well as a moral truth. Conversely, to say that something is good but that there is nothing wrong with harming it is a kind of contradiction, a necessary falsehood.

It is important to see that this way of construing intrinsic value does not commit the naturalistic fallacy. Natural processes, objects, and living beings might be bearers of value even though factual statements describing them do not logically entail value statements. For example, by definition a *good* violin will produce a beautiful tone even though no number of true factual statements about its components and construction will ensure, by dint of logic alone, that it will have a beautiful tone. We learn that it has a beautiful tone, not by reasoning about it but by listening to it when played by a skilled violinist. Similarly for an owl or a wolf: we come to appreciate their beauty by observing them, particularly as they go about their business in the wild, and by learning about their natural histories and ecological roles. Beauty is not always obvious. Frequently it takes special instruction or experience for people to be able to perceive and appreciate the beauty of an artwork, for example, or the complex beauty of an ecosystem.

It is also important to recognize that value assessments that take intrinsic values into account are not normally arrived at through linear chains of reasoning of any kind—deductive or inductive—as you might calculate the cost of building a garage by summing the costs of supplies and labor (deduction), or predict a storm based on present atmospheric data and past experience (induction). (Indeed, the impossibility of deducing truths about value from truths about facts is the whole point of the naturalistic fallacy.) Rather, they are intuitive assessments of what is good, or best, formed after due reflection upon the relevant facts.

AESTHETIC BLINDNESS

Now let's return to Leopold's story about watching the fierce green fire die in the old wolf's eyes and compare it with the following passage taken from a recent *New York Times* op-ed account of an encounter with wolves written by wolf researcher Arthur Middleton, titled "Is the Wolf a Real American Hero?":

> I recognize that it is hard to see the wolf through clear eyes. For me, it has happened only once. It was a frigid, windless February morning, and I was tracking a big gray male wolf just east of Yellowstone. The snow was so soft and deep that it muffled my footsteps. I could hear only the occasional snap of a branch.
>
> Then suddenly, a loud "yip!" I looked up to see five dark shapes in a clearing, less than a hundred feet ahead. Incredibly, the wolves hadn't noticed me. Four of them milled about, wagging and playing. The big male stood watching, and snarled when they stumbled close. Soon, they wandered on, vanishing one by one into the falling snow.
>
> That may have been the only time I truly saw the wolf, during three long winters of field work. Yet in that moment, it was clear

that this animal doesn't need our stories. It just needs us to see it, someday, for what it really is.[7]

Perhaps intentionally, this account is vaguely reminiscent of Aldo Leopold's account of seeing the fierce green fire die in an old wolf's eyes, but one hardly knows what to make of it. Consider the final sentence: "It [the wolf] just needs us to see it, someday, for what it really is." And what, pray tell, is that? What does it take to clear our eyes and see the wolf for what it really is? Unfortunately, Middleton didn't say. Perhaps he didn't know.

One interpretation of his account is that it describes the first time Middleton ever observed wolves in a detached mood—that is, without distraction and without engagement of his will pro or con—and that he recounted the experience accordingly to caution people against getting carried away by their feelings about wolves. Less charitably, it can be interpreted as suggesting that, however interesting wolves might be from a scientific perspective, they have no intrinsic value, positive or negative—there just happen to be different attitudes towards them, that's all, with some people loving and admiring them, and some people hating and reviling them. It is certainly true that wolves evoke wildly different sentiments in different people. There is probably no other species that is more controversial.

One would like to accept the charitable interpretation, but the article as a whole accuses both sides in the debate over wolf recovery of projecting false portraits onto the animal—portraits that are based on myth and emotion—which suggests that Middleton, at least at the time he wrote the article, thought all human valuations of wolves, pro or con, are subjective and arbitrary, and that the accurate and proper stance is one of strict value neutrality: they are neither good nor bad, they just are. This interpretation is supported by the fact that Middleton says nothing to suggest that he found the wolves beautiful or that watching them gave him pleasure, as you would expect from someone who has enjoyed an aesthetic experience. His passionless, matter-of-fact manner of description would as well suit the observation that there was snow on the ground.

Which interpretation shall we accept? Can we make true evaluative judgments about wolves or not? Clearly Middleton was trying to caution us against getting carried away by our emotions with respect to wolves, which is good advice, but the mere fact that he did not realize the ambiguity of his remark suggests that he was himself unclear on this very point. Perhaps, like Leopold, his understanding has evolved since then.

CHICKEN OR EGG?

To paraphrase Socrates's question to Euthyphro in the dialogue by that name: Do things have intrinsic value because we value them for their own sake, or do we value them for their own sake because they have intrinsic value?

As a first step towards answering this pivotal question, we should remind ourselves that "intrinsic value" is commonly understood in two quite different ways. First, it is often understood (misunderstood, really) as the noninstrumental and nonmonetary value that something has *for* a person or persons—something that is enjoyed for its own sake, like a sunset or dancing. This is the way that most people understand it, including—no doubt—most scientists, most economists, and not a few conservationists. On this view, finding something beautiful is all there is to its being beautiful. But "intrinsic value" can also be understood as the value that a thing has just by virtue of its being, like the specific gravity of a block of rosewood or the hardness of diamond—properties that are completely independent of all things human and that might be regarded as essential to whatever possesses them. Philosophers will typically understand it this way, the only difference being that physical properties are measurable.

These two ways of construing intrinsic value, while logically distinct, are also logically compatible. In fact, if a thing has intrinsic value just by virtue of its being, that would be an excellent reason for us to value it for its own sake. Unfortunately, these two conceptions are rarely distinguished but are instead unwittingly conflated, with resulting confusion and uncertainty about what intrinsic value is or whether there is any such thing. Furthermore, upon reflection, one can easily see that the first kind of "intrinsic" value is really not a kind of intrinsic value at all, but a kind of "extrinsic" value, in the sense that it depends upon human valuing. After all, if no one were to value a thing for its own sake, on this view it would have no intrinsic value. So, if you think of intrinsic value this way, you might legitimately doubt that there truly is any such thing, for how can valuing something for its own sake actually imbue it with intrinsic value in the second sense? You might as well wish for a pile of garbage to be a pile of gold, expecting a magical transformation. It would be no more miraculous. Maybe this confusion explains Middleton's diffidence about what it is like to see the wolf "for what it really is."

GRADES OF INTRINSIC VALUE AND KINDS OF BEAUTY

Assuming that intrinsic value is an objective quality of some things, what sorts of things might possess it? Connected with this, we might even ask whether there are some things that possess negative intrinsic value—that are, as it were, evil. While I am strongly inclined to think so—the phenomenon of pain being an obvious candidate—I will leave this question aside to concentrate on "positive" intrinsic value.

In addition to the question about what sorts of things might possess intrinsic value, we need to address two others: What is it about something by virtue of which it possesses intrinsic value? How can we know whether there is such a thing as intrinsic value construed as an objective quality of things? I shall tackle these questions in order, in this and the remaining two sections.

Living beings arguably possess intrinsic value, and some nonliving things too: a Stradivarius violin or Van Gogh painting, for example. A fine violin presumably has intrinsic value as a work of art in its own right, as well as instrumental value for producing beautiful music in the right hands—music that also has intrinsic value by virtue of its beauty. Yet one might wonder, if intrinsic values cannot be reckoned in monetary or numerical terms—if they aren't aggregates of discrete atomic units of equal value—how we can compare intrinsic values when we must decide which of competing ones is the greater. Or is all intrinsic value equal?

I believe we can state some general truths. The concept of intrinsic value certainly does not require that all instances of intrinsic value are equal just because it is a type of value that can't be quantified. There can be grades of intrinsic value nonetheless. For example, I think we can plausibly say that, in general and other things being equal, living beings have greater intrinsic value than nonliving things, and that a human life has greater intrinsic value than a whale's life, and similarly for a whale's life relative to the life of an octopus, and an octopus's life relative to the life of a clam. There can be a hierarchy of grades of intrinsic values.

Among living things, I should think complexity of the nervous system, including the brain, is an important consideration, along with consciousness, sentience, curiosity, the ability to learn new behaviors, the capacity for reasoning, and moral agency. No doubt we still have much to learn in this regard. For example, it is a fairly recent discovery that corvids, such as jays, have prodigious memories for such things as where they stashed thousands of individual pine seeds, each in its own spot; and octopuses are not just strange blobs of protoplasm, but have brains and nervous systems of a kind suggesting that they may experience emotions.

Perhaps it is our prerogative to regard our own species as "higher" and more valuable than others—perhaps we can't help but do so—but it doesn't follow that all the others have no value apart from how useful they are to us. As far as that goes, if there is a serious doubt about the intrinsic value of nonhuman beings, there is no apparent reason why the same doubt would not also apply to human beings, yielding the implication that the value of each person amounts to nothing more than his or her usefulness to some other person or persons. This would appear to license slavery, murder, and rape, which seems counterintuitive to say the least.

The caveat "in general and other things being equal" two paragraphs up is important. Cutting down a fine, old red spruce to build a fire to roast marshmallows would be wrong, but using the wood to produce fine acoustic guitar tops would arguably justify the loss, assuming there are plenty of red spruces left. On the other hand, killing an elephant for its ivory or for a trophy is quite another matter, regardless of how many elephants there are.

Now let's climb to a higher level of abstraction. In his foundational article "What Is Conservation Biology?" conservation biologist Michael Soulé proposed three moral axioms: "Diversity of organisms is good," "Ecological complexity is good," and "Evolution is good."[8] The good ascribed in these axioms is intrinsic and is represented most fully and perfectly in wilderness, where the world is wild, e.g., "self-willed," and is not subjected to our dominating influence. That is where you find each of the three axioms satisfied most fully.

We can group kinds or varieties of intrinsic value into four broad categories exemplified by (1) sentience—that is, the capacity of a living organism to experience simple sensations, such as pain and pleasure, (2) the capacity for "higher" mental processes, such as perception, reason, and the like, as well as emotions, particularly empathy, and the ability to ask (and answer) moral questions, (3) the complex workings of nature (e.g., wild ecosystems and the multitude of organisms and interactions that comprise them), and (4) human artifacts, including such things as musical instruments, works of art, scientific and philosophical theories, and mathematical proofs. This is just one possible taxonomy. But what all the examples have in common, I submit, is that they are beautiful, each in its own way. And this beauty is not just a matter of our finding them beautiful, but rather of them being beautiful.

THE INGREDIENTS OF BEAUTY

What is it that makes something beautiful? I doubt if it is possible to grasp the essence of beauty in all its variety by means of imagination or reason, not because imagination and reason are not up to the task, but rather because there is no such thing as the essence of beauty. Different things, or kinds of things, are beautiful by virtue of being the particular things, or kinds of things, they are (this includes living beings and natural processes). And this has to do with specific and unique facts about each. Beautiful things need not all have some essential "sameness" in common to be beautiful. Nor must we have a general idea of beauty in mind—a universal mental template, as it were—by comparison with which we can judge whether something is beautiful. Familiarity with the object or objects in question is all we can have and all we need. Of course, there can be degrees of familiarity.

THE REALITY OF BEAUTY AND INTRINSIC VALUE

So far this amounts only to an exposition of the concept of intrinsic value *qua* beauty—and one that is philosophically controversial at that. The really important question of whether there are any such things as beauty and intrinsic value, objectively speaking, remains unanswered. By way of addressing it, consider this example: If you have firewood and a Stradivarius violin, and you want to make a fire to heat your cabin, which will you burn first? I dare say that you will burn the firewood, not the violin, even if you are unable to play the violin and the option of selling it is not available to you. Are you being irrational or arbitrary? Why not? Isn't the answer simply that the violin has a lot more intrinsic value than the stick of wood? Surely this thesis has at least as much going for it as the thesis that neither has any intrinsic value at all and that they are merely two potential resources.

Beauty is one kind of intrinsic value and is itself various: the beauty of a fine musical instrument is not qualitatively identical to the beauty of a symphony orchestra performance, which is not qualitatively identical to the beauty of a tiger, which is not qualitatively identical to the beauty of a healthy ecosystem. Indeed, they are so different that I seriously doubt that a satisfactorily unifying and illuminating theory of beauty (or of intrinsic value) can be contrived. But it would be fallacious to conclude from this that beauty is merely an affectation of the mind.

Furthermore, so I maintain, the beauty of each is not merely "in the eye (or ear) of the beholder," but is a real feature of the "mind-independent" world there to be seen and heard. It is silly to ask whether a tiger is still beautiful when no one is looking at it. What sort of doubt can there be? It still has stripes too. Or is there a right way to look at a tiger that will reveal it as having no stripes? The burden of proof is entirely on the skeptic.

I suggest that the skeptical doubt arises from an unconscious tendency, shared by all humans, to reify the contents of our consciousness—in this case, by confusing one's experience of a thing with the thing experienced—as though one's visual experience of a tiger, stripes and all, is some sort of queer entity in its own right, residing in the "mental space" of one's mind, and is the thing that is really striped and really experienced, not the tiger out there in physical space. But I think it is impossible to make coherent sense of such a notion, and therefore hard to make sense of the skeptical doubt. Where is the tiger-simulacrum that is supposed to arise in the mind when a person looks at a tiger? A neurosurgeon won't find it in the brain of someone who is looking at a tiger, though he might find a neural correlate of the experience of seeing it. The closest thing to a tiger-simulacrum that we know anything about is the image on the retinas of the eyes when someone is looking at a tiger. But eyes are still objects in the physical world: we see objects in physical space with them; we don't see our retinas. And even if we did, we would still be seeing something in physical space.

Let's switch to an even simpler example. When you look at the full moon against the dark horizon and hold out a dime next to it at arm's length, you might say that it looks to be about the size of a dime. But the moon certainly isn't the size of a dime (or the shape of a dime, for that matter). So, is your visual image of the full moon about the size of a dime? And where should we look for this visual image in order to measure it and to see if it is the color of the moon and as beautiful as the moon?

Doesn't it make a lot more sense to dispense with the idea of the "inner" mental image and just talk about the moon itself? In reality, the moon is 2,159 miles in diameter and is roughly 238,900 miles from Earth. And it is really beautiful, too. Just look at it and see.

Granted, we do sometimes speak of beautiful experiences, which grammatically speaking has beauty qualifying experience. And isn't experience subjective? Perhaps, but when describing our experiences we don't think of them as some sort of queer thing inhabiting our minds, in total isolation from the physical world. When we describe our experiences, we do sometimes focus exclusively on their subjective aspects— our feelings and thoughts—but typically these feelings and thoughts, which are "internal" to our minds if you like, are connected to things we do, or things that we observe, or things that happen to us in a world of physical objects, including our own bodies—in other words, with things that are not "in" our minds. And these things are normally also represented, along with feelings and thoughts, in our descriptions of our experiences. To see what I mean, ask yourself whether this makes sense spoken in seriousness: "It was a dreadfully smoggy, cold, wet day, and my feet ached as I walked to work. It was really a beautiful experience." That would be sarcasm. Now contrast it with: "It was a beautiful, sunny day, the air was blue, birds were singing and the lilacs were in bloom as I walked to work. It was a beautiful experience." The experience was beautiful because the day was beautiful.[9]

You can't hear beautiful music if you are deaf, or perceive the beauty of a landscape if you are blind, but that doesn't mean they are only beautiful while they are being perceived. Nor does it constitute a reason for doubting that they are beautiful. And if beauty is a real feature of the natural world apart from our perceptions, feelings, sentiments, and thoughts, that is surely reason enough, morally speaking, for us to take good care of our beautiful planet and its myriad creatures. It's not only a good idea, it's the right thing to do. It is in this sense that beauty provides us with a rational "foundation" for conservation ethics.

NOTES

1.   Aldo Leopold, *A Sand County Almanac and Sketches Here and There* (New York: Oxford University Press, 1949).
2.   Ibid.

3. J. Baird Callicott, "Foreword" (unpublished foreword to *A Sand County Almanac*), in *Companion to* A Sand County Almanac, ed. J. Baird Callicott (Madison: University of Wisconsin Press, 1987), 282.
4. Leopold, *A Sand County Almanac.*
5. G. E. Moore, *Principia Ethica* (Cambridge: Cambridge University Press, 1903).
6. Leopold, *A Sand County Almanac.*
7. Arthur Middleton, "Is the Wolf a Real American Hero?," *New York Times,* March 9, 2014.
8. Michael E. Soulé, "What Is Conservation Biology?," *BioScience* 35, no. 11, The Biological Diversity Crisis (1985), 727–34.
9. Barry Stroud, *The Quest for Reality: Subjectivism and the Metaphysics of Colour* (New York: Oxford University Press, 2000).

Altered State

A Place for Wildlife

Monte Dolack

Monte Dolack looks at his native Montana and finds it altered—and sometimes ravaged—but he also finds its altered state an inspiration for his artwork. While he laments the damage imposed by extractive, industrial, and other types of development, he discovers irony and discreet beauty in the juxtaposition of wildlife and human endeavors. Even the colors of the ores and dissolved metals from refining processes find their way into his paintings and sculptures.

Montana has a notable and sometimes volatile relationship with its industrial legacy. Blessed with an uncommon abundance of natural resources and beauty, the Treasure State's heritage includes coal, oil and gas extraction, mining, timbering, ranching, and real estate development. A powerful tension exists between the naturally diverse Montana landscape and the civilization that has established here. Vast wealth for a few and jobs for many have been the result of this significant inheritance, and the condition continues today. Some of Montana's greatest natural beauty has been set aside in national wildlife refuges and parks, forests, and state parks. Our state's abundant rivers and astounding wildlife draw tourists from around the world. Conversely, the by-products of industry and development have contaminated our water and air with toxic waste and resulted in the loss of rare species and the introduction of invasive plants, fish, and animals.

When Lewis and Clark and the Corps of Discovery passed through the area now known as Great Falls in 1805, they described wildlife sightings and encounters that surpassed anything else they would see on their journey. The area, often referred to as the "American Serengeti," was also the buffalo-rich hunting grounds for the Blackfeet Nation. By the 1950s, when I was growing up there, Great Falls was becoming an industrial hub and little of the profuse wildlife in Montana remained. The Great Falls of the Missouri became a series of dams powering the refinery for the Anaconda Company. It boasted the tallest smokestack in the world. The refinery smelted the rich copper ores of Butte and manufactured most of the world's copper wire, helping to create the first major global communication networks.

My grandfather, Steve Dolack, was a Slovak immigrant who, in around 1914, started his own coal mine in Belt, Montana. My father, Mike Dolack, worked for more than thirty years at the Great Falls Anaconda copper refinery. After graduating from high school, I worked summers at the smelter in Great Falls while attending college. It was a good paying job and an education. I learned how mineral-rich ore from Butte's mines was turned into copper and other metals.

Because of my family's history in mining, it seemed natural to me that copper and coal would be interesting materials to assimilate into my art-making process. Just like a painter's palette, a full spectrum of exposed colors is blended on the sidewalls of the colossal Berkeley Pit in Butte. The mine's toxic wastewater, which has a rich concentration of dissolved metals, forms a lagoon in the bottom of the pit. The metal tailings change the colors of the lagoon from red to turquoise, depending on the time of day.

In 1995 a large flock of snow geese alighting on the lagoon's surface died from exposure to the lethal effects of the water. The geese took the toxic lagoon for a natural lake. But surprisingly, the toxic lake is not dead. Something is alive there.

A team of researchers recently discovered microscopic organisms living in the contaminated waters of the Berkeley mine pit. Yellowstone National Park is one of the few places on Earth where similar colors to those of the Berkeley Pit can be found occurring naturally. These vibrant hues are the fabulous results of volcanic activity and the pigmented microorganisms that have adapted to Yellowstone's thermal waters. This naturally occurring phenomenon has long attracted painters and photographers, including Thomas Moran and Ansel Adams, to the park.

Many of my paintings are on copper panels, with the metal's iridescent qualities showing through multiple thin paint glazes. My creative constructions and sculptures are assemblies using found materials from industry that relate to Montana's industrial heritage and our abundant natural resources.

The challenge in creating my paintings has always been in discovering the irony, beauty, and honesty in the subject while not losing my sense of humor. Almost everywhere I look in Montana there is subject matter that speaks of our altered state.

Occurrence. By Monte Dolack. Acrylic painting on copper panel. Copyright Monte Dolack, Monte Dolack Fine Art.

Saving Things, Saving the West

James C. McNutt

James McNutt is a foremost advocate of collecting and preserving the artifacts of human culture in the West. "From the records of collectors, museums, and other institutions," he says, it's easy to see that "we're great at saving things from the past, but not very good at conserving things for the future." He reminds us here that we must never "fail to put our massive collections of creative output, history, and scientific data into motion" on behalf of wildlife and western landscapes.

The Cheyenne, Wyoming, Frontier Days Celebration in 1910 featured horse races, bronco riding, a sham battle between cavalrymen, and a speech by ex-president Theodore Roosevelt—along with lots of handshaking. The next morning Roosevelt met John Avery Lomax, who was seeking an endorsement from the former president for his forthcoming book, *Cowboy Songs and Other Frontier Ballads*.

Lomax got the endorsement. Many of the songs he published in the book began to reach a broad popular audience for the first time, so that by the 1930s pieces such as "Home on the Range" emerged as popular hits.

The meeting of Roosevelt and Lomax in Cheyenne was appropriate because of their shared interest in cowboy songs and the West, and because Lomax's collecting of cowboy songs and ballads had been encouraged by his Harvard professors George Lyman Kittredge and Barrett Wendell, both of whom were known to Roosevelt. In the literary worlds that they inhabited, scholars had frequently treated folksong and ballad as the building blocks of national literatures, and so it was in keeping with this tradition that Roosevelt encouraged Lomax and concluded that "it is therefore a work of real importance to preserve permanently this unwritten ballad literature of the back country and the frontier."[1]

Lomax's life work, collecting songs, was arduous but rewarding labor, prompted by his conviction that the songs themselves belonged to an oral tradition and should be preserved. Whether the songs really belonged to an oral tradition or not would sometimes be questioned. "Home on the Range" was the subject of a lawsuit to which Lomax was party in the 1930s, when an Arizona couple claimed that they had composed it long before Lomax's publication in *Cowboy Songs.* The Arizona couple lost because in the end, as attorneys discovered, the song was actually written and published by a Kansas physician in the 1870s. Much later, but without knowing that background, Lomax collected an oral version from an African American saloon-keeper in San Antonio, and then put it into his book.

In spite of the often-tangled history about oral tradition and printed or recorded music, the passion of a collector to save things resulted in a cultural treasure. Lomax's work and his subsequent collecting of folk song across the country, with his son Alan Lomax and other members of his family, helped develop a major repository, the Archive of American Folk Song at the Library of Congress. The archive, now called the Archive of Folk Culture, includes over three million photographs, manuscripts, audio recordings, and moving images. And the Cheyenne Frontier Days, mind you, is still an annual occurrence.

Somewhat earlier than Lomax's cowboy-song collecting, a leading American photographer also had a hand in contributing to future cultural resources. As I wrote in my introduction to National Geographic's *Greatest Photographs of the American West,* William Henry Jackson engaged in strenuous searches for iconic images. On August 23, 1873, Jackson and his team of assistants—sixteen people and a greater number of mules—labored up a valley strewn with fallen timber, slick rocks, and bogs, west of the Eagle River in Colorado, seeking a route to a view of the legendary Mountain of the Holy Cross. Leaving the valley, Jackson took two members of the team and ascended a ridge to a vantage point on Notch Mountain. Hauling hundreds of pounds of photographic equipment up the last 1,500-foot climb, they spent a day above the clouds that obscured the main subject but that compensated by producing a nearly circular rainbow.

After a restless night at tree line, they arose to a clear, cold morning and a sunrise view of the snow-crossed mountain. Jackson had to wait for snowmelt to produce the water needed to wash his glass plates, then he

Mount of the Holy Cross. By William Henry Jackson, 1873. Albumen silver print. Digital image courtesy of the Getty's Open Content Program.

made eight images—the first ever—of the Mountain of the Holy Cross. His stereographs and prints, slightly altered to extend one arm of the cross, became some of the most popular photographs of the American West in the nineteenth century, symbolizing to many the union of America, nature, and God that fulfilled a romantic destiny.

Jackson's photograph served to his sometime collaborator, the painter Thomas Moran, as a spur to action and a confirmation. Just as their joint works imaging the Grand Canyon of the Yellowstone had prompted congressional action to establish the first national park, the photographer and painter again created paired images that would convince their audiences of the significance of the West. Moran deposited a copy of the photograph of the Mountain of the Holy Cross with the US Copyright Office in 1874 so that he could lay claim to its use for a painting, and then he made the difficult trip himself to obtain sketches. Jackson's photograph and Moran's painting both appeared in Philadelphia's Centennial Exhibition in 1876, where the photograph won seven medals. Upon seeing the image, Henry Wadsworth Longfellow composed a sonnet to memorialize his deceased wife, "The Cross of Snow" (1879, published posthumously), with the lines:

There is a mountain in the distant West
That, sun-defying, in its deep ravines
Displays a cross of snow upon its side.

Proving a legend, Jackson's photography helped bequeath to future generations a sense of the American West as an enormous natural territory in which to explore national and human possibilities. In the words of one writer, "The photographs became as legendary as the mountain itself."

In 1989, *National Geographic* magazine published both images in a retrospective of William Henry Jackson's career. By that time, the pages of the magazine had been carrying stories of western adventure and expansion for over a century. The legends of lost cities of gold, endless deserts, rivers flowing to the Pacific, and enormous herds of wildlife followed by nomadic peoples belonged to the history of the frontier.[2]

The National Geographic Society's Image Collection in Washington, DC, includes millions of images compiled, published, and many not published over the 125-year history of that organization. The Image Collection furnishes a second example of cultural riches, gathered from the work of numerous photographers.

Such cultural riches as the Archive of Folk Culture and the National Geographic Image Collection—often sprung from the isolated efforts of individuals but also organized by numerous historical, artistic, and scientific organizations—have become things we take for granted. Collections of songs, images, and stories about the American West abound at universities, museums, cultural centers, and libraries, not to mention private collections.

The scope and quantity of collections about the West and its landscape are staggering. A nationwide consortium of museums with collections devoted primarily to western art collectively houses over one million items in collections.[3] We quickly realize, however, that it is hard to delimit collections, even for such a magnificent space. Collecting about nearly everything, in fact, has for some time been a global undertaking.

A decade ago, with the support of the Institute for Museum and Library Services, Heritage Preservation estimated that US museums, libraries, scientific organizations, archives, and historical societies hold an estimated

4.8 billion items.⁴ Speaking only about museums, it has become a commonplace that most museums display only about 10 percent of the items in their collections. The other 90 percent remains in storage, the product of years of gathering and collecting, but often unstudied and seldom displayed. The infrastructure problem had become acute already, ten years ago when this data was published. A second study is now underway. But the results are already in: we have built structures and methods of caring for objects that now themselves need rebuilding and constant expansion.

The irony is that we have often lost sight of the purpose of gathering and collecting that was the signal activity of people like John Lomax and William Henry Jackson. I once told my staff at a major East Coast history museum, which held some three hundred thousand objects in its collection, that they could throw the entire collection out but we would still be in business—if we took our business to be listening to and gathering the histories of the people of the state. They were not amused.

After collecting, literally for centuries, one begins to wonder if the records of human creativity could somehow exceed the grains of sand in the Red Desert of Utah.

Something of the contrast that these activities pose comes in the form of two articles that recently appeared in the *New York Times*. The first tells the story of a Brazilian collector of vinyl records. The second warns of the threats posed to the Grand Canyon by developers. These two articles point to a distinction between collecting human-made items, creative or otherwise, and gathering and preserving features of the natural world and the creatures that inhabit it.

Among the most influential museum collectors was a group at the American Museum of Natural History in the early twentieth century: Carl Akeley, William R. Leigh, James Lippitt Clark, and Carl Rungius. Led by Akeley, these artists created the first museum dioramas involving backgrounds painted in deft perspective and taxidermied animals staged in the foreground. In Akeley's words:

> For the first time we have the opportunity to train a group of men not only to practise the various arts which are combined in making modern zoological exhibits, but also to further develop the methods that make this sort of museum exhibition worth while from the scientific and artistic standpoint. In this considerable corps of men I am resting my hope that the

technique of my studio shall be carried on to higher perfection instead of scattering or being carried underground when my part shall be done. This is important not only for Africa, but for all other continents as well, inasmuch as we are making records of rapidly disappearing animal life.[5]

This impetus generated a longstanding motivation by museum workers. For example, a young and accomplished photographer named Michael Forsberg had this to say about his work that was recently featured in an exhibit at the National Museum of Wildlife Art:

The overriding goal of my work is to photograph and build appreciation for what is left of the wild Great Plains, trying to capture on film the fierce spirit and the unique and often overlooked beauty of the creatures and landscapes that still make up these wide-open spaces. Through this work I hope that in some small way the collective spirit of the land and its inhabitants will never be forgotten: that the wild lands that still exist remain left intact and forever preserved: and that someday even more of its wildness may be restored.[6]

The distance traveled during the last century is instructive. Akeley and his colleagues labored in the conviction that the animals they shot, taxidermied, and displayed would one day soon become extinct. Nevertheless, their efforts may have helped draw attention to those very creatures, many species of which yet survive. Forsberg expresses a more hopeful determination that the wildness of the plains may be restored.

From the records of collectors, museums, and other institutions, we can easily gather that we're great at saving things from the past, but not very good at conserving things for the future. This is unfortunate, because frequently the early collectors, documenters, and museum builders—like John Lomax, William Henry Jackson, and Carl Akeley—were busy saving things for posterity. That is, they were saving things with the experience of future people in mind, not with the goal of amassing more things.

Followers of music archives have often lamented the loss of the Edison cylinders on which John Lomax recorded cowboy songs. Examples also abound of the cultural restoration that can occur when such items do survive. The cylinders of Omaha tribal songs recorded by Frances

Densmore in the 1890s later provided access to traditional music that tribal members themselves had forgotten. Nevertheless it seems that we have now burdened ourselves with so much of the past that we frequently feel we cannot afford to look at the contemporary world. Perhaps more critically, we fail to use the past to gauge the future—we fail to put our massive collections of creative output, history, and scientific data into motion.

When it comes to actual spaces and places, our thinking at first seems to be of a piece with the collectors of human creativity. We have maps showing parks, public lands, forests, rivers, and mountains preserved. Among the most poignant and controversial, perhaps, are reservations, places that call to mind both humanity's relationship with nature and man's inhumanity to man.

Here I feel honored to be called to consider strategies in the humanities to inspire people to act on behalf of wildlife and western landscapes. The search for a bridge between the collector's intimacy with an object, a story, a space, or a wild animal, and the complicated process of extending that intimacy to others is one that we now have no choice but to confront. I look forward to hearing the experiences and ideas of others and learning from them.

NOTES

1. John A. Lomax, *Adventures of a Ballad Hunter* (New York: Macmillan Company, 1947), 68–70.

2. James C. McNutt, *National Geographic Greatest Photographs of the American West* (Washington: National Geographic Society, 2012), 15–29.

3. See Museums West (website), https://museumswest.org.

4. See American Institute for Conservation of Historic and Artistic Works (website), http://www.conservation-us.org/home.

5. Carl Ethan Akeley, *In Brightest Africa* (Garden City, NY: Doubleday, Page & Co., 1920).

6. Michael Forsberg, *Great Plains: America's Lingering Wild*, exhibition at the National Museum of Wildlife Art, October 2010–January 2011.

Love Has No Net Zero-Sum

Erin Halcomb

When you ask, "Where are the young people in this fight to save wildlife and wilderness?" look to Erin Halcomb. Her passion drives a commitment to be in the trenches of wildlife preservation at its most fundamental level, and like many of her generation, she taps into a need to get straight to the bottom line. Her message is brief: we save wilderness by never giving up on it and devoting ourselves to the virtues of the humanities in service and story with restraint and imagination. Stay with her, she asks, out of "reverence and generosity and respect" for the wild. The Dalai Lama calls this "loving kindness."

My story? Let's begin at twenty-one, my senior year of college, when I called my mother to complain that I'd be spending my birthday studying for a final exam. She responded, offhandedly, "Well, at least you're not getting shipped to Saigon."

And I heard her for the first time in a long while.

So, after graduation I enrolled in a national service program called AmeriCorps. I moved from Georgia to Oregon and banded tightly with a crew of folks who had come from all across the country to perform, like me, one year of environmental restoration.

Our projects were diverse. We fought forest fires and restored fish habitat. We served across a wide variety of land ownerships and designations, packing in crosscut saws and camping out for weeks to clear trails in wilderness. I gained knowledge, skills, and confidence.

I signed up for another term. And became increasingly more feral.

In fact, when I returned home, my mother, having served as a nurse in Vietnam, saw the areas on my back and arms where the pigment had discolored, and identified it as a fungus. She said soldiers would get it from wearing their soiled uniforms for too long. She asked me just how often was I showering and laundering my work shirts?

This, to a Georgia girl who cried in grade school because her clothes weren't good enough, and who was ticketed in college for littering.

My lesson: never underestimate the power to transform, to transcend. My invitation to you: go feral.

Presently, I'm employed on a research team that questions how forest thinning—to reduce the risk and intensity of wildfire—affects small mammals. I spend the day hiking the hills of southern Oregon, checking hundreds of mini wire-mesh cages for critters.

Often, when I peer behind the spring-loaded door, I am greeted—or scolded, I can never tell which—by the chatter of a chipmunk. Sometimes when I look in I see, curled back in the nest box, the soft glint off the quiet eye of a flying squirrel.

I ear tag what I find and turn the animal over in my palm. If it's a female, I blow across her belly in order to part the fur and determine if she's yet nursed young.

Ultimately, I handle these animals because they are deemed valuable as prey. Flying squirrels and woodrats, in particular, are considered critical meals for the region's threatened Pacific fisher and endangered spotted owl.

But they've given me much fodder too. I wonder how my values would differ had I stayed in Atlanta. What would be my desires? My metaphors?

These days, I desire the durability and pluck of a chipmunk that, after being bear rolled in the night, stands up in its disheveled cage and cheeps at me what is without a doubt the sound of protest.

I desire the stealth magic of a flyer: to glide, with elegance, through the dark.

And when I glance around my room at any time, I am reminded of what a scientist once catalogued inside a packrat's stick nest: feathers, socks, a bar of soap, a bottle, and a jellyroll. I recognize my own compulsion to covet, carry off, and accumulate.

And so I pray.

For restraint: to stop myself from taking, and doing, simply because I can.

For imagination: to redefine what exacts pleasure and valor.

And I try each day to re-dignify myself by re-calculating my own capacity for generosity.

Nesting Trumpeter Swan. Photographer unknown. A historic photograph of a trumpeter swan (*Cygnus buccinators*) nesting in the Red Rock Lakes National Wildlife Refuge. The trumpeter's wingspan may exceed 10 feet (3.0 m). Courtesy of United States Fish and Wildlife Service Archives.

In 2013, the dysfunction in our political system led to the closing of our national parks and refuges, and I thought, What if we had elected to give our lands a rest? For a day? Or a week or two? What if we didn't just divide watersheds into hiking and biking days, but offered wildlife quietude during breeding season? What a lovely gesture.

To date, I think the greatest gesture Americans have made is the preservation of wilderness. We limit our work and play in acknowledgement of our collective disturbance. We've set up a trust fund for the future.

Gary Snyder wrote that grasses photosynthesizing are the ultimate working class. What a humbling thought.

Close your eyes. Forget the labels, the inches and pounds and years that define you.

And think only of the future. Feel how much you want.

I feel at times that I could burn right through my skin, I want so much. And I believe that this is our commonality, our strength.

I believe that now, as always, there is a great hunger within people to understand the wit of their universe. And that through service and story we can cultivate conservationists from all generations.

I believe that "elder" is a title that must be earned. That our movement isn't a "job" that you can "retire" from. It is one of persistence over time, and so I ask all of you to stay in this with me, because the sentiments behind wilderness—reverence and generosity and respect—don't diminish with age, or with how much you give. Trust me. Love has no net zero-sum.

PART 3

Practice

Programmatic Approaches

Managing, Accommodating, and Sustaining the Wild

Wendy Fisher

*Wendy Fisher devotes her professional life to working with landown-
ers and communities to protect open space through conservation
easements, which protect land in perpetuity. She calls her work "an
exercise in hope—hope for future generations; hope for the survival
of species; and hope that this effort will make a difference in the collective conservation needed for the planet." With passion and detail,
she drives home the point that saving the wild is not easy, but when
advocates on all sides of the issue come together and identify common ground, progress on behalf of nature can be made.*

Anticipating the potential future changes to an ecosystem is nearly
impossible, but conservation easements protect land and undeniably
provide the essential intention for safeguarding landscapes and the conservation values we attribute to them. And intention is not insignificant.

It is appropriate that preservation intended to last forever takes time
to craft. How to distill a landscape into a written document is challenging,
to say the least.

Like the intricate ecological systems, family connections, and historical context they are intended to protect, conservation easements are
complex. They are tailor made—specific to the land, the landowner, and
the myriad conservation values that are unique to place, time, and circumstance. They do not happen overnight.

In 1976, Congress recognized the need to promote conservation in
the United States through aiding private efforts to preserve our country's
heritage and natural lands. This intention was first codified in the Tax
Reform Acts of 1976 and 1977. As those acts expired in 1980, Congress

made the incentives permanent by creating Section 170(h) of the Internal Revenue Code. Today, conservation easements are created under the provision of that code. To satisfy this part of the Internal Revenue Code, there must be a public benefit. That public benefit is derived from the preservation of the conservation resources of the land, which the code rudimentarily identifies as: scenic, significant habitat; a clearly delineated governmental policy; historic or cultural significance; and public recreation or education.

Negotiating land preservation utilizing the tool of a conservation easement identified under the rubric of federal tax code sounds mechanical and discounts the emotion and sentimentality that, in reality, accompany land protection efforts. As a land trust, Utah Open Lands has the duty to forever protect public benefits. This intention to indefinitely protect the conservation resources of the land is a promise that is made to the land, the landowner, and the public, and it is not entered into lightly.

I was told early on by other land trust professionals that the reason someone places land under a conservation easement is because, fundamentally, they love their land. I have watched communities pass open space bonds because they love their land. I have watched families, whose disagreements have risen to lawsuits, come together to protect their family lands, because they love their land. And I witnessed a community come together and raise $250,000 in five weeks, because they love their land.

These passionate forces of emotion that demand a landscape be forever saved are hard to balance when considering the largess of a landscape as a whole. Balancing the protection of wildlife habitat, cultural and historic significance, agricultural operations, public use, restoration, and management of a landscape within the four corners of a conservation easement agreement is an exercise in documenting the present while trying to predict the future. It is fraught with unknowns. Knowing how a landscape will react to climate change, how public use will increase with the popularity of a new access and new trail, or the size of an elk herd in successive years is, at best, a guess. Therefore, the art in negotiating the preservation of a landscape becomes an exercise in understanding what draws us to a place from the moment we determine we need to protect it. It is an exercise in hope—hope for future generations; hope for the survival of species; and hope that this effort will make a difference in the collective conservation needed for the planet.

In Summit County, just twenty miles from Utah's largest metropolitan area and fifteen minutes from the resort town of Park City, lies Toll Canyon. The protection of Toll Canyon was and is an evolving discussion about how we enlarge our sense of community to include the voices of future generations of residents, whether they are human, deer, moose, black bear, or cougar. It is a place where passionate forces have the potential to collide.

Toll Canyon has required Utah Open Lands and the eventual landowner, the Snyderville Basin Special Recreation District, to redefine stewardship, refine an understanding of recreational experience, and evaluate how best to adapt management and protection of the land amid safeguarding old-growth forests and concerns over fire protection. The story of saving the land from development and planning for the canyon's protection into the future contemplates the friction that comes from trying to balance the needs of wildlife amid a growing recreational population.

In 1998, driving through a blinding blizzard at seven thirty in the morning, I was seriously questioning my dedication to finding a solution that would preserve Toll Canyon. I was on my way from Park City to Salt Lake to meet the landowner, who was one of the largest developers in the state. In the 1970s he had purchased the 780 acres, now sandwiched between two expansive sprawling neighborhoods with room for approximately nine hundred homes.

That morning was filled with anxiety, not just from slick roads and poor visibility, but from the concern of wondering if this landowner could possibly share a perspective of preservation. We were from different worlds. I imagined that he looked at a landscape with an opportunistic mindset of where the best lots should be located and how to engineer the roads. My view of any landscape didn't include those possibilities, but I feared they were unavoidable.

The meeting went as well as could be expected. Preservation wasn't out of the question, but it would be complicated. The land was held by the development company. I found, though, that the landowner loved the land—not for its development potential, but because the land had become a sanctuary for him. What made it complicated was the reality that a full donation of a conservation easement to protect it was out of the question, in part because of the disposition of the land as part of his larger development portfolio. With no state or local funding options available, the possibility of raising money equivalent to the development value of the land was remote. I hoped at some point there would be a significant source of funding for such an effort.

Years passed by, and the landowner passed away, leaving the land—his sanctuary—in the hands of his estate and the real estate holding company. I inquired with the landowner's attorney I had met at that first meeting. He remembered the meeting and, indeed, remembered the intention to see it protected. The attorney was willing to take a proposal from Utah Open Lands to the holding company. He believed a proposal that compensated the development value would be considered favorably by the new owners.

Purchasing land for its natural value, its attendant conservation value, requires a transaction that recognizes the priceless nature of saving the land as it is for future generations. That recognizes passing along a legacy that enhances and supports the delicate life balance, instead of stripping away its roots.

Conservation in Utah is challenging, as perhaps it is everywhere. As a society we have created regulations for the protection of endangered species, saving habitats, wetlands, and forests for the land's sake, but we also have created trade-offs when money and politics are involved. Conservation is often a fight to protect a landscape for the land itself, pitted against what the land can provide in housing units or board feet. There is no monetary return on investments for donors of land preservation; instead there is the understanding that we are building a broader currency in safeguarding something that cannot be replaced and that is, therefore, priceless. There was hope for Toll Canyon because the Snyderville Basin Special Recreation District had been focusing on land preservation since 2006 and was born out of community consideration for saving the places in which people play, get inspired, and gain a sense of solace. Open space bonds had been approved by voters, and funding to compete with the fair market development value was within the realm of possibility.

There were months and months of negotiation with the new holding company that owned Toll Canyon. The resulting deal would require substantial funding from the Snyderville Basin Special Recreation District's open space bond, a 10 percent donation of the value of the land, and a requirement that Utah Open Lands raise $250,000. Basin Recreation would put up the initial $2 million down payment on the property. When the papers were finally drawn up, and the prospect of the preservation of Toll Canyon could be talked about publicly, Utah Open Lands had five weeks to raise the money. The gears shifted, and now we began enumerating the reasons why the canyon should be saved.

The most obvious reason to protect the canyon was the reality that if it was not protected it would be developed. I had learned early on in my career that zoning rules change and that lawsuits heralding the supremacy of private property rights often won out over community master plans and county ordinances. One of the first conservation projects I was involved in included acreage where the jurisdictional wetlands on the property rendered it, according to the Army Corps of Engineers, undevelopable. Nine months later, the land—where nothing could be built—was slated for a nine-lot subdivision. So the future of Toll Canyon, were it not preserved, was truly unknown and full of many development scenarios.

Development was only a portion of the reason Toll Canyon had a dedicated following. Surrounded by half-acre and acre housing lots, just minutes from the Factory Outlet Stores and the commercial hub of Kimball Junction, Toll Canyon is another world. In the canyon you can engage in a sense of wildness. Moose, deer, and elk leave tracks and signs throughout the canyon. Early-morning hikers often catch sight of a mountain lion. It is common when coming along the trail to flush out a ruffed grouse in a flurry, trying to evade predators and protect its chicks camouflaged somewhere in the brush.

Halfway up the canyon, towering Douglas fir, which haven't been touched since the mining days of the 1860s, are densely packed guardians of the canyon. Toll Canyon Stream flows year round and is fed by ephemeral streams flowing with the rhythm of the spring snowmelt. Toll Canyon is heralded as a refuge for species like the Bonneville cutthroat trout (*Oncorhynchus clarkii Utah*), northern goshawk (*Accipiter gentilis*), and the smooth green snake (*Opheodrys vernalis*), which are designated as sensitive by the Utah Division of Wildlife Resources.

As the story of Toll Canyon unfolded, it was these species, these streams, the pace of nature so close to the daily grinding of cars and commuters and work commitments, that captivated the attention of the public, and soon support began to trickle in. On December 8, 2012, a *Salt Lake Tribune* editorial entitled "Toll Canyon: Magical Place Should Be Saved" defined it this way: "There are few places left not far off the Wasatch Front where a hiker, skier or equestrian rider can easily leave behind the sights, sounds and smells of modern life and luxuriate in nature. Toll Canyon is one of those.... Once trees and other vegetation are removed, the stream is tamed and the canyon walls bulldozed to make way for houses, this magical place will be lost forever. That should not be allowed to happen."[1]

That was how everyone felt. Those who contributed to the effort to save Toll Canyon had stories of how magical it was for them. They told stories of wildlife encounters and how the canyon was their daily therapy, both physically and psychologically. For me, moose had become the harbingers of Toll Canyon. The canyon provides critical year-round habitat for moose that rely on it for forage, especially in the winter months. It seemed that moose were always appearing in this effort, signaling hope and determination and a sense of wariness to ensure that we tread lightly.

At times the work to preserve a piece of land seems dangerously out of control. Funding is tenuous; details, from securing the mineral interests to understanding the water rights, confuse and confound what should be straightforward. The magnitude of preservation intent on surviving generations and the fragile nature of life is a startling reminder that everything we do has a consequence, intended or unintended.

As weeks ticked by and the end of 2012 loomed closer, we were still short of our $250,000 goal. We had scheduled to meet a reporter up on the property, and we were hoping a story in the local *Park Record* newspaper would tip the scales. There was a fresh blanket of snow on the ground as we drove to the canyon to begin our hike. In the car we were discussing the story of Toll Canyon, the wildlife, the potential for wildlife experiences and education, and how, over the years, the canyon had become a sanctuary to many. It was distinct, juxtaposed against the onslaught of development that had built up around it. It was unique because it bordered twenty-six thousand acres of watershed land, national forest land, and a fifteen-hundred-acre property also protected by Utah Open Lands and Basin Recreation.

We parked, got out, and began our journey, and within moments a moose appeared three yards in front of us. The young bull moose ambled out of the brush, paused, and then proceeded off into the forest. A moose at close range is always amazing, but at nine o'clock in the morning, the reporter from the *Park Record* was catching her first glimpse of a moose in the wild. Our journey up the canyon that morning was infused with the glow of that moment, that first impression.

Sandhill Cranes. Photograph by Mary Tull, 2012.

When we finished our hike and began to walk out of the forest, just down the slope from us were two moose, perhaps the young bull and his mother, nestled for a mid-morning nap. Of all the ways we had enumerated the importance of Toll Canyon, nothing we said had as much impact or was as telling as the reporter's wildlife experience. It changed skepticism to wonder.

It was a reminder to me of the difficulty in saving these places. How does an individual come to value the land with an intention of leaving it alone? Is it through an experience on the land, or is there a part of our human experience that intuitively informs us that the carrying capacity of the land is dependent on places untouched? Throughout my work at Utah Open Lands there have been places protected that continue to be working landscapes. There are places that provide vital habitat for threatened species. Amid this preservation there have been critics. There are those who have concluded that without public access, conservation for the sake of a species is not the best use of public dollars. Others argue that placing the protection of certain wild species above the needs of the human species is not in our best interest. This is flawed logic. We are so young in our understanding of a landscape that has evolved over millions of years that we are far from truly understanding the cascading effect of losing one species. What the implications are for our own survival are still unknown.

For five feverish weeks, Utah Open Lands worked around the clock. There were Toll Canyon open houses held by individuals in the neighborhoods adjacent to Toll Canyon. There were more news stories. There was a handful of large donors. Four hundred individual donations later, Utah Open Lands succeeded in raising the $250,000. It was a testament to the story of Toll Canyon.

One of the donors to the campaign had been hiking the canyon for more than fourteen years. Shortly after Basin Recreation and Utah Open Lands announced that we had met the goal and the land would be preserved, he called both offices.

"You need to know about the state of disrepair of the trails in Toll Canyon" was how the donor's conversation started for both Bob Radke of Basin Recreation and me. The donor wanted to know what the plans were for continued public access in the canyon, maintenance of the trails, and more opportunities for recreation. Bob told him that studies were underway and that we were working to balance the wildlife protection, water quality of the stream, and recreational uses. An adaptive management plan was being developed as a vital part of the preservation effort for the canyon. Together, Basin Recreation and Utah Open Lands were gathering data on conservation values in the canyon, determining restoration needs, and employing criteria to aid future decision-making that both tracked and minimized impacts to wildlife. However, stating that the management of the canyon and the development of trails were undergoing a study was not a satisfying answer to someone who had been exploring the canyon for fourteen years.

My response to the donor was similar to Bob's. Trail use would be part of the plan, but balancing recreational uses and ecosystem health would be paramount. Here, again, the friction of perspective and intention and values was forefront. What Toll Canyon means to the more than four hundred individuals who had pledged to save it is very personal.

We had assessed the canyon from many perspectives; first and foremost were the conservation values that were present on the land and hearken back to the IRS code. The careful consideration of the ongoing stewardship of Toll Canyon, which Basin Recreation and Utah Open Lands were firmly engaged in, seemed foreign to some. For many, just saving the land from development seemed to be the essential part of protecting habitat and ecosystem health. The reality that increased use posed a threat to the very protection of the canyon had the potential to dampen the enthusiasm of its preservation.

At the nexus of public benefit lies a fundamental question: How does the public benefit if it is restricted from accessing the property? Some of the answers that spring forward are protecting a species from extinction or leaving a wild place untouched. Still, within the stunning protection of Toll Canyon was the immutable reality that it was saved because of human engagement with the land.

In the twenty-five years that I have been working to preserve land, adaptive management plans have not been standard in the conservation easement template. There is little guidance in the IRS code on managing the potential conflict of conservation values, except to hint that one shouldn't impair the other. There are considerable impacts from recreational use on the conservation values attendant to the natural ecology of an area. Off-leash dogs threaten species of concern, like the smooth green snake, even if the pets are under control enough not to chase larger wildlife. Impacts to stream health are inevitable when trails are adjacent to riparian corridors. The danger of fire increases as the forest is left to be a forest. Managing the potential conflicts has to be adaptable. Regardless of what decisions are made, it is obvious that management will restrict use, and for some there will be a sense that something has been taken away, perhaps even a perceived inalienable freedom to use the land as they see fit.

For both Utah Open Lands and Basin Recreation there continues to be a lot riding on the management plan for Toll Canyon. It will set a precedent for stewardship of this canyon and potentially other open spaces. It will be seen by some as bending to either recreational enthusiasts or wildlife advocates. If done right, no one will be completely satisfied. If done right, it will err on the side of keeping the canyon healthy. Just the discussion of different management ideas for the canyon has angered some of the donors to the campaign.

The final decisions made to restore areas, including the closure of trails in the canyon to improve and protect the stream health and wildlife habitat, have evolved as we become ever more familiar with the land and document the way that species—human, plant, and animal—exist on it. Hiking alongside the stream is considered one of the wonders of Toll Canyon and yet, as a study from the Division of Forestry Fire and

State Lands has determined, "Keeping the riparian zones healthy is of primary concern for the health of the overall ecosystem and most of the associated wildlife. Riparian areas should be left undisturbed as much as possible." That provides a challenge because the current state of the riparian areas is not one of nondisturbance.

Working on any management plan necessitates time on the land. At one point, Basin Recreation put together a potential trail connection and we headed out. The focus of the hike was to determine how much a new trail connection would impact sensitive wildlife habitat, in an effort to determine how best to minimize impacts. We began the hike amid the sounds of a nearby kids' summer camp. The beginning of the trail was in a populated area, not far from an adjacent multifamily development. In our periphery a gangly, graceful figure danced into view. It was a young moose. This young one was alone and nervous as it danced up the hill, keeping us in his sights. I couldn't help but see its appearance as something of an ambassador for striking a balance in the canyon.

The time out on the land, documenting and assessing it, was matched with outreach to the public. The donors of Toll Canyon comprised those four hundred direct contributors and the donors who voted to approve the Basin Recreation open space bond that provided the bulk of the funding for its preservation. As part of our outreach, Utah Open Lands conducted a survey of what the public values in Toll Canyon. One of the questions asked was: What natural characteristics of Toll Canyon do you most appreciate? Solitude and quiet enjoyment of the canyon ranked highest in the survey, as did scenic views and wildlife. Overwhelmingly, hiking and backcountry skiing were the activities the public felt were most appropriate in the canyon. According to the survey, the most commonly seen wildlife in the canyon is far and away moose. It became apparent that as much as the public was concerned about their access to Toll Canyon, there was a subtle, yet higher, percentage of those respondents who clearly saw a need to safeguard a place for wildlife.

After almost a year of Utah Open Lands and Basin Recreation studying and contemplating the management scenarios for Toll Canyon, the donor concerned with the state of disrepair of the trails called again.

Frustration had surfaced regarding the inaction on the part of Utah Open Lands and Basin Recreation in maintaining trails. Eroding the euphoria that surrounded the five weeks of furious fundraising was the ire of many who felt that access should be improved and that the experience on the land was impeded by downed trees, willows along the stream growing out of control, and grasses and brush encroaching on the trail along the creek. There was the threat that the effort made to preserve this place would be tainted.

It is no surprise that Basin Recreation had received the calls as well. It was time for another hike. The natural cycle of a forest, of a stream, of an ecosystem is one of a constant flow of energy. Fallen trees provide habitat in the wake of their decay; thickets of willows hold stream banks in place and become impenetrable places for moose to hide. On the day Basin Recreation staff and I went out, we didn't see moose. My thoughts and view of the canyon were clouded by the complaints. And it dampened the typical enthusiasm that usually accompanies heading out on a protected property.

There was no question that there were areas along the trail where nature had become wilder, and though there was a well-worn path, there were places where downed trees and limbs had caused rogue trails by those heading up to higher meadows. This was not desirable, but in some areas maintenance of the existing trail only encouraged an intolerable impact to the stream corridor. We didn't decide on any action, but rather decided to talk further with the donor. At the end of the hike things were frenetic. We shuttled cars and rushed to get to meetings. The fascination, the frustration, the magnitude of needing to craft the right document rushed in. Up ahead lights were flashing; someone was pulled off of the side of the highway and a moose lay by the side of the road.

Making good decisions for the management of Toll Canyon amid competing interests seemed impossible at that moment. When competing ideologies remain unresolved, the unintended consequences are never desirable. I determined that we needed to hike with this donor.

The beginning of the hike was tenuous. The heated conversation over the phone was tempered by the reality of hiking together for the next two hours. Walking to the edge of the canyon, we engaged in typical polite conversation to provide context, and I realized this individual had a connection to the natural world based on his spirituality. He was older than me, and in better shape. He told me that he hiked the canyon on a daily basis for many years. Bob from Basin Recreation joined us, and I was struck at that point by how committed Basin Recreation was to the successful management of the canyon.

Prior to heading out on the hike, I had wondered what the donor saw when he looked at the land. I wondered how many shared his perspective.

Was it merely a place to recreate? We begin talking about the moose in the canyon. He shared story after story of his encounters with moose and how one cow seemed to know when he would be hiking there and showed up in the same place for several days in a row. We came across the willow thicket that had been a source of contention in our previous conversations. To me the willows were a barometer of riparian health—a sign that we were being the kind of steward that puts the canyon and the stream first. But the donor talked about how the willows soaked you from head to toe with early-morning dew. Then we talked about how they are the perfect hiding place for moose. We talked about how the willows provided cover for the stream, how it was protected by the willows' dense nature. We talked about the shade they provided along the trail. We agreed, respectfully, that the willows should remain untouched.

The rest of the hike was full of moments like that, as we discussed alternatives of removing trees or cutting back brush. Remarkably we came to the conclusion that most of the forest and riparian area should be left alone. There were some areas where removing downed trees would divert the path away from the stream, and though it would be a fairly passive restoration, it would allow for the impacted areas to begin to recover and achieve the goal of moving activity out of the stream corridor.

There is a frustration that mounts when we try to balance needs, wants, uses, and what is right. As we hiked, I recognized that our mutual appreciation for this canyon, though different in nature, was equally deep. From a broader perspective, I wondered if we could get past the fear of what we perceived would be taken away, if maybe we would be able to see the land from each other's perspective. I began to recognize that what is truly priceless and astoundingly beautiful about these lands we save is what draws us, each of us, to them. And what draws us to many places is intrinsically tied to that intricate web of life, to the shades and colors, tones and textures that magically provide individual experience, which is as sacred and unique to us as we are to one another. Treading lightly requires that we stand back and adjust our perspective, make room for nature amid our desire to pursue it. It requires us to see that our connection to the land is a greater connection to what has come before and what will survive after.

Fundamentally, preserving a landscape safeguards the potential for an ecosystem left untouched, an experience yet to be had—a refuge. Most precious in these protected lands is the hope that we will evolve, become more open, gain new perspective, and through our experience on the land share a connection to each other that transcends our differences.

Over the years, I have become convinced that successful and sustainable land protection is dependent upon two things. The first is a conservation easement that is well crafted and inclusive of management strategies for the long-term stewardship of the land, and legally unflinching. The second is a community dedicated to its conservation.

The over fifty-six thousand acres of land that Utah Open Lands has worked to protect tell stories of communities coming together to save what they treasure, and accounts of successfully safeguarding habitats for threatened species such that they have a chance at survival. They tell stories of generations connecting through the land—even in places where arguments once prevailed—and how we, as residents, embrace the prosperity provided by the land by ensuring that it is saved.

Utah's population is expanding: The Governor's Office of Planning and Budget anticipates that two decades from now the Wasatch Front will add another 1.7 million residents. Summit and Wasatch Counties will more than double their populations. By 2050, the entire state will see an increase of 2.5 million residents; the majority of the growth anticipated to occur within a 75-mile radius of Salt Lake City.[2]

Open space is a natural resource. Utah's recreational opportunities and scenic beauty attract people who choose to live in or visit Utah because these natural resources exist. Once we attribute value to these spaces and give them meaning, they become places. Our landscapes provide stories of today in the experiences we have on the land, and they hold an understanding of the past. As we engage in the landscape, we become part of the landscape, and we gain a sense of place.

If there is a place for wildlife, a place where the interplay of the ecosystem can function unfettered, it has to be protected with that intention. Whether it is in the public interest to preserve these habitats, these wild lands, canyons, meadows, streams, and forests, in a manner where little to no public engagement is allowed, may always be debated. However, encouraging responsible engagement with a landscape will require that we learn from mistakes, that we provide the ability to experience nature and that we evolve and enlarge our perspective in a manner that fosters a community committed to this end. In the case of Toll Canyon, there are opportunities. There is the possibility to reclaim, restore, and respect the canyon for the sake of the canyon. And there exists the possibility to change our perspective, but only through creating that responsible engagement. I believe that all who work to sustain places for wildlife will benefit from the experiences people have in places like Toll Canyon.

What Utah will become two decades from now is uncertain, but it can be hoped that its society is informed as much by the grandeur of the mountain peaks, solace of aspen forests, and sanctity of desert streams as it is by the commerce that those resources invite. What we easily envision is that Utah will have lost its grace if it has lost the lands that feed, inspire, and rejuvenate its citizens.

NOTES

1. "Toll Canyon: Magical Place Should Be Saved," *Salt Lake Tribune*, December 8, 2012, http://archive.sltrib.com/story.php?ref=/sltrib /opinion/55422411-82/canyon-toll-open-park.html.csp.
2. See Governor's Office of Management & Budget (website), https://gomb.utah.gov.

Conserving Wild Bison in the Twenty-First Century

Robert B. Keiter

"I wish to speak for the bison," says Robert Keiter, and that simple declaration sums up his eloquent history of that great symbol of the North American western plains. Keiter's important essay chronicles the bison's complicated story of improbable survival since the European settlement of the West. He details the complex interplay of science, politics, culture, and economics that have brought the bison to an existential moment in the twenty-first century.

I wish to speak for the bison, a magnificent animal steeped in the history of the West. Almost prehistoric in appearance, the bison is symbolic of our frontier heritage, including our often depressing relationship with Native Americans. It appears on the US Department of the Interior's seal and on the Wyoming state flag. It represents an extraordinary wildlife conservation success story tied to our national parks and the heroic efforts that went into saving the species from extinction a century ago. But the bison's story is also awash in irony, as reflected in the manifold controversies that surround the animal as it wanders the Yellowstone landscape, oblivious to the jurisdictional boundaries that dictate its fate. Indeed, the bison has been much maligned as a disease vector and is not even regarded as wildlife in some quarters, at least not as the state of Montana defines it. This essay reflects on our bison conservation efforts in the Yellowstone ecosystem, the ironies embedded in it, and the challenges that persist.

When did I first encounter bison? Almost certainly as a child growing up on the East Coast during the 1950s, in the western movies that captured my fascination with the old West of cowboys, Indians, and vast landscapes. The buffalo—as bison are known by Native Americans—was regularly present in these films, usually connected to the Indian tribes that were confronted with the onslaught of white settlers moving westward and the loss of their way of life on the Great Plains. Though more enamored as a child with the conflict between the Native Americans and white civilization, I was aware that bison numbers were dwindling from scenes of buffalo hunters killing these animals with abandon for their hides. I probably first encountered a real bison in the National Zoo, along with stuffed ones at the Smithsonian's Natural History Museum, where I was regularly enraptured by the nature dioramas.

A car trip across the West during college was my first exposure to real bison, when a friend and I traversed Yellowstone, though we were more interested in seeing the park's notorious bears and meeting girls than anything else. My first clearly recollected encounter with bison still resonates in my mind's eye; it came during 1984, when my wife and I visited Yellowstone in the winter to ski around the Old Faithful area. We were amazed to find these stolid shaggy beasts standing placidly in subzero temperatures, persistently swishing their huge heads to and fro in order to reach the dry forbs that lay encrusted beneath the 3-foot-deep snow covering the thermal basin. Blanketed themselves in ice and snow, their nostrils periodically blasting steam into the frozen air, these solitary bison appeared oblivious to onlookers like ourselves as we snapped photos from a few feet away before retreating to the warmth of the nearby lodge. We marveled at their capacity for survival in this harsh winter climate, wondering why they remained in the snow-covered park rather than seeking food in the lower-elevation areas adjacent to the park.

Since then, my understanding of the bison's story has deepened, as has my appreciation for this iconic creature that is such a prominent feature of the Yellowstone landscape and so reminiscent of the West and its history. My favorite time to visit the park is late spring, when the bison are on the move, the cows accompanied by their newborn calves, whose cinnamon coats stand in sharp contrast to the shaggy, dark brown coats of the mature animals. The thrill of running into a bison herd on the roadway and waiting while it passes is still palpable even after many such encounters. That same thrill is also obvious among the legions of enthralled park visitors who are having their initial experience with this emblematic creature, mostly unaware of the controversy that surrounds the park's bison as they seasonally move about in search of food.

I first started digging deeper into the plight of the bison during the early 1990s, upon realizing that it was generating more legal conflict in the Greater Yellowstone Ecosystem than any other matter, even as the park wrestled with nearby mining and energy development proposals, escalating snowmobile visitation, clear-cut logging on its perimeter, and growing sentiment supporting wolf reintroduction. Unlike every other park animal, the bison was not allowed to move outside the park on pain of being shot. Approximately 50 percent of the park's bison have been exposed to the *Brucella abortus* bacteria, which it was feared might be transmitted as brucellosis to the domestic livestock maintained on the private and federal lands surrounding the park. Brucellosis can trigger spontaneous abortion, costing ranchers dearly and potentially costing the state of Montana its brucellosis-free status as determined by the US Department of Agriculture, which could embargo cattle across the state and thus preclude ranchers from moving their herds to the interstate markets.[1]

Faced with these consequences, the Montana legislature had designated bison "a species in need of special management" and vested the state Department of Livestock with management authority over any bison that left the park.[2] As a result, several hundred bison were annually being killed when they left the park, prompting such a loud public uproar that the Montana legislature was forced to repeal a recently enacted law permitting bison hunting. The situation, from my vantage point, seemed both unreasonable and untenable, and certainly inconsistent with the bison's historic and ecological importance. After all, Yellowstone's bison represent our only genetically pure wild bison population, and by far our largest free-ranging bison herds. What had happened to create this regrettable situation in our nation's first national park, and how might this matter be resolved to restore the maligned bison's dignity as a free-roaming wildlife species?

It is the 1750s, Euro-American settlement is unfolding in western North America, and bison teem throughout the Great Plains. The bison's ancestors arrived more than three hundred thousand years earlier, having migrated across the Bering ice bridge. Though originally found primarily in the continent's northern reaches, the plains bison now regularly inhabit much of the central United States, stretching from the Rocky

Mountains to the Mississippi River and from Canada into Texas. Native American tribes also populate North America, and the bison has become a key element in the daily life of the Plains Indians, who depend on it for food, shelter, clothing, utensils, weaponry, and other essentials. Spanish colonization has spread from Mexico northward, and horses have come into the hands of the Plains tribes, giving them an efficient way to hunt bison from horseback with the bow and arrow. Before the horse, the Indians hunted the bison on foot, stampeding whole herds toward buffalo jumps, where the unwary animals plunged to their death. It was a nomadic life for most of the Plains tribes, who were often at war with one another over hunting grounds, but the bison assured them a steady source of food and other necessities, a fact that gave the animal a mythological status in native cultural and religious beliefs.

The year is 1805, and the Lewis and Clark expedition is afield in the western United States, where they are encountering an array of Indian tribes on their journey across the Great Plains, as well as an astonishingly rich assortment of wildlife. Meriwether Lewis's June 3, 1805, journal entry captures the prevailing scene: "The country in every direction around us was one vast plain in which innumerable herds of Buffalo were seen attended by their shepherds the wolves; the solitary antelope which now had their young were distributed over its face; some herds of elk were also seen; the verdure perfectly clothed the ground, the weather was pleasant and fair."[3] By most recent estimates, the bison population exceeded thirty million animals; early travelers recounted seeing massive herds that took days to pass across the landscape.

Now move to 1832, and the westward migration is getting underway. Americans are being lured across the continent by the prospect of free land and tales of abundant natural riches. That year, the artist George Catlin journeyed up the Missouri River to observe the region's native inhabitants, where he was dumbstruck at the impact the early pioneers were already having on the region's native tribes and wildlife. As Catlin related in his 1841 account of his travels, *Letters and Notes on the Manners, Customs, and Condition of the North American Indians*, "Nature has nowhere presented more beautiful and lovely scenes, than those of the vast prairies of the West; and of man and beast, no nobler specimens than those who inhabit them—the Indian and the buffalo—joint and original tenants of the soil, and fugitives together from the approach of civilized man; they have fled to the great plains of the West, and there, under an equal doom, they have taken up their last abode, where their race will expire, and their bones will bleach together."[4] In an effort to forestall this looming extinction, Catlin proposed "a nation's Park, containing man and beast, in all the wild and freshness of their nature's beauty," which historians widely regard as the first reference to the national park idea that would not take hold for another thirty years.[5] Just over a decade later, in 1843, John James Audubon made his own journey up the Missouri, where he confirmed Catlin's earlier premonition: "Even now there is a perceptible difference in the size of the herds, and before many years the Buffalo, like the Great Auk, will have disappeared; surely this should be not permitted."[6]

Jump forward a mere forty years, and it is 1872. A transcontinental railroad system is now in place, western settlement under the doctrine of manifest destiny is in full swing, and the once-profuse bison that graced the Great Plains are verging on extinction. Market hunters seeking fortune from buffalo robes have relentlessly stalked the animal across its range and are decimating the herds. Figures like Buffalo Bill Cody are making themselves into legends by adeptly dispatching as many as 4,280 bison for their hides in a single season. (The evident individual daily record was 120 bison killed in one stand during a forty-minute period, stopped only by an overheated rifle.) Rail passengers take sport in shooting the bulky creatures from moving trains with no intent of utilizing the carcasses.[7] In 1873, Colonel Richard Dodge, who commanded Fort Dodge in Kansas, reported that "the air was foul with a sickening stench, and the vast plain, which only a short twelve months before teemed with animal life, was a dead, solitary, putrid desert."[8] Though efforts were afoot in Congress to stop the slaughter by legislation, the military succeeded in blocking its passage, arguing that the demise of the buffalo would finally force the Indians to accept their fate on federal reservations. But Congress did act on other legislation and created Yellowstone as the world's first national park, little knowing that this new federal reservation would soon become the last refuge for the buffalo.

It is 1901, and Yellowstone National Park is being overseen by the same US Army that had resisted earlier legislative efforts to save the bison from extermination. A decade earlier, fewer than one thousand bison were still roaming the western landscape; some two hundred of them had found refuge in Yellowstone. But by 1900, the park's bison population had fallen to just twenty-three animals, the result of rampant poaching. To forestall an imminent extinction (and perhaps sensitive to the unseemly recent history of the bison), Yellowstone's military caretakers proceed to supplement the herd with imported bison from Texas and Montana, and they construct the Buffalo Ranch to breed more bison in secure surroundings.[9] At the ranch, the park's bison are put on display for visitors, and they are managed much like the ranchers who now dominate the Great Plains manage their cattle.

In less than half a century both the buffalo and the Native Americans have been removed from the landscape and consigned to a few reservations under the watchful scrutiny of the federal government. The frontier is closed, and the era of buffalo and Native Americans living in freedom and harmony on the western landscape is over. The park's military caretakers are soon replaced by the National Park Service, which comes into existence in 1916 with responsibility for Yellowstone and a dozen other fledgling national parks. Expressly charged by Congress to conserve wildlife in the new park system, the Park Service continues to corral and intensively manage Yellowstone's growing bison population, regularly culling the herds to meet the park's supposed range–carrying capacity. Although the Yellowstone bison population grows to over 1,000 animals by 1930, marking an extraordinary wildlife restoration accomplishment, it then falls by 1967 to just 397 animals. From 1925 to 1967, it is estimated that the agency has slaughtered and removed 9,016 animals.[10]

The year 1963 looms large in National Park Service lore, representing the date of the seminal "Leopold Report," which fundamentally altered national park resource management policies and ultimately freed Yellowstone's bison from the agency's heavy-handed management policies. According to a respected group of scientists commissioned by the secretary of the Interior to review Yellowstone's wildlife management policies, the Park Service should change course: "As a primary goal, we recommend that the biotic associations within each park be maintained or where necessary recreated, as nearly as possible in the condition that prevailed when the area was first visited by white man. A national park should represent a vignette of primitive America."[11] The report further explained that "the maintenance of naturalness should prevail" in the parks, requiring a new science-based approach to managing natural park ecosystems.

When Interior Secretary Stewart Udall gave his blessing to the report, he launched the Park Service on a new era, one that gives precedence to protecting park ecosystems with minimal human interference. For the bison this meant the end of the Park Service's culling efforts and a return to their free-roaming status, which enabled them, as their population grew, to begin moving during the winter months from the high-elevation park habitat to lower-elevation adjoining lands, where adequate snow-free forage was available. Of course, this also placed the bison on nonpark lands that were either owned by private individuals or managed by other agencies not necessarily committed to preserving wildlife. In either case, the bison were in closer proximity to domestic livestock, making them a nuisance at best and a potential disease threat at worst. They also were under the jurisdiction of the state of Montana and not the federal government once they strayed beyond the park's northern and western borders.

By the mid-1980s, the federal government was seeing an end in sight for its expensive decades-long campaign against the livestock disease of brucellosis, but the Yellowstone bison and elk populations constituted an extant pool of infected animals that threatened to undermine its brucellosis eradication achievement. In a cruel twist of fate, the bison, having just recently secured its freedom to roam, was once more the target of an intensive federal campaign designed to safeguard the same ranching interests that had previously supported its removal from the plains to make way for white settlement and a new livestock industry. Sadly reminiscent of the earlier buffalo destruction era, one of the proposed solutions was extermination of the Yellowstone bison population in order to eradicate brucellosis from the park's wildlife and ensure a disease-free area. Though that proposal ultimately failed to gain much traction, Yellowstone's bison found themselves the target of local anger within the agricultural community and faced a veritable firing squad when they set foot outside the park. The state of Montana sought to address the situation by essentially declassifying the bison as wildlife and declaring it "a species in need of special management," which vested the state's livestock department with jurisdictional authority over any wild bison "that pose a threat to persons or livestock in Montana through the transmission of dangerous disease."[12] Despite the presence of commercial bison ranching operations, no one suggested that Yellowstone's genetically pure wild bison resembled these domesticated animals. Curiously, the same level of outrage was not directed toward the region's elk population, which also harbored the brucellosis bacteria.

During the 1990s, a virtual avalanche of lawsuits showered down, pushing federal officials to come to grips with the problem, which was obviously exacerbated by the complex jurisdictional arrangements that prevailed as well as the political realities and scientific uncertainties that attached to bison and brucellosis. The jurisdictional map included the National Park Service, with sole management responsibility for bison while they were in Yellowstone; the US Forest Service, which managed habitat on national forest lands; the Montana Department of Fish, Wildlife and Parks, which ordinarily oversaw wildlife and hunting within the state's borders; the US Department of Agriculture's Animal, Plant, and Health Inspection Service (APHIS), charged with preventing disease transmission within the nation's livestock herds; and the Montana Department of Livestock, given responsibility for managing bison as "a species in need special management."[13] Although the Park Service was committed to allowing nature to take its course with bison and other wildlife within the national parks, the state of Montana and other federal agencies were pushing for more intensive management for disease-control purposes.

The bison found itself once again center stage in a legal-political tug of war that largely ignored the region's ecological realities and discounted much of the scientific evidence. Most scientists now believed that brucellosis was originally transmitted from cattle to bison, but the park's buffalo were nonetheless being targeted to safeguard ranching interests, even in the absence of any documented case of transmission from bison to cattle in the wild. The pressure to eradicate rather than control brucellosis in Yellowstone's wildlife populations ignored the immense practical difficulties of identifying and capturing diseased animals in the park's two-million-acre wilderness environment, while calls for a vaccination program ignored the fact that no vaccine had yet proven effective in wildlife. Nor did anyone seem to acknowledge that it would be much easier to manage and control the region's livestock herds than its wildlife populations. No one wanted to address the related elk brucellosis issue, evidently because elk were a highly valued wildlife resource with a strong hunting and outfitting constituency that also included members of the ranching community. And even if brucellosis were eradicated from the bison population, the diseased elk would almost immediately re-infect them. Nor was anyone paying much attention to Native American tribes, who were beginning to reconnect with their buffalo heritage and to consider restoring bison to some reservation lands. No wonder when Rutgers

University professors Frank and Deborah Popper proposed creating a "buffalo commons" on the northern Great Plains in the late 1980s, the idea met with intense opposition locally even though their research suggested that bison restoration might rejuvenate the region's flagging economy and populace.[14]

The year 2000 represents yet another milestone in the Yellowstone bison saga, being the year that the federal and state agencies finally agreed on an interagency bison management plan that has ever since governed how the park's bison are managed. The plan is designed to control, not eradicate, the risk of brucellosis infection by separating—both spatially and temporally—bison from cattle outside the park. The long-term goal, however, remains elimination of the disease within the region. The plan allows bison to roam freely within the park and provides limited room for bison outside park boundaries through a series of management zones where a few bison are more or less tolerated depending on the likelihood of contact with domestic livestock. It establishes a bison population goal of three thousand animals, and employs capture, test, and slaughter protocols to reduce the population size when bison wander outside the park into forbidden areas or at the wrong time of year. It permits some bison to be quarantined, tested for brucellosis over an extended period, and then released back into the park or transported elsewhere if they test negative. It also contemplates the eventual vaccination of the park's bison to prevent brucellosis infection.[15]

The plan did not, however, address the issue of elk brucellosis and possible transmission by these animals. Nor did it contain any measures designed to manage livestock more intensively, even though cattle can be managed much more easily than wildlife by, for example, delaying the date on which cows are turned out on the range in order to eliminate the likelihood of contact with bison as they seasonally move back into the park, or by altering grazing allotments to eliminate intermingling opportunities. In short, the plan called for intensive management of Yellowstone's bison outside the park, affording them only limited tolerance during their seasonal quest for nourishment at lower elevations in Yellowstone's notoriously harsh wintertime.

Since then, much has transpired on the ground that not only lays the groundwork for a new bison management plan but also heralds the advent of new bison restoration opportunities that could restore the buffalo more widely across its native habitat. Following several mild winters, the Yellowstone bison population reached fifty-five hundred animals in 2016, but has since been reduced by aggressive culling to roughly four thousand animals. Since 2001, when the management plan was implemented, there have been no reported cases of brucellosis transmission from bison to cattle in the area, but elk have been identified as the culprit in twenty-two cases. Since 2003, limited hunting of bison as a control measure has been allowed outside the park without any major incidents. APHIS has revised its rules governing a state's brucellosis-free status to allow states to subdivide themselves to address wildlife-related brucellosis reservoirs, thus isolating disease outbreak problems to the affected area. In 2010, a cohort of eighty-seven quarantined brucellosis-free bison was transferred without much fanfare from federal quarantine facilities to Ted Turner's nearby ranch for further surveillance, representing the first time that the state of Montana has allowed any Yellowstone bison to be transported outside the park. After completing a comprehensive environmental review, the Park Service has rejected remote bison vaccination as a disease management tool inside the park, concluding that this approach would be impractical and ineffective in the Yellowstone setting under current circumstances.[16]

The region's Native American tribes have become engaged in the bison management effort, and three tribal entities are now included as interagency partners. In 2012, the state of Montana transported sixty-one quarantined disease-free bison to the Fort Peck Indian Reservation, and another thirty-four disease-free bison were transported in 2013 to the Fort Belknap Indian Reservation. Faced with litigation by ranching interests, the Montana Supreme Court ruled that the state had adequate statutory authority to transfer Yellowstone bison to the reservations, seemingly paving the way for additional transfers as a means to relieve population pressures in the Greater Yellowstone Ecosystem.[17] The Department of the Interior has consulted with several tribes and tribal organizations to assess the interest in receiving brucellosis-free Yellowstone bison on reservations and in assisting to reestablish bison herds on other suitable federal lands.[18] And the Park Service has completed an environmental analysis that recommends transporting Yellowstone bison to the Fort Peck quarantine facility for observation, and then offering the disease-free animals to tribes and landowners interested in restoring bison.[19] But the Montana legislature killed the bill that would have permitted the transport of bison from the park before being determined to be disease-free.

Conservation groups have worked with the National Park Service, the state of Montana, and others to expand bison habitat opportunities outside the park. They have secured easements and leaseholds on strategic ranchlands, opening thousands of acres of additional habitat for bison north of the park, and they have retired key grazing allotments on national forest lands to open habitat in the upper Gallatin River Basin and the Gardiner Basin. With these arrangements, Yellowstone bison are now allowed seasonally to roam as far north as Yankee Jim Canyon in the Gardiner Basin and onto Horse Butte in the Lake Hebgen region west of the park. In 2015, Montana's governor opened three hundred thousand acres west of the park to bison year round.[20] The American Prairie Reserve, several tribes, and other groups are actively pursuing bison restoration initiatives elsewhere in the state,[21] further legitimizing the presence of wild bison outside the Yellowstone region. The Park Service, in conjunction with the state of Montana's wildlife department, has begun the process for revising the Interagency Bison Management Plan, which should include more nonlethal control options and identify potential bison restoration sites, while also finally addressing elk brucellosis concerns.[22] Though slowly, the door appears to be opening to a more enlightened and tolerant management policy for the park's beleaguered bison, one that not only provides expanded local habitat but also contemplates a broader bison restoration effort.

Wildlife management on the western landscape regularly presents complex issues involving a mix of science, economics, and culture as well as law and politics. A defining characteristic of the American West, according to the writer Wallace Stegner, is the presence of federally owned lands, which creates an obvious jurisdictional tension between the federal land management agencies and state and local governments.[23] Outside of the national parks, wildlife management is the responsibility of the states, but federal agencies like the Forest Service and Bureau of Land Management administer wildlife habitat as part of their multiple-use mission, and these agencies must adhere to an array of federal legal mandates. As the Yellowstone bison controversy so vividly illustrates, most wildlife species do not respect conventional jurisdictional boundary lines, which means they are subject to conflicting legal management standards; they may be fully protected when within the national parks, but subject to being hunted (or even just shot on sight) under state law when they venture beyond park borders, even if the animal is still on federal land.

During the past century, Congress has extended federal wildlife management responsibilities by the adoption of such laws as the Endangered Species Act, Wild Free Roaming Horses and Burros Act, Bald and Golden Eagle Protection Act, and Migratory Bird Treaty Act. This extension of federal authority into the traditional state realm of wildlife management has been met with suspicion and resistance, particularly in the case of the Endangered Species Act, which places certain species trending toward extinction under stringent federal control and can be invoked to block economic activities on both public and private lands. Although the bison does not enjoy federal endangered species status, conservation groups have petitioned the US Fish and Wildlife Service to protect Yellowstone bison as a "distinct population segment" of genetically pure wild bison—a prospect that would surely provoke considerable local angst.[24] One way to minimize the prospect of such a listing is to establish additional populations of Yellowstone's wild bison on receptive Native American reservations and elsewhere, which would reduce the risk that a rampant disease outbreak or other catastrophic event could decimate this genetically unique population. In this same vein, the Department of the Interior has recently endorsed "the goal of restoring bison herds to their ecological and cultural role on appropriate landscapes within the species' historical range."[25]

While the federal government's foray into wildlife management has been largely for protective purposes, western state governments have traditionally viewed wildlife as a valuable harvestable resource. During the early twentieth century, in response to the unregulated slaughter that decimated the bison population as well as other wildlife species, the states established professional wildlife management agencies, charging them with employing scientific principles to regulate hunting and to rebuild depleted wildlife populations. Most state wildlife agencies were—and still are—overseen by politically appointed commissions, injecting an overt political element into wildlife management decisions. The policy that emerged is the so-called "North American model" of wildlife management, where hunters and fishers who use these resources pay to help maintain them through license fees and various taxes. This model has

Wildlife Conservation–American Buffalo Stamp. Designed by Robert Lougheed, Bureau of Engraving and Printing, 1970. US Postal Service, National Postal Museum.

been remarkably successful at maintaining and restoring big game species and sport fisheries, including providing the financial resources necessary to acquire critical habitat as needed to sustain individual species.[26] It has done little, however, to address contemporary biodiversity conservation concerns, which endorse the holistic view that conservation efforts should extend to all species regardless of their economic value and that the maintenance and restoration of healthy ecosystems is crucial to the effort.

Put in this context, the Yellowstone bison-brucellosis controversy can be understood in basic political terms. Driven by ranching interests, the Montana legislature's political decision to split legal authority for bison management between the state's wildlife and livestock agencies has essentially given economic considerations priority over scientific facts and ecological realities, which explains why the focus has been entirely on bison (not cattle or elk) management. Because the bison has not been regarded as a valuable species for hunting purposes, it does not enjoy the same powerful hunting and outfitting constituency that elk and other big game species enjoy, surely accounting for the fact that elk, unlike bison, have not been central in the brucellosis controversy even though every confirmed case of disease transmission has involved elk not bison. The fact that the region's livestock interests lost the Yellowstone wolf reintroduction controversy has reportedly made the ranching community less willing to compromise on bison, where its political and legal position is much stronger in the absence of directly applicable federal law. But now that APHIS has acknowledged its authority to divide a state for brucellosis status purposes,[27] much of the political pressure coming from the entire state's livestock community should be reduced, because eastern Montana ranchers are no longer at immediate risk in the event of a Yellowstone-area brucellosis outbreak. Moreover, the Montana Supreme Court ruling permitting the intrastate transfer of park bison removes a legal impediment to nascent bison restoration initiatives across the state.

The situation on the ground in the Yellowstone region continues to evolve, with both political and policy implications. With the successful quarantine program, the absence of any bison transmission cases, the successful transport of bison outside of the area, and grazing allotment retirements and easement purchases, local resistance to bison outside the park has diminished. Over the past thirty years, the Greater Yellowstone Ecosystem concept has taken hold; most federal officials, along with their state and local counterparts, now recognize the Greater Yellowstone Ecosystem as a practical entity, and the corresponding need to coordinate resource management across boundary lines, as manifested in the Interagency Bison Management Group.[28] At the core of the ecosystem is Yellowstone National Park, where federal national park policy dictates preserving wildlife and ecological processes on the landscape. The park, adjacent wilderness areas, and nearby public lands play a vital role in the region's economy as magnets for tourists as well as new residents and businesses. During the past couple decades, resource priorities on the neighboring national forests have shifted away from logging, grazing, and other commodities toward the forest's recreational and amenity values, which puts a premium on wildlife conservation. The park's neighbors, however begrudgingly, have come to recognize that they live in a wilderness-like setting, where natural forces and processes are a primary feature of the landscape. This includes seasonal wildlife migrations, predation, periodic wildfires, floods, and other natural phenomena, all of which predate white settlement in the region and therefore necessarily temper property ownership expectations and rights.[29]

These shifts in the political and regional landscapes seem to have opened the door for a more realistic, science-based strategy to control, not eradicate, brucellosis within Yellowstone's bison population. As we have seen, some bison are now being allowed to roam more widely outside the park, disease-free bison have been relocated outside the Yellowstone region without incident, and plans are afoot to revise the 2000 Interagency Bison Management Plan. Further changes to bison management should include revising Montana state law to treat the park's bison as wildlife, placing some responsibility on ranchers to more closely manage their cattle, and permitting transport of brucellosis-free bison to Native American reservations and other locations outside the state where these animals are welcome. Such changes would not only help to reduce the intergovernmental friction that has fueled the controversy, but would relieve the pressure to wantonly kill bison on the park's perimeters, thus tempering the humane treatment concerns that animal rights groups have injected into the conflict. Such changes would also legitimize the budding bison restoration efforts and enhance Native American culture, returning the animal to some of its historic range and also dignifying it once again as wildlife.[30]

Given the intermixed pattern of federal, state, and private land ownership that prevails across the West, wildlife management will inevitably generate controversy, regardless of who has final decision-making authority. The appropriate strategy for addressing the Yellowstone bison and similar wildlife controversies in this larger context is the emergent concept of landscape-scale conservation, which builds upon closely related ecosystem management concepts. Though difficult to define with precision, large landscape conservation entails integrated planning and management at an appropriate scale to address biodiversity concerns, climate change adaptation, and socioeconomic matters; it therefore involves intergovernmental collaboration, the use of science-based information, and public engagement opportunities.[31] Indeed, the federal government has endorsed landscape conservation as a guiding management principle, as displayed in the Department of the Interior's 2014 "Bison Report" and other policy statements. The report identifies more than a dozen possible bison restoration sites across the West; promotes building the necessary collaborative partnerships with tribes, states, and landowners; and explains how quarantined brucellosis-free Yellowstone bison can contribute to the broader conservation of the species beyond its current range. It specifically calls for building "partnerships with other land-owners to weave together landscapes large enough to cultivate the full interplay between bison and the surrounding ecology, which would also help promote biological diversity of other plant and wildlife species."[32]

Irony abounds throughout the history of the bison and only recently shows any sign of abating. Originally found swarming across the Great Plains in staggering numbers, the bison is now largely confined to the high-elevation Yellowstone plateau without license to roam, its numbers reduced to a minuscule fragment of the original population. Much like the Native Americans who relied on it for their livelihood, the bison has been relegated to federal reservations and denied ready access to its historical territory. The same ranching interests that originally supported the demise of America's free-roaming bison population to make room for cattle are again in the vanguard, supporting an aggressive federal wildlife disease-control program that keeps the Yellowstone bison largely confined within the park's artificial boundaries. While one arm of the federal government—the National Park Service—is committed to preserving bison as vital free-roaming wildlife, another arm—APHIS—sees the animal as a disease vector and has treated it like domestic livestock in order to complete its brucellosis eradication campaign. The state of Montana, though avidly promoting Yellowstone's wildlife and other natural attractions to draw tourists to local businesses, legally treats the bison as something other than wildlife, denies the animal its basic instincts, and ignores the serious elk brucellosis problem.[33]

If there is not room for wild bison in the Yellowstone country, then where in our increasingly populated and homogenized world? Having been engaged in the bison's fate for nearly twenty-five years, it is heartening to see some progress in recent years toward acknowledging that this wild animal has a place in the Greater Yellowstone Ecosystem as part of the region's natural and cultural heritage. Where official policy was once to destroy the bison to control Native Americans, this policy is now shifting toward facilitating bison restoration on native reservations. And official policy is slowly moving toward granting bison more room to roam outside the park, so long as cattle are not present, manifesting a degree of tolerance and collaboration that has long been missing. If so, the saga of the bison is coming full circle, though only after more than a century of controversy. Saving the bison from extinction at the dawn of the twentieth century was a remarkable wildlife conservation achievement; restoring the bison to portions of its historic range would be an equally remarkable twenty-first-century wildlife conservation achievement.

NOTES

1. 21 U.S.C. § 134a(a); Robert B. Keiter and Peter H. Froelicher, "Bison, Brucellosis, and Law in the Greater Yellowstone Ecosystem," *Land & Water Law Review* 28(1) (1993): 21–23.
2. Mont. Code Ann. § 87-1-215 (1991); Keiter and Froelicher, "Bison, Brucellosis, and Law," 25.
3. William Kittredge and Annick Smith, eds., *The Last Best Place: A Montana Anthology* (Helena, MT: Montana Historical Society Press, 1988), 145.
4. Ibid., 179.
5. Ibid., 181.
6. Ibid., 191.
7. Dayton Duncan, *Out West: An American Journey* (New York: Viking, 1987), 201.
8. Ibid.
9. H. Duane Hansen, *How the U.S. Cavalry Saved Our National Parks* (Bloomington: Indiana Univ. Press, 1971), 165–67; Aubrey L. Haines, *The Yellowstone Story* (Boulder: Colorado Assoc. Univ. Press, vol. 2, 1977), 54–77.
10. Zachary L. Lancaster, "Restraining Yellowstone's Roaming Bison," *Journal of Land Use & Environmental Law* 20 (2005): 423, 427.
11. A. Starker Leopold et al., "Wildlife Management in the National Parks," in *America's National Park System: The Critical Documents*, ed. Lary M. Dilsaver (Lanham, MD: Rowman & Littlefield, 1994), 239, 243.
12. 21 U.S.C. § 134a(a); Keiter and Froelicher, "Bison, Brucellosis, and Law," 25.
13. For an overview of the agencies engaged in the Yellowstone region brucellosis controversy and related litigation, see Keiter and Froelicher, "Bison, Brucellosis, and Law"; Peter Morrisette, "Is There Room for Free-Roaming Bison in Greater Yellowstone?," *Ecology Law Quarterly* 27 (2000): 467; Zachary L. Lancaster, "Restraining Yellowstone's Roaming Bison," *Journal of Land Use & Environmental Law* 20 (2005): 423.
14. Anne Matthews, *Where the Buffalo Roam: The Storm Over the Revolutionary Plan to Restore America's Great Plains* (New York: Grove Press, 1992), 1–38.

15. US Dept. of the Interior, National Park Service, et al., Final Environmental Impact Statement and Bison Management Plan for the State of Montana and Yellowstone National Park (2000).

16. National Park Service, US Dept. of the Interior, Record of Decision, Remote Vaccination Program to Reduce the Prevalence of Brucellosis in Yellowstone Bison (March 2014).

17. Citizens for Balanced Use v. Maurier, 303 P.3d 794 (Mont. 2013).

18. US Dept. of the Interior, National Park Service, DOI Bison Report: Looking Forward (2014).

19. National Park Service, The Use of Quarantine to Identify Brucellosis-free Yellowstone Bison for Relocation Elsewhere Environmental Assessment (2016).

20. Governor of Montana, Decision Notice: Year-Round Habitat for Yellowstone Bison Environmental Assessment (November 15, 2015).

21. Dan Flores, *American Serengeti: The Last Big Animals of the Great Plains* (Lawrence: Univ. Press of Kansas, 2016), 179–82.

22. Indeed, the recent National Academies of Sciences update report on brucellosis in the Yellowstone region recommends against further aggressive action toward the region's bison until the agencies and states address the burgeoning elk brucellosis problem. National Academies of Sciences, Engineering, and Medicine, Revisiting Brucellosis in the Greater Yellowstone Area (2017): 5.

23. Wallace Stegner, *The Sound of Mountain Water* (Lincoln: Univ. of Nebraska Press, 1980), 32–38.

24. US Dept. of the Interior, Fish and Wildlife Service, Endangered and Threatened Wildlife and Plants: 90-Day Findings on 17 Petitions, 81 Fed. Reg. 1368 (Jan. 12, 2016).

25. US Dept. of the Interior et al., DOI Bison Report.

26. Martin Nie et al., "Fish and Wildlife Management on Federal Lands: Debunking State Supremacy," *Environmental Law* 47(4) (2017): 811–14.

27. 9 C.F.R. § 78.40 (2017).

28. For information on the Interagency Bison Management Group, see http://www.ibmp.info/index.php (last visited Jan. 7, 2018).

29. Joseph L. Sax, "Ecosystems and Property Rights in Greater Yellowstone: The Legal System in Transition," in *The Greater Yellowstone Ecosystem: Redefining America's Wilderness Heritage*, eds. Robert B. Keiter and Mark S. Boyce (New London: Yale University Press, 1991), 77–84.

30. For a comprehensive scientific and cultural review of Yellowstone's bison and related management concerns, see P.J. White, Rick L. Wallen, and David E. Hallec, eds., *Yellowstone Bison: Conserving an American Icon in Modern Society* (Yellowstone National Park: The Yellowstone Association, 2015).

31. Matthew McKinney et al., *Large Landscape Conservation: A Strategic Framework for Policy and Action* (Cambridge, MA: Lincoln Institute of Land Policy, 2010).
32. US Dept. of the Interior et al., DOI Bison Report.
33. National Academies of Sciences, Engineering, and Medicine, Revisiting Brucellosis in the Greater Yellowstone Area (2017).

Ranching Communities and Conservation Must Be Combined

Yvonne Martinell

Yvonne Martinell's deep respect for generations-old traditions in Montana's Centennial Valley resonates in her description of a year in the life of her cattle-ranching family. Her family's lives are inextricably tied to the cycle of their animals' lives, to the seasons, and to various regulatory systems; thus, Martinell gives voice to the frustrations, tedium, exhausting effort, and anxieties of ranching in the twenty-first-century West. She recounts the ways contemporary ranchers collaborate with conservationists and governments, with varying degrees of success. Ultimately, she reveals the joy, pride, and satisfaction she finds in her family's wise ranching practices.

Elmer Martinell, the paternal grandfather of my husband, Allen, got off the train at Dell in 1889—the year Montana became a state. Elmer worked on a ranch in the area and then became a property owner in Beaverhead County in 1893. He was a risk-taker. Allen's maternal grandfather, Ras Hansen, came from Denmark in 1902. They must have found something they liked here in Dell because both stayed in the county throughout their lives and became successful businessmen.

The house Elmer and his father, Mitchell, built in 1898 is where Allen and I live and where Elmer and Addie raised three sons and two daughters. Their daughters, May and Ethel, married neighboring ranchers and the sons went into business with Elmer and Addie. Allen's father and his brothers took over the ranch at Dell and expanded it up Big Sheep Creek. In the early 1960s they dissolved their partnership—the eldest brother retiring, one taking the property up Big Sheep Creek, and Allen's father, Lee, taking the ranch at Dell. With that change, Lee then needed summer pasture. That was when Allen's family first bought property in the Centennial Valley.

Lee and Ethel Hansen had four children: Byron; twin girls, Janice and Carol; and Allen. Byron and Allen stayed on the ranch. Byron retired in 2010, and we are buying his interest in the ranch. Janice and Carol both left the ranch after college but still had a financial interest. We just finished buying them out.

I grew up on a wheat ranch north of Great Falls on the Bootlegger Trail. My family moved to Hilger in 1963, when my parents bought a cattle operation. Allen and I met at Montana State University in Bozeman; he was a teaching assistant in a horsemanship class I was taking. My degree was in business education and his was in animal science. We married in 1973. I taught at the high school in Lima the first two years of our marriage. We have three children—Heath, Carlen, and Kristen. Heath and his wife, Kiley, have three children. Kiley is an embryologist and works part-time for a vet. We are blessed that they are on the ranch with us.

Carlen and her husband, Brett Keaster, live in Belt. She is a CPA with Anderson-Zurmuellin, and he sells financials and insurance for the Farm Bureau. We haven't put the burden on her of being our accountant yet, but we ask her a lot of questions. They have two little girls. Our youngest, Kristen, and her husband, Ryan Bailey, will move to the ranch in September. She is a vet tech, and he has been employed by FLIR, working with lasers and crystals. They have two sons. We hope this move will be good for them and positive for the family and the ranching business.

In 1960, the Martinells bought the "Mayberry Place" above Lima Dam. About that same time, they acquired the Gobel (1965) and Buck (1968) places, both currently with conservation easements on them. All of these properties were purchased the good, old-fashioned way—with a mortgage. The cows would go to the Mayberry Place but the two bands of sheep would go on up the road to the Gobel and Buck places, on their way to the forest lease by Elk Lake and Lion Mountain. A herder was a necessity, to stay with each band of sheep. Coyotes and bears were the larger predators, with eagles working on the lambs when they were smaller. Wildlife officials from Yellowstone Park would bring problem bears and release them in the proximity of the sheep, and the bears would frequently raid the herders' camps, leaving them without groceries until the next time the camp tender came. That usually happened once a week, if all was well.

Shortly after Allen and I were married, the Martinells sold the sheep. The increase in predator problems and the lack of sheepherders were cited as the reasons. We then started increasing the cow herd and took the cows on up to the Gobel and Buck places. The cows thought we were crazy the first couple of years. Now they start looking up the way, wondering when we are going to open the gates. In the mid-1980s we added more property near Dell and two more fields in the Centennial. One was called the Monte Kent, about 460 acres in the valley floor. We moved a little house to the property. Mostly we use it to stay overnight on our way up country. The other field we call the Barney Green. It is between the Gobel and Buck places. As you have probably figured out, they are named after previous owners, and not necessarily the most recent ones either.

One of the first questions we usually hear from people when they realize we are ranchers is: "How many acres do you own?" or "How many cows do you have?" This is equivalent to asking what your net worth is or what your gross income is. Most don't mean to be rude, and we try to respond politely. In some cases we give a direct answer, and sometimes we tend to beat around the bush. Folks usually don't understand the hours we put in working and that we can't remember being gone for more than two or three nights in a row. Those times are usually to attend meetings. Vacations seem to be few and far between.

This family has been in the Dell area for 125 years. We are in this for the long haul and want the next generation to have something to care for. If we aren't good stewards of the land and ecosystem then we won't be able to make a living and we degrade our property resource.

Living at a higher elevation like we do presents its own set of challenges. A local joke about the growing season is that we usually have three frost-free days but they may not all be in a row. In other words, we have a short growing season for crops. We can't depend on getting a second cutting on hay crops, and it makes growing grain challenging. We live in a relatively dry area and must depend on irrigation for crop production. This is very labor-intensive—especially flood irrigation. For a number of years a lot of agencies and conservationists have been pushing sprinkler irrigation as a way to extend the water use.

We use both flood and sprinklers on our property. It does allow for more acres to be irrigated; however, these agencies and conservationists are just figuring out what most long-time ranchers understand—that the sprinkler usage is consumptive because the groundwater does not get recharged. This affects the next year's crops as well as the groundwater and streams down the watershed. With flood irrigation, you have ditches and head gates and must have an irrigator to move the fabric dams up and down the ditches. The ditches and head gates must be maintained, and the fabric dams have to be built. All of this takes time and equipment, but flood irrigation recharges the groundwater!

Depending on the year, it will take two to two and a half tons of hay per cow. This does not include what they graze from the residue on the fields that regrows after the hay was removed (we are taxed on that feed when they do assessments for property taxes). Someone must be on hand to feed the animals, so again, you have labor and equipment costs. Cows are like us; they like to have shelter, fresh feed, and water daily. With the higher elevation, we sometimes get more extreme weather, and that cold means it takes more feed just to keep the animals warm.

Many people are moving their calving to a later season, when the temperature is a bit warmer and the cows' nutritional needs during their pregnancies are different. We haven't been able to figure out how to get our cows to a place to calve later in the spring and then still get them to their summer range. Also, we don't feel that having those younger calves at that higher elevation and in greater proximity to the larger predators would be good for us or the predators.

We calve our heifers starting about the tenth of February. Most of them will go through the barns because of the time of year. We try to let them calve on their own but closely monitor them. At night, someone stays with them to make sure all is well and to assist as necessary. Sometimes the assistance equates to getting them into the barn, out of the wind and cold. They are all tagged and records kept for identification purposes. Any calving problems or mothering and health issues are noted.

Our older cows calve out in the hay fields. They begin about the first of March. Our goal is to have the heifers done calving by the time the older cows start. We live along the Red Rock River, where there are willows and tall grass along ditches that provide protection. These cows are checked at least twice daily for problems. The calves also are tagged and records kept. We vaccinate all of the calves as soon as possible following their birth. When we get about 250 cow/calf pairs in a field, we move the cows that have not calved to an adjacent field. This makes checking them easier, improves calf health, and also makes a group size that works for us for branding in April and May. We try to check every calf every day

Montana Cattle Rancher. Photograph by Leslie Miller, 2013.

for their health and to make sure they look like they are being fed. The cows also are checked for the same issues. "Bags and butts," as Allen says.

We have some issues with eagles and coyotes. We have had calves that have just disappeared. One of the neighbors in the past year had calves carried out of their field by wolves. They have had fences crashed and calves tromped by mother cows trying to protect them. One day a neighbor saw a coyote pull a calf under a fence right after the cow had it, consuming it alive before the cow even got up. All nature isn't pretty.

The calves are branded and vaccinated, and the cows also are vaccinated. Once this is done, we move some of them across the interstate, where we have fresh ground for them. Spreading them out is beneficial to their health. They will still need to be fed hay for quite some time.

We don't usually go into the Centennial until about the middle of June. This gives that higher-elevation feed a chance to get started. We go to the Mayberry Place and then on to pasture that we have been renting from a neighboring ranch for the heifers and from The Nature Conservancy for some of the cow/calf pairs. We are in our second year of a grazing plan with the National Resource Conservation Service and the Sage Grouse Initiative. We are rotating our grazing and resting some. The money we receive from the Sage Grouse Initiative goes to rent pasture, to allow this rest to be more affordable. The remainder of the cows go up from Dell in July. From that lower place we go on up to the Gobel and the upper ground. We have state leases that are all in one field, and we go to those about the middle of August. They are even higher yet in elevation.

One of the priority jobs of the employee who stays with the cows all summer and fall is to keep a prescription mineral and salt out at all times. This helps with the larkspur poison problems. He also must check and maintain waterlines, tanks, fences, and more. Wildlife also consumes the salt and mineral. The employee doesn't see all of the cows every day because of the size and terrain of the landscape. He is responsible for doctoring sick animals and removing any carcasses he may find to an area away from routes the other cattle use. If he needs help, he lets us know so we can assist him.

Allen and Heath help regulate the water on the state ground. Some of the water system we share with a grazing association and some we do not. All of it comes with a significant financial investment and takes constant monitoring.

We move the cow/calf pairs out of that area towards the end of the third week in October. This is just prior to the general rifle big-game season. We have been shipping the calves to a feedlot by Billings and sending the heifers to the ranch at Dell. We keep the steers at that feedlot and sell them anytime from mid-December until the first part of February.

Immediately after the calves are gone, we will pregnancy test and vaccinate the cows, mark any that are open (not bred), and put them on pasture in the valley floor. The cows that are open will be retested and those that don't pass will be sold. Our cows will remain in the Centennial through November most years, and into December if the feed and water are available. They will then be trailed to Dell.

Any sexually intact animal we sell must be blood tested for brucellosis because we are in the Designated Surveillance Area (DSA)— an imaginary line that is expanding out on an annual basis. We don't interact with the elk during their calving season; however, if we should have an animal test positive in the spring while the cattle are at Dell, we could be quarantined there and not be able to go to our summer pasture. We could not afford to feed them hay all summer. Also, it would be a lot more disruptive to sort the cows from their baby calves in the spring. With the continual movement of the elk and their access to brucellosis through the bison in Yellowstone Park and feeding grounds in Wyoming, the contamination seems to be spreading. The DSA is drawn not so much by where infected cattle are found but by where infected elk are found. The disease is transmittable to humans through contact with contaminated milk or animal fluids. The milk is mostly taken care of by pasteurization. If a hunter comes in contact with diseased fluids while gutting an elk and has a sore or cut, he or she can contract undulant fever, a condition that never goes away. A number of years ago, one rancher in the Madison Valley contracted it that way and when the disease was discovered, his herd was quarantined and tested. He had no infected cattle.

We keep all of our heifer calves. After they have had time to adjust to being weaned and have received their vaccinations and are healthy and able to handle it, we vaccinate them for brucellosis. Allen and I have been married for forty-one years, and they had been vaccinating here before that time. Then, it was voluntary. Now it is mandatory because of the DSA, but it is still our bill to pay.

We artificially inseminate 250 heifers and bull breed the rest in mid-May, when they are a year old. We will ultrasound them in late July to get estimated calving dates. The earlier calving heifers we have been keeping and we sell the remainder. The ones that don't breed we sell with the smaller ones that we spayed. Those will go the end of September or the first part of October. The past several years we have been renting pasture for about six weeks for the yearling heifers. They then go to the Gobel until about mid-November, when we will head them back down the road to Dell. We trail all of our cattle into the Centennial and out. Only the calves and bulls get hauled in the fall, and any animal that is sick or lame.

Caring for the cattle, work prepping for irrigating and haying, mechanical work, building maintenance, spraying weeds, attending meetings, doing financial reports for lenders, paying bills, staying on top of regulations—all are part of the things we do. That completes the yearly cycle; we get one finished and begin the next. Many of our neighbors have similar scenarios, with tweaks that make things fit their own systems. The main point being that we take care of our animals and our resources.

Since the wolves have become more prevalent, we have moose that reside in the river bottom and tributaries. They are fun to see but not to have in the corrals, lots, or yard. I try to remember to warn the fishermen, who we mainly let in free of charge, to watch out for the moose. Safety for our employees is more of an issue with larger predators and ungulates on the landscape. We try to operate in a safe, common-sense way.

We live with our animals. We are so accustomed to seeing the wildlife that we often take the vision for granted. We don't record every time we see a deer with pretty little twin fawns, a raccoon or skunk, or the eagles flying up and down the river fishing. We have seen a change in the habits of the elk these past years. They travel in larger groups in the fall and winter. Many ranchers have had grass that they held in reserve for winter or spring use wiped out by the elk moving in and camping. The fences are wiped out, and sometimes an elk gets hung up in fencing. Some have the elk and deer come into their calving pens, use the bedding, eat the feed, and graze the riparian areas. The elk feel safer around humans than they do out in the larger landscape. We don't see many on our upper summer and fall range, but we used to. The elk numbers are supposed to be good. Their habits have changed for good or bad.

We are a part of our community. Allen is on the Vigilante Electric Cooperative Board and has been president of the Water Users Irrigation Company that manages Lima Dam. I was on the school board for eighteen years. Heath just termed out from the state Stockgrowers Board and Kiley is on the school board. She also is on the state beef board. We are also active in our community church.

Allen and I have been involved with the Centennial Valley Association (CVA) from the beginning. Allen served as an officer on the first board and now I am the chairwoman. At inception, the CVA served as a mechanism to bring neighbors in the Centennial together, but its major project was taking action to address the growing noxious weed problem in the valley. More issues and needs seem to pop up on a regular basis. CVA doesn't take action on them all, but tries to keep the neighborhood informed.

Allen's father used to tell a story about taking a break at a cabin when they had been trailing cattle up Big Sheep and seeing a wolf hamstring a five-year-old gelding. The horse was, of course, ruined. He wasn't left for the wolves to finish off easily, since he had been severely lamed. One of the wolves' techniques for taking down larger animals, we have been told, is to injure them and then come back when they have had time to stiffen up and slow down.

An analogy I recently heard is that predators are like shoplifters. The merchandise—in our case, livestock—is stolen. We are not able to add it to the cost of the next item sold, like Walmart and other merchants do. We sell a commodity. You only get paid for what you take to the sale.

In 2013 we were missing over forty calves. Eight carcasses were found. Where did the rest go? Ranchers can get reimbursed for their losses from wolves and bears, but you must have a body to be examined before you can even think about making a claim.

We were also missing eight cows. Six of them we believe were stolen. They found the carcass of one, and that last one was never found. We keep very exacting numbers on our cows. We try to take exceptional care of our animals. We like animals.

In 2014, the CVA began a pilot project, the Range Rider Program, to help the ranching community and agencies determine what wildlife, predators, and people we have on the landscape. Primarily, the project is providing an additional tool in the Centennial for predator coexistence. Participating ranches joined the program voluntarily to test a new practice that would protect their business while also allowing wildlife and predators to thrive in the ecosystem. We want to know what inhabits our system and how to best get along. If we can't get along all the time, then what steps do we take to change patterns?

We participate in the block management program with Fish and Game. We believe it affords local people a better chance to have access to hunt and gives those from out of state an opportunity to see some beautiful country. We could make more money by leasing out the hunting rights to a guide. Currently, we receive about $7,700 annually. By the time hunting season is over, I hate to answer the phone or the door. Ninety-five percent of the hunters are fine. The other 5 percent, however, are careless and give the "good" hunters a bad reputation. Occasionally we find the rule breakers, dead livestock, and bullet holes in our buildings. (Are two-legged hunters like four-legged hunters?)

When I am around a group of people who are new to the area and a local mentions seeing an antelope, we are usually reprimanded by the visitor, who declares them to be "pronghorn." We know what they are! Fish, Wildlife and Parks sells "antelope" tags for hunting purposes. Maybe the education should begin there.

We sometimes feel that visitors just think we aren't very sharp. However, if the people who have been in the Centennial Valley in the past hadn't been good stewards, you wouldn't be enjoying a lot of what you see in this valley today. When we burn sagebrush in an area, the elk camp on it in the spring, long before we try to access it. Water projects are a benefit to all. Our range rider recently got close-up pictures on the motion-activated camera of a couple of moose drinking at one of our tanks. The wildlife like fresh feed, just as we do. They don't camp out where the vegetation is old and stagnant.

We don't just ranch with wildlife, we ranch with a whole set of rules, regulations, and people—just like every other occupation does. Some rules are beneficial and some are not. A person has to wonder about the thought processes behind some of them. Sometimes it seems that there is no concept for what is real. The wildlife side is usually the pleasant distraction that we enjoy seeing, just like everyone else.

Ranching with wildlife—what does that mean? It means that we feed a fair number of animals and receive little or no financial receipt. It also means that we live where we get to sometimes view them. They add to our work and finances by tearing down fences, stressing and sometimes killing our livestock, consuming salt and mineral and other feed. We are required to do additional testing of our animals, which also adds to their stress. Do we want to sell out and move away? No! Having wildlife wanting to utilize your pastures and fields means you have a viable and productive habitat—not only for wildlife, but for the cattle as well.

We believe that the ranching community is an asset to the situation, not a problem. We, the ranching community, are a part of a larger community. We help feed a growing population and utilize a resource that would otherwise produce little. We are proud of what we do and of our contribution to a safe food supply for our nation. The best product farmers and ranchers raise is upstanding, hardworking, dependable kids who become the adults who hold their communities together and make them stronger, which in turn makes our whole country a better place.

Keeping people on the land is also beneficial to law enforcement—they know who is out there—and generates essential specialized skills and knowledge about land and resource management. Protecting what we love—open space, healthy ecosystems, wildlife habitat, clean water and air—must be an active pursuit, not a passive one. You all know what comes with subdivisions in rural areas. It would be wise to look carefully at what you are trying to change before you make the leap.

Conservation goes beyond just this valley. It also goes to where the rest of our community is. All practices haven't been successful, but it is not just the agricultural community that makes mistakes. The conservation community hasn't always gotten things right. We are human, and we will make mistakes. Hopefully we can learn from them. It is easy to cite problems but much more important to develop workable solutions to them. Solutions must be effective and manageable for all involved. If you cite a problem, are you ready to help develop a solution?

Successful, thriving agricultural communities partnering with conservation communities is wildlife's best shot. Communities and conservation must be combined.

Managing and Sustaining the Wild

Kerry C. Gee

Kerry Gee comes to the wildlife-protection conversation from a unique orientation. As a geologist with a long career in the mining industry, he has wrestled with the obligations of his profession, the demands of governmental regulations, and his own human desire to make right a natural world that is often disrupted and occasionally defiled by one interest or another. Gee argues that proper land management is best achieved when the land itself is returned to sustainability, a process that requires landowners and regulatory agencies to work together.

As human populations expand, there will be continued pressure to encroach upon wild lands. Places of exceptional beauty and serenity make wild landscapes desirable. Interaction with the natural world is an important part of everyday life. We human beings need time to interact with wild nature in order to recharge and reflect on our own existence.

In our lifetime, massive incursions by mankind have had devastating impacts on the wild: sediment containment dam breaks that caused hundreds of thousands of tons of sediment to contaminate the flow of a river in America's Southeast, oil spills in Alaska and the Gulf of Mexico, and nuclear accidents that have killed thousands and devastated wildlife on a global scale are but a few examples.

New ways of looking at nature are needed to curb these manmade intrusions and the negative impacts on wildlife.

Negotiating is crucial to securing and protecting habitat from human ingression. As new subdivisions and real estate developments are planned, an awareness of the impacts urban development has on wildlife and habitat is essential in negotiating responsible project approvals. Protecting

Trumpeter Swan Eggs. Photographer unknown. Almost driven to extinction in the twentieth century, the trumpeter swan's healthy comeback is considered a conservation success story. Courtesy of United States Fish and Wildlife Service Archives.

the elements of wildlife—water and expanse to thrive—is critical to sustaining it.

A negotiation for the wild can take many forms and present demanding levels of complexity. Every negotiation is different. Negotiating to acquire open space from a current owner can be challenging when opposing sides have different agendas or are not particularly motivated. However, given the right information exchange it's possible that all parties can, and often do, reach an accord.

Once a price for the open space has been agreed upon, it is purchased by an entity that wants to protect and manage the land. Usually, city or county governmental agencies are engaged to help safeguard open space and lessen the tax burden by establishing a specific zone or conservation easement.

Negotiating with federal agencies can be cumbersome. These discussions are generally not along the lines of an acquisition, but rather focus on managing or accommodating remediated and restored lands. When the environment is damaged due to pollution, part of the Comprehensive Environmental Response, Compensation, and Liability Act (CERCLA) process allows for natural resource trustees to negotiate for restoration of the damaged resource. Depending on the particular circumstance, trustees can try to set aside the environmentally damaged land to protect the resource.

As an example, United Park City Mines, a company located about thirty miles east of Salt Lake City, recently completed a remediation and restoration program under a CERCLA remedial design / remedial action consent decree. To minimize costs, the restoration was done at the same time as the remediation. Environmental damages were determined using what's called a habitat equivalency analysis, which established baseline conditions with detailed analysis to determine the level at which the resources had been restored. Debits (damages) or credits were resolved based on the analysis. The company then completed the primary remediation, which improved water quality and restored services back to baseline.

In the instance of the remediation and restoration project for United Park, the analysis resulted in a credit of 1,860 Discounted Service Acre Years (DSAYs), or the equivalent of fifty-three acres of wetlands—a considerable value. The credits are slated for the next remediation project, already underway in the Silver Creek watershed. How these credits are applied depends on to what degree the company is willing to protect the restoration that was completed. Negotiations are ongoing, as they have been for the past several years. The lines of communication remain open and have not completely broken down.

When it comes to negotiating agreements, governmental agencies differ from private entities. As with most agencies dealing with environmental issues relating to the wild, the Environmental Protection Agency (EPA) operates under Superfund or CERCLA, which is in turn guided by the National Contingency Plan. The EPA also operates under the Clean Water Act. There are scores of laws governing the EPA and Fish and Wildlife Service.

When protecting human health and the environment, the EPA, Fish and Wildlife Service, and Bureau of Land Management (BLM) have very strong negotiating positions because of CERCLA laws. The Fish and Wildlife Service has its own set of far-reaching laws for protecting wildlife, but together, the EPA and Fish and Wildlife Service powers are formidable. For example, there is currently a proposal for a mine at Bristol Bay, Alaska. Environmental groups, the EPA, and Fish and Wildlife Service have engaged the proponent of the mine and have asked for public comment on the project. The state of Alaska favors the mine, as do many of its residents. However, the mine could potentially impact commercial fisheries and salmon-breeding areas, which further complicates the project negotiations.

The EPA can at times be very difficult to deal with, particularly if it involves land or water resources where the law has been blatantly violated. Agency personnel are generally passionate about their charge and work hard on environmental restoration projects. However, the cost of restoration generally does not concern them, especially when it is a project driven by a potentially responsible party. In these cases, unlike with a government agency, a private entity pays for remediation.

Currently, United Park is in the process of submitting plans to begin an Engineering Evaluation / Cost Analysis (EE/CA) for the Silver Creek drainage near Park City, Utah. This project has a "natural resource damage" component, which is being formulated at the beginning of the EE/CA process rather than at the end.

Negotiating an agreement with the EPA to clean up a floodplain contaminated with metal-laden sediments can be fairly straightforward. But if the CERCLA-driven project puts the natural resource damage assessment and restoration portion of the program at the *front* of the CERCLA (non–time-critical removal action), then negotiations become increasingly difficult. It took the government and corporate parties almost a year just to negotiate Administrative Orders on Consent for the project. That was after more than two years of negotiating a similar three-party agreement that ultimately failed.

The Fish and Wildlife Service is another difficult federal agency when it comes to negotiating because agency managers are highly educated, intelligent scientists who can get mired in detail. Federal environmental agencies take the position of being the true stewards of the wild, so progress can be slow.

United Park City Mines also owns a large parcel of land near Park City that includes a 160-acre tailings pond. Covering the exposed tailings began in 1983, shortly after the mining company that formerly leased and operated the Ontario Mine abandoned it. The land had been proposed for inclusion on the Superfund National Priority List on two separate occasions.

The 258-acre site, and eventual remediation and restoration study area that contained the tailings pond, was in terrible condition. Acres of exposed tailings were visible. Contaminated material in a surface-water diversion ditch carried polluted runoff to and around the tailings pond. The poisonous ditch contained a load of over two parts per million of zinc. Finally, in 1999, United Park City Mines agreed to perform a remedial investigation / feasibility study (RI/FS) on the site.

Many years prior to the RI/FS, when the site was originally being covered, mallards or cinnamon teal dabbling in snowmelt puddles near the pond were common sights. Some of the puddles were only a few inches deep and formed in less than 6 inches of clean soil on top of the mine tailings. Still, the ducks returned each spring.

According to a Fish and Wildlife Service biologist, the toxic site had a great deal of potential. A consent decree was lodged in court in 2007, and the remediation process commenced. The primary remediation activities and restoration construction were concluded in 2011.

Since completion of United Parks' remediation and restoration project, the former mine tailings site is visited by nearly sixty varieties of birds, nine varieties of ducks, and numerous mammals and birds of prey. Mallards, cinnamon teal, American widgeon, American shoveler, and gadwall nest on the restored site, along with a diverse mix of songbirds. Thirty-one Canada goose goslings hatched on the site last year.

Current oversight puts an emphasis on weed control and erosion, but bird counts, vegetation and macro-invertebrate monitoring, and water-quality sampling continue to be a significant part of the management program. Even so, the site is subject to an EPA five-year review provision and could be reopened should there be an issue.

Careful management of open spaces in the American West is essential. Watching weeds, monitoring precipitation levels, and observing wildlife—particularly avian species—is like taking the land's temperature. It helps in determining the health of an ecology. The lack of water and aggressive weed growth typical in arid western states can impact the land and require almost constant attention. Certain weeds, like spotted knapweed, devastate large landscapes and crops. It is so intrusive in Montana that it causes millions of dollars of damage to cropland and poisons the soil. As land-monitoring trends emerge to help drive future management decisions, diligence will pay off.

If adequately funded and left to do its job, the BLM performs well. The agency, however, is saddled with a number of difficult issues and is under constant bombardment from a variety of groups. Since the BLM is a federal agency, it manages many controversial programs that can be manipulated by politicians. Horses were introduced to North America over five hundred years ago and should remain viable, but the federal wild horse and burro program is extremely difficult to manage. There are many people who think the BLM is doing a good job with the program, and many who think otherwise. Regardless, wild horses and burros need to be responsibly managed.

Federal laws created to manage wild animals, like the Endangered Species Act, protect animals in decline and in danger of becoming extinct. There are many successes and some failures with this legislation and its related programs. An increase in populations of native species that include America's California condor, bald eagle, and gray wolf are examples of Endangered Species Act victories. Saving the gray wolf from extinction not only required a better understanding of the species by federal agency regulators, but also from western ranchers, who for years demanded the wolves' decimation. Negotiating terms between farmers, ranchers, and regulators for a control program that manages wild wolves has increased wolf pack numbers and allowed a place for them back in the wild, where they once reigned.

Regrettably, there are more species in danger of annihilation right now. The greater sage-grouse and American pika are two wild animals indigenous to the American West whose populations are in a downward spiral. Extinction looms large unless something is done to remedy this modern-day wildlife reality. Not long ago, sage-grouse in large numbers inhabited the vast grounds of sage surrounding Park City. The last grouse seen here was in February 2011. Habitat destruction has all but eliminated the greater sage-grouse, a native resident of Park City. Watching the American pika antics was once common in Park City's mountains and boulder fields. Like the sage-grouse, the American pika has not been seen in Park City in years. While the greater threat to the sage-grouse is habitat destruction, it has been speculated that the decline of the American pika has been related to climate change. Widely accepted in most circles, climate change is still a controversial topic in the West. Linking the decline of western wildlife with the politicization of climate change may explain why there is still great opposition to adding these species to the endangered species list.

As human population expands across the western United States, we must make accommodations for the wild to exist on land taken for development and land set aside for preservation. Many entitling agencies require new subdivisions to designate a certain percentage of the land as open space. This practice needs to be improved by requiring that the land set aside is managed and maintained into perpetuity. Importantly, there must be wildlife corridors so that animals can pass safely through developed as well as undeveloped parcels. While this may appear to be an excessive burden for developers, it is a concept essential to assuring lands set aside with wildlife in mind are productive habitats and viable open spaces. New open space laws prompted by concerns for wildlife may cause a reduction in developers' earnings, but the gains for local communities and the wild are worth it.

Because developers make a great deal of money building on open land, a program similar to those designed for mining and oil production could be established for urban development. Intrusive types of industries and urban developers share a responsibility in accommodating, managing, and monitoring lands set aside for wildlife. Open land strategies like these should be introduced at the college level because educating students to think along these lines is key to making broad, sweeping changes in wildlife management. This won't happen overnight.

Today, "sustainable" is a word that is thrown around for virtually anything. "Sustainable development" is one that I find particularly interesting. Sometimes the way the term is used seems almost ridiculous. The one thing I know for sure is there has been a long and sustainable attack on the wild, our western landscapes, and the environment by industrial and urban development. The deterioration is clear. Until habitat restoration, remediation, and conservation programs increase, and wild lands are brought back to a productive state, we cannot make the claim that something is sustainable. If lands are healthy, they should be self-sustaining.

Along with the attacks on our environment by expansive industry and development, the other ecological factor is the increase in human population. Habitat loss due to unchecked human expansion is colossal.

Unfortunately, the increasing rate of population growth will put pressure on decision-makers to change western land-use status. The impact on our natural resources will be profound. Accelerated demands for water can radically increase and decrease available water levels. In addition, a warming climate will negatively influence the health of our western landscapes.

Private landowners and government entities have to hold various concepts of land use with typical land-management issues. However, wild lands must be protected against intrusive development with legislative acts and government programs. It is the only way to assure open land sustainability. Proper management and monitoring practices, which look to and learn from the natural resources provided by the land, are very important. They are the barometers of healthy landscapes that reflect real sustainability.

The stewardship of wild lands is one of the most rewarding pursuits imaginable. In spite of ongoing responsibilities that include weed control, trash removal, trespass issues, and erosion abatement, wild lands oversight offers the satisfaction of knowing that a beautiful, natural resource is forever protected. Having had the experience of taking land that was gut-wrenchingly damaged, like United Parks' contaminated tailings pond, and restoring it to a state that provides scenic views and natural habitat for birds and other animals is immensely gratifying.

Wildlife Encounters

Michael Blenden

Michael Blenden speaks from experience. Three decades of working for the Fish and Wildlife Service and the National Wildlife Refuge System have given him a rare perspective regarding ways the disciplines of science and the humanities are inspired by encounters with wildlife and wild places. The spark of inspiration happens not only for scientists, humanists, and artists, but for the average person— if she or he will be open to it. The crucial factor, according to Blenden, is not necessarily the scientific insight, prose, or imagery that wild encounters inspire, but the deeper understanding of nature we derive from our encounters, and how it enables wise decision-making.

Although I was trained in the biological and physical sciences, I believe the practice of fusing humanities and science is not some intellectual or entertaining exercise, but a necessity if we expect broad public appreciation and understanding of landscapes, natural resources, and sustainable land-use practices. Encounters with wildlife continue to inspire not just scientific questions but my basic emotions. The challenge in developing and maintaining broad public appreciation and understanding is inspiring those who do not have the luxury or opportunity to live and work on the land or some other direct connection to the land. I have some thoughts, no real answers.

My perspective comes from my experience with the National Wildlife Refuge System (NWRS), administered by the United States Fish and Wildlife Service. The mission of the NWRS is to administer a national network of lands and waters for the conservation, management, and— where appropriate—restoration of fish, wildlife, and plant resources and their habitats for the benefit of present and future generations of Americans. The system encompasses approximately 150 million acres of lands and waters of the United States and is the largest such system in the world devoted to wildlife and wildlife habitat. The system manages habitats including, but not limited to, prairie pothole grasslands, seabird nesting islands, tall-grass prairie, bottomland hardwoods, arctic tundra, intermontane desert, coastal estuaries, and important riparian habitats throughout the country. Although this system includes an incredible diversity of wildlife and fish habitat, all of its units contribute to the perpetuation of migratory birds, endangered or threatened species, or other species or populations where law and international treaties require federal involvement.

The operation of the NWRS is supported by a number of laws, the most recent of which is the National Wildlife Refuge System Improvement Act, which requires every unit of the system (536 refuges and 37 wetland management districts / conservation areas) to:

- Fulfill the mission of the Refuge System;
- Fulfill the individual purposes of each refuge;
- Support the biological integrity, diversity, and environmental health of the Refuge System;
- Recognize that wildlife-dependent recreation activities, including hunting, fishing, wildlife observation, photography, environmental education, and interpretation, are legitimate and priority public uses;
- Retain the authority of refuge managers to determine compatible public uses; and
- Fulfill the requirement of developing a comprehensive conservation plan for each unit of the Refuge System and fully involve the public in preparation of these plans.

Additionally, the wildlife and habitat vision for each unit of the refuge system supports the following principles:

- Wildlife comes first.
- Ecosystems, biodiversity, and wilderness are vital concepts in refuge management.
- Habitats must be healthy.
- Growth of refuges must be strategic.[1]

Coyote Moonrise, 1920. By Frank Tenney Johnson (American, 1874–1939). Oil on canvas. 30 x 40 inches. JKM Collection, National Museum of Wildlife Art, Jackson, Wyoming.

I have had the fortune of managing national wildlife refuges for thirty years. My career interests were certainly shaped by personal encounters exploring and growing up in Missouri. I watched the stunning colors of long-eared sunfish and rainbow darters in Ozark streams, listened to a chorus of countless spring peepers mating in pothole ponds, and experienced the fantastic dance of the greater prairie chicken attracting mates from a grazed-off prairie hilltop. I remember the musky smell on my hands after catching a disturbed garter snake and hearing the deafening roar of periodic cicadas calling on a hot August night. These and other innumerable direct encounters in nature shaped me.

I was fortunate. Not only was my life rich with wildlife encounters, I was also exposed to influential wildlife artists, such as Charles Schwartz, the illustrator for Aldo Leopold's *A Sand County Almanac* and a producer of early motion pictures that featured Missouri wildlife species. As the creator of wildlife drawings used by proponents of a successful landmark ballot initiative, Schwartz used his artistic talent to help ensure a modest sales tax devoted to state wildlife and fishery conservation efforts.

Throughout my life, my encounters with wildlife and wildlife artists have influenced and inspired me. My time in the bush and maritime Alaska was full of fascinating spectacles. I saw brown bears on the Alaska Peninsula, thousands of swarming seabirds along a Pribilof Island nesting cliff, breeding rock sandpipers displaying from tundra hummocks, and streams choked with spawning salmon. These sorts of encounters not only stir scientists like myself but artists too. Photojournalists and videographers, weavers, painters, wood carvers, musicians, writers—creative people from every discipline are inspired by the very wildlife and landscapes that the refuge system and its employees work to perpetuate. A stroll through the shops lining Pioneer Avenue in Homer, Alaska, will verify this if you have any doubts.

Encounters in the lower forty-eight states may be less exotic but are no less inspirational. Clouds of snow geese lifting from North Dakota wetlands, piping plover chicks teetering along wetland shorelines, or thousands of elk raising a dust cloud as they move across spectacular landscapes are not that different from scenes of wildlife encountered by Lewis and Clark, John Fremont, and Kit Carson.

These experiences elicit fundamental emotions in everyone—scientists, ranchers, hunters, anglers, and outdoor enthusiasts alike. However calculating it may seem, it is true that in American democracy the voter ultimately determines land-use and environmental policies. It is also true that those with direct connections to the land and wildlife are not an unchallengeable majority. Without a broader and deeper understanding on the part of the public—many who will never see or be inspired by the Porcupine Caribou Herd, a desert pupfish, or a manatee—I am not confident the best or most sustainable land-use decisions will be made.

Our challenge in protecting and sustaining our natural resource heritage is to keep the public connected, not just with a few charismatic species but with entire ecological systems. Beyond developing a relationship with the natural world, society must be linked to the economic, social, and political systems that can either support or detract from nature, wildlife, and cherished landscapes. As one of our regional directors once stated, "We need to educate our publics. It's fundamental to nurturing a strong land ethic and critical to developing people's appreciation and participating in decisions affecting wildlife and habitat conservation. We must act now."[2]

The National Wildlife Refuge Improvement Act, passed in 1997, recognizes the value of wildlife-dependent recreation activities, including hunting, fishing, photography, environmental education, wildlife interpretation, and wildlife observation. These interests are popular, and many of our refuges are heavily visited by those pursuing these activities, but the need to reach out to more people, more deeply, cannot be overstated.

Frankly, I don't know anyone who does not generally like wildlife, fish, spectacular vistas, and open spaces, but we don't always know or understand the harmful consequences of our actions, such as dam construction, the conversion of native prairies into croplands, wetland drainage, and so on. Practitioners of the humanities and those who study human culture are in a unique position to assist private and public land managers, policy makers, politicians, and educators in effective ways to maintain connections between local, regional, and national communities and their landscapes. As an example, the National Wildlife Refuge System is asking the question, "How can we inspire Americans to care, visit, and learn about wildlife and refuges?" To start answering this question, the Fish and Wildlife Service has hired a social scientist and established a branch called Human Dimensions, which "examines the complex relationships between people and the wildlife and habitats the Refuge System protects." This work has been extremely valuable already but there is much to do.

As a nation we simply cannot count on wise land-use policy and practices resulting from a shallow understanding by the public. "Understanding" cannot be limited to those who have the fortune to live, work, or spend time thinking about our American landscapes and everything that comes with them. Wildlife encounters inspire, and inspiration leads to curiosity, followed by the development of a deeper understanding of our ecological place in the world.

NOTES

1. See "National Wildlife Refuge System Improvement Act of 1997," US Fish and Wildlife Service, last updated August 19, 2009, https://www.fws.gov/refuges/policiesandbudget/hr1420_index.html.
2. See "Conserving the Future: Wildlife Refuges and the Next Generation," US Fish and Wildlife Service, October 2011, https://www.fws.gov/refuges/pdfs/FinalDocumentConservingTheFuture.pdf.

PART 4

Ethos

Wither Humanities?

Restoring Transcendent Humanities Values as a Step to Reimagine Western Landscapes

Timothy Bywater

To conclude this collection, two passionate humanists make the case for the role of the humanities in "reimagining" our western landscape and our relationship to its wild inhabitants. Each argues in his own way that the humanities may best answer the question of what it means to be human and to set right our fractured relationship with nature and the wild.

Timothy Bywater, Professor of English and humanities at Dixie State University, invokes a number of prominent humanists, poets, and social critics in his provocative polemic. In an era when many are rushing to embrace and defend science as the answer to existential challenges we face, Bywater makes a heartfelt plea for the humanities. He concludes by writing: "[M]aybe sometime in the future, the natural world will be seen as a place we don't escape to but as a place that dwells in our hearts, constantly influencing our daily lives, the lives of others, and the landscapes where we live. [The humanities help] us discover an inroad to reimagine our western landscapes and the landscapes of our hearts."

We spend our days filling out forms, begging the stamps of official approval and permission, currying the favor of a foundation grant, an academic appointment, a government contract, counting it our duty to strike attractive poses, to pass vaguely through a room while displaying the finery of our moral sentiments, finding our way in the world by saying to a succession of masters, "Make of me what you want; I am what you want me to be."

—Lewis Lapham

American life, driven by market capitalism's perpetual motion machine, runs on fast-forward. There is little chance to regroup—the pause button has been jammed. If we turn for relief to movies and television, we are accosted by the capitalist's version of mind-numbing "entertainment": made-for-profit helpings of sex, violence, and death; if we try to find some semblance of serious intellectual engagement by participating in the democratic process, we have no choice but to indulge in politics as a polarizing blood sport: "Hardball," "Crossfire," or "Firing Line." If we try to escape to the natural world, the specter of land development run amok and carbon-driven global warming confront us. Many of our western landscapes have been mortally injured by rising temperatures, floods and droughts, excessive wildfires, declining wildlife populations, and deforestation. If we look to the classroom to find humanities values in academic study, we encounter the mind-set of business school elites who endorse cutthroat competition as the ultimate value—a value that has transformed much of academia into a monstrous business school. It is no wonder that in the last ten years Harvard University has lost 35 percent of its humanities majors—which echoes a national trend.

America's compulsive race to the bottom line is well documented. The damage to western landscapes as a result of this compulsion convinced Leslie Miller to stage the first Reimagine Western Landscapes symposium. Miller invited renowned environmentalists, western scholars, biologists, wildlife managers, academics, and community leaders—all with diverse environmental interests and experience—to the University of Utah's Taft-Nicholson Center for Environmental Humanities Education in Centennial Valley, Montana. Participants were encouraged to draw on their unique expertise and begin formulating "a new environmental paradigm and a reimagined vision for the future of the West."

The paradigm would be based on "renewed respect for the preservation and restoration of western landscapes." The Reimagine model would include creating imaginative humanities-based projects for transforming landscapes "into places where humans and wildlife not only interact but thrive." Perhaps just as important, the hope was that the Centennial Valley setting would allow the participants to transcend their political and social differences and defenses and replace them with feelings of empathy for the natural world and all those who live there.

At first glance, Centennial Valley appeared to be the perfect place for this transformation to begin—a place where symposium attendees could hit the pause button, slow down, begin to unwind and regroup. The landscape is magnificent: the sky never ends, the air is sweet, wildlife abounds, the "win-at-all-cost" mind-set vanishes, the dollar seems to be less of a distraction. But freeze the frame; look a little closer: Moose, deer, and elk are hunted and killed in the valley and on the refuge (which challenges the meaning of the word "refuge"), a half mile from the Red Rocks National Wildlife Refuge headquarters. Trumpeter swan enthusiasts fight fishery biologists over who should control the watershed in the wildlife refuge—the swan supporters, led by the Audubon Society, want to preserve what is left of Centennial ponds as trumpeter swan habitat; the fishery biologists, supported by Trout Unlimited, want to drain more of the remaining ponds to restore spawning streams for Arctic grayling. The Koch brothers' private ranch encloses the heart of the valley. Can oil fracking be far behind? And, ironically, the symposium could only happen after enough money was raised to pay expenses. Even in magnificent Centennial Valley, the symposium participants faced a daunting predicament similar to that described by William Wordsworth over two hundred years ago:

The world is too much with us; late and soon,
Getting and spending, we lay waste our powers:
Little we see in Nature that is ours;
We have given our hearts away, a sordid boon![1]

Under these conditions, including an epic rainstorm that dumped historic amounts of water nonstop for three days, there was a distinct possibility that the symposium could offer nothing more than a brief escape from capitalism's reach by providing conservationist Band-Aids to ease the pain of wounded spirits before returning to the fast-forward status quo.

Curtis White, professor emeritus of English at Illinois State University, in his remarkable book *The Barbaric Heart*, makes a strong case that the status quo may be impossible to change.[2] White compares market capitalism's power to jam the pause button to the power of the barbarian throughout history: the Roman conquests, the Goths sacking Rome, Gitmo soldiers waterboarding prisoners, Wall Street bankers triggering a worldwide financial collapse. Alan Greenspan, as he testified before Congress after the financial meltdown, is compared by White to an "astonished Goth." According to White, from time immemorial, when the human heart is driven only by the bottom line, eventually it will calculate that if it takes violence to win, then violence is justified. The result is barbarism. In White's judgment, America's sell-out to market capitalism's values has meant undreamed-of prosperity for the few, with violence unleashed on most of the human and natural world. The opening chapter of *The Barbaric Heart*, "Naked Force Clothed in Beauty," sets the tone of the book. Here White cites evidence of market capitalism's need to damage everything it touches in the natural world while at the same time praising the damage as "progress" and proclaiming that free markets are all that matter since they create "jobs for working people." But more frightening yet is White's belief that

> the Barbaric Heart cannot be punished for its excesses. It cannot be disciplined. It cannot be brought within the boundaries of decency, legality, or ethical behavior. It cannot be persuaded, cajoled, or "shown the light of day." The proposals of the environmental community for better systems of transportation, cleaner smokestacks, purer foods, and jail time for corporate polluters, none of that changes the Barbaric Heart. If it is frustrated by the activities of others (those troublesome tree huggers), it simply concludes that it will be more cunning and violent the next time.

One of White's main concerns is that environmentalism uses the same science to save the planet that the barbaric heart uses to destroy it. He labels this strategy "green capitalism." If science invents and capitalism promotes the internal combustion engine, a main cause of global warming, reason suggests that better science can be used to save the planet—replacing the gasoline engine with an electric engine. White cites Al Gore's documentary *An Inconvenient Truth* as the perfect example of this fallacious reasoning. Gore's film "may have distressing things to say about global warming, but at the level of consciousness, it is an extended apology for scientific rationality, the free market, and our utterly corrupted democracy." White anticipates that with reasoning like Gore's— using only the best science, with capitalism's blessing, to solve our most serious environmental problems—the ice caps will melt faster than predicted. "A more adequate response to our true problems," he contends, "requires that we cease to be a society that believes that wealth is the accumulation of money (no matter how much of it we're planning on 'giving back' to nature), and begin to be a society that understands that 'the only wealth is life,' as John Ruskin put it. That is the full dimension and the full difficulty of our problem."

A small group of environmentalists speaking at the three-day symposium would seem to have little chance of making many inroads to solve the problems manifested by the overwhelming power of the barbaric heart. And White offers little encouragement. He believes there will be no adequate solutions until the environmental movement stops depending solely on its alliance with science for its sense of itself.

> It should look to create a common language of *Care*, (a reverence for and a commitment to the astonishing fact of Being). Through which it could begin to create alternative principles by which we might *live*. The establishment of those principles... would begin with three questions. First, what does it mean to be a human being? Second, what is my relation to other human beings? And third, what is my relation to Being as such, the ongoing miracle that there is something rather than nothing?

White acknowledges this radical notion is risky. It is the risk to "return to our nobility. We should refuse to be mere creatures, mere functions of a system we cannot in good conscience defend. And we should insist on a recognition of the mystery, the miracle, and the dignity of things, from frogs to forests, simply because they are."

White's advice to accomplish this poses a real challenge, not only for environmentalists, but for every human being. We all must, he believes, begin to rethink our "relations with nature," not in scientific or Darwinian terms but in transcendent humanities parlance: "In spiritual terms or poetic terms, or with Emerson and Thoreau in good old American transcendental terms." Unfortunately, over the past forty years those terms have been replaced in humanities studies by what White calls "a lower common denominator: the languages of science and bureaucracy." Consequently, humanities curricula today offer a bevy of pseudoscientific subjects: semiotics, linguistics, critical theories (such as deconstruction, gender, and queer theory), historiography, cultural studies, and rhetoric. Some humanities professors, shored up by language theory, claim—unbelievably—that the spiritual, poetic, or transcendental language of the human imagination has the same human value as a British Petroleum commercial.

In the 1970s, the English curriculum began to concentrate aggressively on theory; studying literature for its power to touch human spirit gave way to studying literature as a sort of complex computer program written by those deluded enough to believe they were using words to express human feeling. Years ago, Pulitzer Prize–winning author and master creative writing teacher Wallace Stegner warned of the danger presented by some professors at major universities led by the "deconstructionist magi of Yale," who "declared themselves superior to fiction, and to literature in general." Stegner dismissed the idea as "a joke," comparing a professor who espoused literary theory at literature's expense to a "snake that took hold of its own tail and swallowed itself."[3]

So far, anyway, the theories have proved to be no joke. Predictably, in fact, deconstruction theory has now slithered into the environmental movement, where influential cliques of professors are questioning the very idea of the word "wilderness," claiming that it is nothing more than what American environmental writer Kenneth Brower calls "an abstraction, illusory, a construct." In a 2014 *Outside* article, Brower warns that these academics are bringing "to the study of environmental history what deconstructionist theory brought to English departments across the land: surpassingly beautiful subject matter—great works of literature on the one hand, wilderness on the other—is subjected to barren formulas and rendered a wasteland."[4] Naturally, Wordsworth was one of the first to condemn the arrogance of believing that human reason could transform nature into a measurable commodity:

> Sweet is the lore which Nature brings;
> Our meddling intellect
> Mis-shapes the beauteous forms of things:—
> We murder to dissect.[5]

As the dissection of humanities' values and the dissection of wild nature's values merge, owing partly to the debasement of language, the immediate solution seems obvious: to become cognizant of and practice using a common language of care. But what exactly does this imply? An answer can be found in Laurence Sterne's groundbreaking 1768 novel anticipating the Romantic movement, *A Sentimental Journey through*

France and Italy.[6] The novel flies in the face of most prose written in the age of reason. Voltaire this isn't. In a section of the novel entitled "A Fragment," the narrator, Mr. Yorick, describes the violent atmosphere in Abdera, "the vilest and most profligate town in all Thrace," with "poisonings, murders, tumults, libels and assassinations" common both day and night. One evening, Euripides's play *Andromeda* is performed. The barbaric audience listens and is delighted by the performance, "but nothing operated more upon their imaginations, than the tender strokes of nature, which the poet had wrought up in the pathetic speech of Perseus, *O Cupid, prince of Gods and men etc.*" Later that night, on every street and in every house could be heard the words repeated, "Cupid! Cupid! Prince of Gods and men." Yorick explains what happened next:

> The fire caught—and the whole city, like the heart of one man, open'd itself to Love. No pharmacopolist could sell one grain of hellebore—not a single armorer had a heart to forge one instrument of death.—Friendship and Virtue met together, and kiss'd each other in the street—the golden age return'd, and hung over the town of Abdera—every Abderite took his oaten pipe, and every Abderitish woman left her purple web, and chastely sat her down, and listen'd to the song.

Yorick concludes that "'twas only in the power…of the God whose empire extendeth from heaven to earth, and even to the depths of the sea, to have done this." Although the scientist and the linguist may be skeptical, perhaps our best chance to escape an environmental catastrophe will be to adopt the language of care, "tender strokes of nature," in narratives that draw on an empathic power, greater than the power of the barbaric heart.

According to one of America's most prescient thinkers, Lewis Lapham, the founders of the republic based the American experiment on the core belief that narratives from all people were a main source of strength that unites us as a nation:

> What joins Americans one with another is not a common nationality, language, race or ancestry (all of which testify to the burdens of the past) but rather their complicity in a shared work of the imagination. My love of country follows from my love of

its freedoms, not from my pride in its fleets or its armies or its gross national product. Construed as a means and not an end, the Constitution stands as the premise for a narrative rather than a plan for an invasion or a monument. The narrative was always plural. Not one story but many stories.[7]

Lapham uses the past tense to draw attention to the disaster that has resulted by replacing the many-story narrative with an elitist, one-story narrative imposed by the least imaginative among us (the capitalist oligarchy)—conformity; lock-step obedience; saying to the masters, "I am what you want me to be"—resulting in, among other things, ruin of our western landscapes and those who live there.

One of the major objectives of the Reimagine Western Landscapes symposium was to replace this one-voice narrative with a variety of conservationist perspectives. This was accomplished to perfection. The keynote speakers and other speakers on the various panels spoke convincingly about the serious problems facing the environment, and they proposed novel solutions to help restore our western landscapes. *New York Times* columnist and author Timothy Egan argued for reclaiming devastated land rather than for securing more wilderness areas, and writer Terry Tempest Williams honored the diverse insights and ideas presented by symposium speakers. However, with the exception of the symposium's opening prayer offered by Native American and former Montana poet laureate Henry Real Bird, a transcendent power of empathy silencing our barbaric hearts seemed to be in short supply. That is, until the epic rainstorm christened the symposium.

In his poem "Voice of the Rain," Walt Whitman translates this sacred message and the transcendent power of empathy:

> *And who art thou? said I to the soft-falling shower,*
> *Which, strange to tell, gave me an answer, as here translated:*
> *I am the Poem of Earth, said the voice of the rain,*
> *Eternal I rise impalpable out of the land and the bottomless sea,*
> *Upward to heaven, whence, vaguely form'd, altogether changed, and yet the same,*
> *I descend to lave the drouths, atomies, dust-layers of the globe,*
> *And all that in them without me were seeds only, latent, unborn;*
> *And forever, by day and night, I give back life to my own*

origin, and make pure and beautify it;
(For song, issuing from its birth-place, after fulfilment, wandering,
Reck'd or unreck'd duly with love returns.)[8]

Before reciting the poem, Whitman would probably have taken the audience outside, into the rain, to hear, see, taste, smell, and touch its message.

The latent seeds planted by speakers at the symposium began to grow, owing not only to their words but to the voice of the rain, which "duly with love" returned daily. Nature's deluge inspired feelings of empathy. Participants smiled in the face of the downpour, acted kinder to one another, and were more open to different conservationist perspectives. Speaking in the language of care, the rain repeated its message for three days: "You're all in this together."

Were it not for the fact that wireless access was unavailable in the wilds of Centennial Valley, this truth may have been ignored and replaced by self-absorbed text messaging. But the rain's persistent voice called for a human, not a Wi-Fi, connection.

Celebrating and interpreting our relationship with the natural world and with one another have always been the responsibilities of the humanities, as expressed by the sentiment in Whitman's poetry and sometimes in the authentic voice of rain. Regrettably, the joining with nature, as

Trumpeter Swan, Lower Red Rock Lake. Photograph by Mary Tull, 2014.

imaginatively construed by the humanities, has been replaced by capitalist values and by scientific "truths."

To restore our connection means to pay attention to those transcendental voices who genuinely use the language of care. Here, for example,
is Ralph Waldo Emerson, the father of transcendentalism, in his poem
"Each and All," reminding us that in order to live in harmony with our
fellow humans we must set aside those scientific "truths" we have learned
as adults and return to the mystical ties to nature we knew in childhood:

> Then I said, "I covet truth;
> Beauty is unripe childhood's cheat;
> I leave it behind with the games of youth:"—
> As I spoke, beneath my feet
> The ground-pine curled its pretty wreath,
> Running over the club-moss burrs;
> I inhaled the violet's breath;
> Around me stood the oaks and firs;
> Pine-cones and acorns lay on the ground;
> Above me soared the eternal sky,
> Full of light and deity;
> Again I saw, again I heard,
> The rolling river, the morning bird;—
> Beauty through my senses stole;
> I yielded myself to the perfect whole.[9]

Wordsworth, in a similar vein, speaks to the power of childhood to
first connect us with nature and then to place the connection securely in
the heart as a touchstone to guide us spiritually through life:

> My heart leaps up when I behold
> A rainbow in the sky:
> So was it when my life began;
> So is it now I am a man;
> So be it when I shall grow old,
> Or let me die!
> The Child is father of the Man;
> And I could wish my days to be

Bound each to each by natural piety.[10]

Nathaniel Hawthorne, in *The Scarlet Letter,* creates a child as "father of the man," seven-year-old Pearl, who stands at the moral center of the novel partly because of her ties with nature. Rejected by the society into which she was born out of wedlock, she is nurtured not only by her mother but by Mother Nature. Pearl's creativity, her imagination, her innocence, her need to seek truth, and her free spirit are recognized and sustained in the forest, as it "puts on the kindest of moods to welcome her." Even the most fearsome animals identify with her:

> A wolf, it is said—but here the tale has surely lapsed into the improbable—came up, and smelt of Pearl's robe, and offered his savage head to be patted by her hand. The truth seems to be, however, that the mother-forest, and these wild things, which it nourished, all recognized a kindred wildness in the human child. And she was gentler here than in the grassy-margined streets of the settlement, or in her mother's cottage.[11]

Emerson, in his essay "Self-Reliance," compares the unsullied minds of children, like Pearl, and brutes, like the animals that befriend her, with the conflicted minds of adults:

> What pretty oracles nature yields us…in the face of children, babes, and even brutes. That divided and rebel mind [of adults], that distrust of sentiment because our arithmetic has computed the strength and means opposed to our purpose, these [children] have not. Their mind being whole, their eye is as yet unconquered, and when we look in their faces we are disconcerted. Infancy conforms to nobody.[12]

James Joyce, in his story "The Dead," portrays perfectly how the conflicted adult mind that "distrusts of sentiment" discovers what it means to be a human being, owing to the power of nature's voice.[13] While attending his aunts' Christmas party, Gabriel Conroy, accompanied by his wife, Gretta, masks his distaste for many of the other all-too-human partygoers—their self-deception, drunkenness, arrogance, academic pretension, mock sentimentality, prejudice, concerns about sex and money, and religious and political dogmatism—forcing him further into his defensive shell. He ignores his connectedness with other human beings, partly to hide the fact that he, too, is human.

Later that evening, in a hotel room, Gretta tells Gabriel that a song she heard at the party, "The Lass of Aughrim," was the same song sung to her long ago by a young lad, Michael Furey, who, she believes, died because of his love for her. Obviously, this disclosure is a blow to Gabriel's male ego. Nevertheless, as he looks at his wife, asleep, a "strange, friendly pity for her entered his soul." That this feeling of "friendly pity" is "strange" to Gabriel is all we need to know about his lack of feelings for others. Using his well-honed defenses, he blocks that feeling with self-pity: "It hardly pained him to think how poor a part he, her husband, had played in her life."

At that moment, however, he lets his defenses down and "generous tears filled Gabriel's eyes. He had never felt like that himself towards any woman, but he knew that such a feeling must be love." His generous tears are a sign of change, as his own identity begins "fading out into a grey impalpable world." Then, as "a few light taps" of snow "upon the pane made him turn to the window," he imagines snow falling hauntingly throughout the land and falling in the "lonely churchyard on the hill where Michael Furey lay buried. It lay thickly drifted on the crooked crosses and headstones, on the spears of the little gate, on the barren thorns." Caught up in his transcendent reverie, Gabriel's soul "swooned slowly as he heard the snow falling faintly through the universe and faintly falling, like the descent of their last end, upon all the living and the dead." By escaping his own identity, Gabriel has translated the snow's faint yet powerful message: "We're all in this together," both in life and in death. His imagination has made this transcendence, affirmed by his swooning soul, possible.

The Reimagine Western Landscapes symposium's transcendent message, "We're all in this together," was not lost on its participants. In a questionnaire asking what they took away from the symposium, words like *listening, perseverance, collaboration, integration, community, passion, compassion, knowledge, empathy, vulnerability, balance, restraint,* and *service* emphatically confirmed that message. As the memory of the first symposium fades, can we keep the images of the Centennial Valley landscape bathed in rain as well as the empathic personal connections alive so the seeds of Reimagine continue to grow? Henry David Thoreau provides the path to accomplish something like this. We must, he believes,

> treat our minds, that is, ourselves, as innocent and ingenuous children...and be careful what objects and what subjects we thrust on their attention.... Even the facts of science may dust the mind by their dryness, unless they are in a sense effaced each morning, or rather rendered fertile by the dews of fresh and living truth.[14]

How exactly to choose what objects and subjects to thrust upon our attention was the topic of a brilliant 2005 commencement speech by the late English teacher and novelist David Foster Wallace.[15] At a time when escaping to nature is not as convenient a choice as it was for Thoreau, Wallace admits that choosing correctly will be difficult because the "so-called real world...of men and money and power hums merrily along in a pool of fear and anger and frustration and craving and worship of self," which has produced a culture of "extraordinary wealth and comfort and personal freedom." Wallace contends that if it's "personal," it's not freedom, and that real freedom "involves attention and awareness and discipline, and being able truly to care about other people." He then provides a practical example of how this care can be demonstrated in the most unsexy way imaginable:

> It's the end of the work day and the traffic is apt to be very bad. So getting to the store takes way longer than it should.... [T]he store is hideously lit and infused with soul-killing Muzak or corporate pop and it's pretty much the last place you want to be but you can't just get in and quickly out.

Wallace knows that everyone has had this experience, and that we will be faced with it almost daily for the rest of their lives, "week after week, month after month, year after year":

> [I]f I don't make a conscious decision about how to think and what to pay attention to, I'm gonna be pissed and miserable every time I have to shop. Because my natural default setting is the certainty that situations like this are really all about me.

About MY hungriness and MY fatigue and MY desire to just get home, and it's going to seem for all the world like everybody else is just in my way.

He then describes, in a brief narrative, how one might make the transcendental choice while being faced with a situation that couldn't be worse—the store's checkout line, behind a horrible, "dead-eyed" woman screaming at her child and trying get fifty dollars' worth of coupons or food stamps out of her purse to pay for her two weeks' supply of groceries. Now comes the transcendent moment—choosing to think empathically, using the language of care:

> [I]f you're aware enough to give yourself a choice, you can choose to look differently at this...dead-eyed, over-made-up lady who just screamed at her kid....Maybe she's not usually like this. Maybe she's been up three straight nights holding the hand of a husband who is dying of bone cancer. Or maybe this very lady is the low-wage clerk at the motor vehicle department, who just yesterday helped your spouse resolve a horrific, infuriating, red-tape problem through some act of bureaucratic kindness.

Although Wallace admits that "none of this is likely," it represents a clear choice to determine what "objects and subjects" we thrust upon our attention. Most of the thinking options in the grocery store line will concentrate on the "annoying and miserable." However, imagining the experience using the language of care can transform "a crowded, hot, slow, consumer-hell type situation as not only meaningful, but sacred, on fire with the same force that made the stars: love, fellowship, the mystical oneness of all things deep down." We will have avoided the status quo of "the default setting, the rat race, the constant gnawing sense of having had, and lost, some infinite thing," and, as a result, we will find the true answer to White's question "What does it mean to be human?" Multiply this small but transcendent moment that repeats, "We're all in this together," and maybe sometime in the future the natural world will be seen as a place we don't escape to but as a place that dwells in our hearts, constantly influencing our daily lives, the lives of others, and the landscapes where we live. Then the power of the rain's message will have helped us discover an inroad to reimagine our western landscapes and the landscapes of our hearts.

NOTES

1. William Wordsworth, "The World Is Too Much with Us," in *The Norton Anthology of British Literature: The Major Authors, 6th Edition*, general ed. M. H. Abrams (New York: W.W. Norton, 1996), 1394.

2. Curtis White, *The Barbaric Heart: Faith, Money, and the Crisis of Nature* (Sausalito, CA: PoliPoint Press, 2009). The subsequent five quotations are from the same text.

3. Wallace Stegner, *On Teaching and Writing Fiction*, ed. Lynn Stegner (New York: Penguin, 2002).

4. Kenneth Brower, "Leave Wilderness Alone," *Outside*, October 13, 2014, https://www.outsideonline.com/1926421/leave-wilderness-alone.

5. William Wordsworth, "The Tables Turned," in *The Norton Anthology*, ed. Abrams, 1335–36.

6. Laurence Sterne, *A Sentimental Journey through France and Italy*, Bartleby.com, https://www.bartleby.com/303/1.

7. Lewis Lapham, *Lights, Camera, Democracy: Selected Essays!* (New York: Random House, 2001), 155.

8. Walt Whitman, *Leaves of Grass*, in The Walt Whitman Archive, eds. Ed Folsom and Kenneth M. Price (Center for Digital Research in the Humanities, 2002). https://whitmanarchive.org/published/LG/1891/poems/349.

9. Ralph Waldo Emerson, "Each and All," Bartleby.com, https://www.bartleby.com/370/2.html.

10. William Wordsworth, "My Heart Leaps Up," in *The Norton Anthology*, ed. Abrams, 1394.

11. Nathaniel Hawthorne, *The Scarlet Letter*, in *American Literature*, *vol. 1*, ed. William E. Cain (New York: Pearson Education, Inc., 2004).

12. Ralph Waldo Emerson, "Self-Reliance," in *American Literature*, ed. Cain.

13. James Joyce, "The Dead," in *Dubliners* (Ware: Wordsworth Editions, 2000).

14. Henry David Thoreau, "Life Without Principle," in *American Literature*, ed. Cain.

15. David Foster Wallace, "Transcription of the 2005 Kenyon Commencement Address," May 21, 2005, https://web.ics.purdue.edu/~drkelly/DFWKenyonAddress2005.pdf.

The Environmental Crisis and the Ecology of the Environmental Humanities

Jeffrey Mathes McCarthy

Jeffrey McCarthy directs the University of Utah's Environmental Humanities Graduate Program and makes an eloquent argument for the program's work. Environmental humanities' role is "to inform the unfolding collision between human necessity and natural limits," and McCarthy believes the need is urgent. While acknowledging the university's role in positioning students for the workplace, he maintains that the real work of the university is in shaping "that temperament and disposition people call character" so that, ultimately, we may "acknowledge ourselves as parts of a bigger-than-human world."

Here we are in the American West, this ground an inflection between nature and culture, a meeting point of the environment and the university. With that all about us, let me begin with a familiar quote from Utah alumnus Wallace Stegner, a quote you will recognize and a quote this essay will develop.

> One cannot be pessimistic about the West. This is the native home of hope. When it fully learns that cooperation, not rugged individualism, is the quality that most characterizes and preserves it, then it will have achieved itself and outlived its origins. Then it has a chance to create a society to match its scenery.[1]

Have we made any progress toward this society of cooperation? Could the environmental humanities be the solution? Let's talk about what universities do and about strategies to reimagine the collision between nature and culture.

Despite Stegner's optimism, the United States seems more invested than ever in an exploitative relation to landscape, and more troubled than ever by the role higher education will play in either accelerating that exploitation or objecting to it. Indeed, universities are themselves coming under fire for being insufficiently linked to the needs of industry and too apt to waste their students' money on rarified inquiry. Higher education does much more than prepare students for jobs. Yes, we are committed to positioning our students for success in the workplace, but that workplace changes so rapidly that higher education's more pressing role is actually building that temperament and disposition people call *character*. The problem is it's not always clear which character higher education actually reinforces. Amidst the glittering monuments of new gymnasiums, luxurious dormitories, and manicured lawns, it's no surprise students indulge their narcissism, self-regard, and personal advantages. However, another version is available to us, and that version foregrounds cooperative engagement, it foregrounds service to the community, it foregrounds generosity, and it molds students toward recognizing each self as part of a bigger whole. Obviously, this latter version of character is more appealing, more aligned with Stegner's "hope," and, I would argue, the environmental humanities is a field uniquely positioned to make this version a reality.

Others in higher education are troubled by the values our universities advocate. Wesleyan University president Michael Roth observes, "Many undergraduates now behave like consumers, intent on building resumes. Parents often want their children's education to be useful" in "a dramatically shrinking job market."[2] From another perspective, entrepreneur Peter Thiel offers fellowships of $100,000 to talented students so they'll leave college entirely and devote themselves to commercial initiatives that pay right away. For him, higher education is insufficiently vocational.

Thiel's vision is fine for a select group of driven minds satisfied to trade broad understanding for profitable focus. But education can do more than that, and graduate education in particular can develop students toward participation in their communities and contributions toward the greater good instead of self-regarding careerism. A fundamental lesson of ecology is that organisms interact with, depend on, and even transform their environments. From this starting point we can map a powerful role for the bright minds who join us to study environmental humanities.

The basic message is that thinking about the environment positions us to see the world as something bigger than ourselves. American biologist Daniel Botkin summarizes the science nicely: "Life is sustained only by a group of organisms of many species...a certain kind of system composed of many individuals of different species and their environment, making together a network of living and nonliving parts that can maintain the flow of energy and the cycling of chemical elements that, in turn, support life."[3] Botkin describes a dynamic, interactive realm we exist within, not somehow atop. The environmental humanities focuses on the interaction between human thinking and the natural world. Poems, plays, religions, political parties, and symphonies all exist within the overlapping mesh of natural forces and human constructs. Thus the power of the environmental humanities as a discipline is its celebration of natural forces, its insistence that human culture sits always within the physical actuality of the natural systems that surround us, and its enthusiastic appreciation of both. For instance, something as simple as a night in the desert offers students the lesson of dryness and the clear truth of cold amidst the clattering night animals and the wagtail cursive snakes and beetles mark upon the ground. I'm thinking of last year's trip to the San Rafael Swell with a van-load of environmental students. The place is itself a study in cooperation. Temperature differential creates a frost to appease local thirsts, while owls nest in prairie dog dens, and lichens and mosses knit the soil together into a living ground cover. Around the campfire, poems and quotes and amateur astronomy fill the night. The point for observers is the interactions, the relationships, the living together that joins organisms into a whole bigger than themselves.

But these are not just lessons of ecology, they are likewise lessons of culture. What the environmental humanities interprets is human expression in relation to nature, and in doing so the environmental humanities repeatedly challenges the claims of anthropocentric, instrumental humanism. To see humans in nature is to destabilize the western tradition of human preeminence, while also offering other epistemologies, other ontologies, to take its place. Another look at ecology will demonstrate the foundational rethinking the environmental humanities makes possible.

Ecology takes as its object the relationship between organisms and their environment. What we find when we press these relations is an interaction between beings and the places they live, an interaction between the various inhabitants of an ecosystem and a healthy dependence of one group of inhabitants on other groups—as seeds depend on birds, and farmers depend on bees, or mountains depend on wolves. In his book *The Great Work* Thomas Berry observes that "for a species to remain viable it must establish a niche that is beneficial both for itself and for the larger community."⁴ To study environmental humanities is to absorb the fact that community is the foundation of individual health. This is a long way from Thiel's me-first careerism. My point, I suppose, is that when we talk about community in environmental humanities something special happens because we acknowledge ourselves as parts of a bigger-than-human world. Henry David Thoreau once asked, "Am I not partly leaves and vegetable mold myself?" This community extends beyond people. D. H. Lawrence wrote that to become healthy western society must "re-establish the living organic connection with the cosmos, the sun and earth." Education can either perpetuate an alienating dualism or work toward erasing it—erasing it and pursuing Lawrence's "living organic connection to the cosmos."⁵ In our field of study, the notion of community extends beyond our borders, beyond our family, beyond even our species to celebrate the ways human health is tied to the context it sits within.

The world's leading biologists and ecologists warn of collapse, of a sixth extinction, and the blame lies with a culture that disunites people from natural communities that surround them. You can point to Bacon, you can point to Descartes, you can point to the Old Testament, but the problem is playing out right now, right here, for us to take up or to sidestep. E. O. Wilson says, "In the end it will all come down to a decision of ethics, how we value the natural word in which we have evolved and now—increasingly—how we regard our status as individuals."⁶ For Wilson, an individualism that obscures natural communities is the problem. What happens in the environmental humanities is the solution—the constant destabilizing of anthropocentric assumptions and the constant reimagining of what Wilson terms "our status as individuals." For example, contemporary environmental critic Stacy Alaimo identifies "trans-corporeality" as the human condition, meaning that people are produced by the material interactions between our physical selves and the physical world around us. For Alaimo existence is bodily, and she frames our community as "the interconnections, interchanges,

Prong-Horned Antelope, 1865. By Albert Bierstadt (German, 1830–1902). Oil on canvas. 13 ½ x 19 ¼ inches. Gift of the Stonehollow Collection, National Museum of Wildlife Art, Jackson, Wyoming.

and transits between human bodies and non-human natures."[7] These are commonplaces in ecology textbooks but bold fighting words in a political climate wed to human supremacy and American exceptionalism.

Let me bring us toward a conclusion by saying that these environmental insights are significant to the unfolding debates about higher education in the United States. Thomas Berry laments, "As now functioning, the university prepares students for their role in extending human dominion over the natural world, not for the intimate presence to the natural world."[8] Education is more and more slanted toward individual achievement, individual career preparation, while the field of environmental humanities makes students see themselves as part of a community. Indeed, the big payoff is that environmental humanities puts students into a community beyond just humans. This is Berry's "great work." He encourages a reordering of ethics where "[t]he ecological community is not subordinate to the human community.... The basic ethical norm is the well-being of the comprehensive community and the attainment of human well-being within that community."[9] A core tenet of the modern humanities is the effort to see things from other points of view, and so a fundamental imperative of the environmental humanities must be bringing more-than-human points of view into the conversation, into the community.

To conclude, our students are entering a crucial fifty-year span in the story of American environmentalism. Not since Muir and Pinchot and Roosevelt have the stakes been so high for the planet and for the way we think about humans in the environment. We have the data about climate change, about species extinction, about habitat loss, but our community needs the stories that extend our version of community to include the natural bodies that surround and interconnect with us. Stegner asked that the West build "a society to match the scenery." Perhaps environmental humanities is building character matched to the ecological actuality we inhabit. If so, now is the time for the environmental humanities to inform the unfolding collision between human necessity and natural limits. This is the work that needs to be done, and the University of Utah's Environmental Humanities Program is the nation's best chance for doing it.

NOTES

1. Wallace Stegner, *The Sound of Mountain Water: The Changing American West* (New York: Random House, 1946).
2. Michael Roth, "The Case for a Liberal Education," *New York Times,* May 9, 2014.
3. Daniel B. Botkin, *Discordant Harmonies: A New Ecology for the Twenty-First Century* (New York and London: Oxford University Press, 1990), 9.
4. Thomas Berry, *The Great Work: Our Way into the Future* (New York: Harmony/Bell Tower, 1999), 105.
5. D. H. Lawrence, *Apocalypse* (London: Penguin Classics, 1995), 204.
6. E. O. Wilson, ed., *Biodiversity,* (Washington, DC: National Academies Press, 1988), https://eowilsonfoundation.org.
7. Stacy Alaimo, *Bodily Natures* (Indiana: Indiana University Press, 2010), 2.
8. Berry, *The Great Work*, 72.
9. Ibid., 105.

List of Contributors

Michael Blenden, recently retired, was the National Wildlife Refuge supervisor for the United States Fish and Wildlife Service in Utah, Montana, and Wyoming. He worked as a wildlife biologist for the Bureau of Indian Affairs at the Izembek National Wildlife Refuge in Alaska, the Alaska Maritime National Wildlife Refuge during the 1989 Exxon Valdez Oil Spill, and at the Des Lacs and Lostwood National Wildlife Refuges in North Dakota. Blenden was refuge manager at San Luis Valley National Wildlife Refuges in Colorado.

Timothy Bywater is a professor of English and film at Dixie State University, where he has taught for over thirty years. He served as dean of the Division of Humanities and Social Sciences before taking his sabbatical as a visiting scholar at Cambridge University. He worked many summers as a park ranger at Yellowstone and Grand Teton National Parks and is currently the director of the National Endowment for the Humanities Challenge Grant.

Julia Corbett is an author and professor in the Department of Communication and the Environmental Humanities Graduate Program at the University of Utah. She has worked as a reporter, park ranger, naturalist, natural resources information officer, and press secretary. Her background in journalism and environmental studies informs her academic research and creative nonfiction about human relationships with the natural world.

Monte Dolack is an artist and a native of Great Falls, Montana. He was selected by the *Missoulian* as one of the 100 most influential Montanans of the twentieth century. Blending mythology, technology, and elements from nature, his work is infused with a sense of humor and irony. Dolack's keen interest in environmental issues has led to commissions for the Nature Conservancy, Defenders of Wildlife, and Trout Unlimited.

Louise Excell is professor emeritus of English and humanities at Dixie State University in St. George, Utah. She volunteers with a number of educational and environmental projects, and is a board member of the Mesa Retreat Center for Writers and Artists in Springdale, Utah, and the Reimagine Western Landscapes Initiative. She lives in Springdale with her husband, photographer David Pettit.

Wendy Fisher is executive director of Utah Open Lands, a statewide land trust that has protected over sixty thousand acres in Utah. Fisher has served on the governor's Agricultural Lands, Natural Lands, and Recreational Lands task force. In 2014 she spoke at the Columbia Law School, State Attorney General Program, Conservation Easement Conference. She was recently given the Park City Rotary Club's Citizen of the Year award.

Kerry C. Gee is vice president of United Park City Mines Co., and manages three CERCLA program cleanup projects in and near Park City, Utah, restoring previously toxic tailings ponds to wetlands habitat. He grew up in Park City and has worked as a mine geologist in the Park City Mining District; Butte, Montana; Bingham Canyon Mining District; Cripple Creek Colorado; and the Tintic Mining District.

Erin Halcomb is the associate director of the Taft-Nicholson Center for Environmental Humanities Education in Lakeview, Montana, and a graduate of the Environmental Humanities Program at the University of Utah. She conducted wildlife surveys for fishers and flying squirrels, and was a fire lookout for the United States Forest Service in southern Oregon.

Robert B. Keiter is the Wallace Stegner Professor of Law, a University Distinguished Professor, and founding director of the Wallace Stegner Center for Land, Resources, and the Environment at the University of Utah's S.J. Quinney College of Law. He has served on the boards of the National Parks Conservation Association, Greater Yellowstone Coalition, and Rocky Mountain Mineral Law Foundation, and has authored several books on public lands, ecology, and the West.

Harvey Locke is a conservationist, writer, photographer, and recognized global leader in the field of parks, wilderness, and large landscape conservation. He is cofounder of both the Nature Needs Half Movement and the Yellowstone to Yukon Conservation Initiative. At the World Parks Congress in 2014, Locke was awarded the IUCN World Commission on Protected Areas Fred M. Packard International Parks Merit Award. He lives in Banff National Park, Canada, where his family has deep roots.

Yvonne (Maberry) Martinell married into a multigenerational Montana ranching family. She graduated with a degree in business education from Montana State University. Martinell raised three children while helping her husband, Allen, manage the family's cattle ranch in Dell and Centennial Valley, Montana. She chairs the Centennial Valley Association, a community group that takes action on a diverse array of issues affecting the valley.

Jeffrey Mathes McCarthy is director of the University of Utah's Environmental Humanities Graduate Program and introduced the Reimagine Western Landscapes 2014 symposium in Centennial Valley, Montana. He asserts that humanities education gives students the ethical, humanist, and scientific tools to create a new environmental paradigm that challenges the "anthropocentric, instrumental humanism" of the past.

James C. McNutt is past president and CEO of the National Museum of Wildlife Art, located in Jackson, Wyoming. During his decade at the museum McNutt developed projects and partnerships with organizations including the National Geographic Society, the Smithsonian, Museums West, Yellowstone to Yukon, and Earth Vision Trust in the service of expanding access to and understanding of art depicting wildlife and the natural world. He now lives in Austin, Texas, and consults with museums and other nonprofits.

Leslie Miller has lived in the Wasatch Mountains since the early 1970s. The unspoiled lands of the West were a template for her outdoor pursuits and community service on the Park City Council, where she advocated for open space conservation. As past publisher of the *Wasatch Mountain Times* and a writer for regional magazines, her stories explore historic and contemporary topics of western culture. She is a twelve-year veteran of the University of Utah College of Humanities Partnership Board and organized the Reimagine Western Landscapes symposium in

Centennial Valley, Montana. Essays from her selected symposium presenters inspired this anthology.

Steve Primm is a conservationist specializing in coexistence between people and big predators. From a Missouri farming family, Primm grew up with twin passions for wild nature and sustainable agriculture. Since 1992, he has worked in all facets of carnivore conflict prevention on ranches and farms, in rural developments, and in the backcountry. Primm earned his master's degree in environmental policy from the University of Colorado-Boulder.

Kirk Robinson has spent much of his life exploring the deserts, plateaus, rivers, and mountains of the West. In 1997 he founded Western Wildlife Conservancy, a nonprofit wildlife conservation organization, in Salt Lake City. He currently serves as the organization's executive director. Before that, he was a professor of philosophy and taught at several colleges and universities in Montana and Utah.

Jeremy Schmidt is author of nearly twenty books and hundreds of magazine articles. He writes about natural history and adventure travel, with a particular interest in the winding frontier between the modern world and what's left of the natural and indigenous. Assignments have taken him to all continents, including Antarctica, where he recently began a natural history of Weddell seals, the world's southernmost breeding mammals. His latest book, *Looking for Tao Canyon*, is set in the slickrock country of America's desert Southwest. He lives in Jackson Hole, Wyoming.

Christopher Smart has been a journalist in Utah for more than three decades. He earned a bachelor's degree in biology from the University of Utah. He served as editor of the *Wasatch Mountain Times* and *Salt Lake City Weekly*. He currently covers social justice issues for the *Salt Lake Tribune*.

Gregory E. Smoak is director of the American West Center and associate professor of history at the University of Utah. He specializes in the native and environmental history of the American West, and public history. His most recently completed book, a public environmental history of Little Bighorn Battlefield National Monument, is forthcoming. Smoak has conducted numerous research projects for American Indian Nations as well as the National Park Service.

John Varley is a biologist who spent thirty-three years with the National Park Service, in Yellowstone National Park. He began his career as a field researcher and retired as the founding director of the Yellowstone Center for Resources. Varley is the author of the award-winning book *Freshwater Wilderness* (1983) as well as *Yellowstone Fishes: Ecology, History and Angling in the Park* (1998). Following his retirement from the National Park Service, he worked as a senior research biologist with a team researching the biodiversity of Yellowstone Lake.